P9-EEO-236

INSTITUTE OF PUBLIC ADMINISTRATION LIBRARY
55 West 44th Street
New York, New York 10036

B89-0102

Professionalizing
the Organization

Guy Benveniste

Professionalizing the Organization

Reducing Bureaucracy to Enhance Effectiveness

NOV 27 1989

INSTITUTE OF PUBLIC ADMINISTRATION LIBRARY
55 WEST 44th STREET
NEW YORK, NY 10036

Jossey-Bass Publishers

San Francisco   •   London   •   1987

302.3
B344

PROFESSIONALIZING THE ORGANIZATION
Reducing Bureaucracy to Enhance Effectiveness
by Guy Benveniste

Copyright © 1987 by: Jossey-Bass Inc., Publishers
433 California Street
San Francisco, California 94104
&
Jossey-Bass Limited
28 Banner Street
London EC1Y 8QE

Copyright under International, Pan American, and
Universal Copyright Conventions. All rights
reserved. No part of this book may be reproduced
in any form—except for brief quotation (not to
exceed 1,000 words) in a review or professional
work—without permission in writing from the publishers.

Library of Congress Cataloging-in-Publication Data

Benveniste, Guy (date)
    Professionalizing the organization.

    (The Jossey-Bass management series)
    Bibliography: p. 271
    Includes index.
    1. Organization. 2. Organizational effectiveness.
3. Professional employees. 4. Bureaucracy. I. Title.
II. Series.
HM131.B437   1987   302.3'5   86-27567
ISBN 1-555-42039-7 (alk. paper)

Manufactured in the United States of America

The paper in this book meets the guidelines for
permanence and durability of the Committee on
Production Guidelines for Book Longevity of the
Council on Library Resources.

JACKET DESIGN BY WILLI BAUM

FIRST EDITION

Code 8706

The Jossey-Bass
Management Series

For Karen

Contents

    Responsibility   195

8. How External Controls Adversely Affect Today's
    Organizations   225

9. Beyond Bureaucracy: Why Profession-Oriented
    Organizations Are More Effective   254

    References   271

    Index   293

Preface

This is a book about professionals in organizations: why they are important, how they can be managed effectively, and how their effective management can contribute to increased productivity. It is also a book about two strategies of managerial control—one based on expanding the routines of work, the other on increasing professional discretion. My interest in the phenomenon of bureaucracy and its impact on professionals grew out of considerable practical experience. I have worked for a large private electric utility, a nonprofit research think tank, and several American and international government organizations. I have always been fascinated by bureaucracy, both its positive and its negative aspects. I believe that professionals will play an increasingly important role in organizations in coming decades. Management will design organizations around professionals in an attempt to reduce excessive bureaucratization. This book is my attempt to present a positive alternative to bureaucratization by pointing to the potential utility of professionalization.

The central question, therefore, is how to design adaptive organizations that will fully utilize the talents of the professionals who work in them. How can these organizations encourage problem-solving, risk-taking, client-oriented behavior? What role can professionals play in achieving these aims? How can managers adopt conscious policies to enhance the level of professionalization in their own organizations? When is this desirable, and when is it not?

These questions are not new, but they have become increasingly important in these last decades of the twentieth century. The current distrust of government and of large national or multinational corporations is indicative of a general malaise that affects all aspects of organizational life on this planet. This distrust translates into very specific realities—such as fewer resources for government and disenchantment with organizations in general. This book addresses some of these issues: my purpose is to suggest a way of reducing the unnecessary evils of bureaucracy.

I emphasize governmental and nonprofit organizations more than profit-making firms because most of my experience and research comes from these organizations. But the distinctions between private and public or profit and nonprofit are not that significant. Two other variables are more important: knowledge and complexity. This book is concerned with organizations that depend on the knowledge and skills of their professional staffs to pursue complex activities. These may be engineering firms, research organizations, social service agencies, museums, philanthropies, hospitals, schools, universities, think tanks, or regulatory agencies. And this list could be made much longer.

For Whom Is the Book Intended?

Professionalizing the Organization is aimed at managers who are interested in organizational design. By design I mean the structure that affects the behavior of people inside and outside the organization. I do not address the psychological dimensions of these issues; this is not a book about how to improve one's leadership skills or achieve better interpersonal relations. Instead I focus on structural dimensions: how the organization's hierarchy is set up and tasks are assigned, how people are evaluated and rewarded, what the prevailing culture and assumptions of management are, how rewards and punishments are made, and what the main power relations and communication networks are.

My arguments mainly derive from organization theory and thinking. Sociologists of organizations have developed a set of concepts—authority, power, dependencies, and so on—that can be used quite profitably to clarify managerial issues. My purpose, therefore, is to explore the issue of professionalization, to clarify what its advantages are, and to point out the benefits it offers both professionals and management. Throughout the book, I have provided text references for further reading. These make this book a valuable introductory text for students of organization theory and management.

Overview of the Contents

We begin by discussing why professionals are important. In the first chapter I contrast two management approaches: bureaucratization and professionalization. I explain why bureaucratization is so prevalent and discuss ways routines are unfortunately often used for other purposes—particularly as defensive strategies. This chapter examines the strengths and limitations of routinization in an effort to increase management's understanding of the value of professionalization.

Chapter Two, examines how professionals differ from conventional workers. I discuss the great variety of professions and the levels of professionalization. How do we recognize a profession? What kinds of behaviors are associated with the role of a professional? Are these desirable or undesirable? When? I analyze professional attitudes and values in an attempt to define managerial styles that can motivate greater professional performance.

Chapter Three explores the relationship and the potential conflicts between professionals and managers. I discuss the governance of the profession-oriented organization and introduce the concepts of envelope supervision and of joint managerial-professional tasks. I then present five governance models: partnership, senior staff, dual governance, collegial, and conventional bureaucratic. My concern here is with power and authority.

What are the relations of power between managers and professionals? What kind of participation enhances the authority of
management and the effectiveness of professionals? When is participation desirable and when is it not? What kind of governance
structures make sense for what kind of organization?

In Chapter Four, our focus shifts to the future, to managing what the organization will become. First, I clarify the difference between professed and operational goals. Then I present a
model for managing ambiguity and discuss the importance of
symbols, trust, and consensus building. I conclude with a discussion of planning, emphasizing the benefits of partial or incomplete planning over comprehensive or strategic planning.

In Chapter Five, I focus on control and on the use of management tools to exercise control. I explore the link between
management tools such as programming, management by objectives, and performance-monitoring systems and the system of
rewards and punishments. Then I examine the benefits and haz-
ards of various management tools and conclude with a focus on
the six dangers inherent in overuse of these tools.

Chapter Six tackles the important structural issues: how
to choose a governance structure that will enhance professional
effectiveness and how to manage incentives. This chapter offers
new ways to encourage the participation and commitment of
professionals. Too many managers forget that professionals have
to be committed and enthusiastic about their work to perform
well.

In Chapter Seven, I turn to the issues of risk taking and
professional responsibility. Three important concepts in managing risk taking are loose coupling, organizational slack, and redundancy. These are discussed, as is the concept of error management—some level of error is needed for organizational
learning and adaptability, and management must both encourage
and control error making and risk taking. I stress the important
difference between evaluation used to learn and adapt and evaluation used to reward or punish. We also spend time on the inevitable professional conflicts engendered by risk taking and
organizational renovation.

Chapter Eight takes us away from internal matters to focus on external controls. This chapter explores the ways government and other organizations control and examines the principal characteristics of "good" and "bad" external controls. It concludes with suggestions on how managers of profession-oriented organizations can protect their organizations and their professional staffs from the bureaucratization of external controls.

The concluding chapter discusses the future of bureaucracy and of profession-oriented organizations. Can we really expect to find ways to reduce natural propensities toward routinization? Can we expect trust to replace control? Yet, as this chapter shows, the bottom line is effectiveness. The profession-oriented organization is more effective than a bureaucratic organization, so it should win out in the long run.

Acknowledgments

I would like to thank many people who have helped me with this book: Moshe Alafi, Bo Anderson, Stephanie Beardsley, Charles Benson, Paul Berman, Barbara Bruser, Susan Callahan, Ladislav Cerych, Nathan Cohen, Philip H. Coombs, Ellen Davies, Sandra Elman, Bernard Gifford, Robert Girling, James Guthrie, Charlene Harrington, Jo Farb Hernandez, Ricardo Diez Hochleitner, Andrew M. Kamarck, Sherry Keith, Edward M. Kersh, Charles H. Levine, Gilda Loew, Gregory Loew, David Losk, Marilyn McGregor, Gustave Maryssael, Arnold Meltsner, William Moran, Karen Nelson, Raymond Poignant, Edward Prentice, Rodney Reed, Allan Sindler, David Stern, and Ben Yerger. Many students in the Graduate School of Education and in our Academic Program in Public and Non-Profit Management have also provided insights and advice.

I also wish to thank the management and professional staffs of Applied Research, Florence's Refuge, and the other organizations described in the text. Although the names are fictitious, the individuals and conditions described are not. Joyce Paysour produced the manuscript with great professional accomplishment. I am also indebted to the Committee on Research at the University of California at Berkeley for a small grant that facilitated data collection.

My last, and most important, remerciement goes to a professional woman who keeps talking with me as we age gracefully together.

Berkeley, California   Guy Benveniste
January 1987

The Author

Guy Benveniste is professor of policy planning in the Graduate School of Education at the University of California at Berkeley. He was born in France and received his B.S. degree (1948) in engineering science and applied physics and his M.S. degree (1950) in mechanical engineering, both from Harvard University. Between 1950 and 1965, he worked for Mexican Light and Power Ltd. in Mexico City; the Stanford Research Institute in Menlo Park, California; the Department of State in Washington, D.C.; the International Bank for Reconstruction and Development, also in Washington, D.C.; and UNESCO in Paris. He was instrumental in the creation of a new international research and training institute affiliated with UNESCO.

In 1965, Benveniste obtained a major fellowship and returned to the United States for further study. In 1968, he received the first Ph.D. degree in the sociology of planning granted by Stanford University. His dissertation was subsequently published under the title *Bureaucracy and National Planning* (1970). Also in 1968, he was appointed to the faculty of the Graduate School of Education at the University of California at Berkeley.

Benveniste teaches courses in organization theory, planning, and management in the School of Education and in the campus Academic Program in Public and Non-Profit Management. He has edited and authored several books dealing with professions, education, and bureaucracy, including *Agents of Change: Professionals in Developing Countries* (with Warren Ilchman, 1969), *The Politics of Expertise* (1973), *From Mass to Universal Education* (with Charles Benson, 1976), *Bureaucracy* (1977), and *Regulation and Planning: The Case of Environmental Politics* (1981). He is also the author of several dozen articles.

Benveniste's main research interest involves the area of debureaucratization and professionalization. He has traveled widely and has consulted and lectured in the United States and abroad.

Benveniste lives with his wife, Karen Nelson, in Berkeley and Carmel-by-the-Sea, California. He is also an accomplished painter and has had several showings of his work.

Professionalizing
the Organization

1

From Bureaucratization to Professionalization: Why Professionals Are Essential to Modern Organizations

Why are professionals important in organizations? One obvious answer is that they are exceptional workers. They have access to specialized knowledge. They tend to be well educated, creative, and well socialized for work. Professionals include not only the obvious categories of doctors, lawyers, scientists, and engineers, but also many less prestigious groups such as teachers, nurses and other health workers, social workers, park rangers, museum curators, and many, many other occupations that require considerable expertise in a given field. In most firms or government agencies, professionals have an important contribution to make, so it is not surprising that much has recently been written about managing them (Guy, 1985; Kelley, 1985; Miller, 1986; Shapero, 1985). These books are mostly concerned with straightforward, yet important, management tasks such as hiring, supervising, motivating, and evaluating professionals. We have to be interested in these issues, but they are not the central concern of this book.

Another answer to the question of their importance is that professionals have become the largest single category of American workers. Also, most American workers today aspire to some of the privileges, style of life, work experience, status, and culture of professionals. A recent report states: "Workers, particularly better educated workers, are becoming more insistent on securing more freedom in the workplace. It is increasingly true that the measure of a good job is high discretion as much as high pay. Americans are less likely to see work as a straight economic transaction providing a means of survival and more likely to see it as a means of self-expression and self-development" (Committee on the Evolution of Work, 1985, p. 31).

This idea has been around for a long time. Wilensky, in a seminal paper published in 1964, recognized a trend toward the professionalization of all workers. But he argued that no more than thirty or forty occupations were fully professionalized, depending on how many of the scores of engineering and scientific specialties of the time were included in the estimate. He was not particularly sanguine about massive professionalization in the workplace and concluded that, given the realities of organizations, very few additional occupations would achieve the kind of authority and autonomy of established professions such as medicine and law.

Be that as it may, the fact is that today professionalization is pursued as a valued goal within the workplace. This shift of attitude primarily reflects greater opportunities for higher education. Bledstein (1976), in his excellent historical study of the culture of professionalism, shows us the link between middle-class values, the development of higher education, and the rise of professional authority during the nineteenth century. What we observe today is a continuation of these trends. As access to higher education spreads, there is continued aspiration toward more professionalization in the workplace. Obviously, these trends are relevant and interesting but, once again, they are not the central preoccupation of this book.

Professionalization: A Tool to Reduce Bureaucratization

We want to understand how professionals in any organization can help reduce bureaucratization; that is the primary focus of this book. Of course many bureaucrats are also professionals. The core question is, how can management use professionals as problem solvers instead of paper pushers? In any organization there are several ways to control: one can give direct instructions, but unless the organization is very small, it is not possible to instruct everyone. Therefore, control has to be exercised at a distance. There are two principal options for exercising control at a distance—to routinize or to delegate. Of the two, delegation is particularly appropriate for professionals and serves to enhance organizational problem-solving capability.

Ordinary tasks that are predictive and repetitive can be routinized. More complex (and more interesting) tasks that require adaptation and problem solving are not easily routinized. These are the tasks that are particularly suited to professional workers, because they have the necessary training and experience to take on-the-spot responsibility. Moreover, they will be more committed if the work is interesting and challenging.

Why is professionalization important in this context? Because professionals behave predictably in uncertain and complex situations. Because problem solving and adaptability are crucial to most organizations. In the recent literature about excellence in organizations one finds, over and over again, the theme of action-oriented, problem-solving, adaptive organizations (Peters and Waterman, 1982; Peters and Austin, 1985). This is not surprising. Technological change, modernization, and the emergence of an integrated world economy affect all organizations. Routines work well in predictive task situations, but they are not well suited to situations where task variability and complexity prevail.

In the private sector there is a strong trend away from routinization and toward increased professionalization. This trend reflects, among other factors, the substitution of highly sophisticated, automated, and continuous production processes for old-fashioned assembly-line work. Modern production workers no longer simply tighten the same bolt over and over again on the production line. They manage complex equipment, monitor performance, and solve problems to keep production flowing.

In government and in the nonprofit sector, technological changes are also taking place, but the spread of routinization

seems to go on unabated. There is considerable talk about problem solving and adaptability, about achieving excellence and
maintaining high standards, but there is a less visible shift
toward professionalization.

Most managers understand about routinization and discretion. They understand that either work can be routinized or
more discretion can be given to professionals and trained workers. They may even be able to describe when discretion is necessary and when it is not. Implementation of these concepts is
another matter. Even when management espouses a strong pro-
professional rhetoric, reality suddenly appears to be quite different. We may find that professional workers do not feel they
have much discretion, that they are not encouraged to solve
problems, that they are not rewarded when they do, and that
the organization is quite different from what it pretends to be.

A Case Example: Applied Research

Several years ago, I studied a nonprofit organization that
I will call Applied Research, run by a manager who spoke con-
vincingly about professional work but actually delegated very
little and supervised very closely the work of all his professionals. This was a relatively small government organization that
produced social science research reports for various other government clients and conducted short-term training programs for
government employees. The small permanent staff of professionals was supplemented by short-term consultants. Most of
the time, Applied Research produced policy reports. The reports required teamwork and usually took several weeks or
longer to prepare. There was considerable time pressure to meet
deadlines, and this problem became acute when sponsors' needs
overlapped.

The manager knew how difficult it was to attract good
people, and showed, when interviewed, that he was extremely
concerned about the reputation and demonstrated expertise of
his staff. "There is no way to do this kind of job without top-
notch social scientists," he said. "We seek to find the best people and give them a lot of responsibility." But, when we inter-

viewed the professional staff, they described the manager as "solitary, keeps everything close to his chest, wants to supervise everything, wants to decide who we hire, who we do not hire, reads every report, rewrites most of them, changes commas, and is a detail freak." Dissatisfaction among the staff was high, and there had been considerable turnover.

When we confronted the manager with these comments, he explained that he was aware of these sentiments but that the staff did not understand the larger political problems he faced. He argued that he delegated as much as he could but that he could not afford mistakes. "You say something you should not say, and you are in hot trouble with the report out in the open and your sponsor pounding on you." He pointed out that turnover had nothing to do with dissatisfaction. "These people get visibility in this job and get hired right and left." He concluded that there was no other way to run that operation. Two years later, having served a total of four years, he was replaced.

Interestingly, his successor also lasted four years, but she ran the operation using a completely different style. She paid much more attention to the needs and aspirations of the professional staff. The staff was involved in some hiring decisions, there were weekly management meetings, project managers were responsible for their reports, and a professional editor was hired. As we shall see in subsequent chapters, the first and second managers pursued totally different management strategies, and these strategies had direct consequences for the success and effectiveness of the organization.

To be sure, the second manager still faced a difficult environment. She did not relinquish her control and responsibility; all reports still had to be approved. Some of the tension did not abate. Staff turnover continued to be high, but for different reasons. Eventually, we recommended more coordination among the various sponsors so that the research load would be more evenly distributed. This would reduce some of the work pressures on the staff. In time, the sponsors assumed greater responsibility for coordination through their representatives on the board, and the situation was stabilized.

Applied Research was a typical professional organization

operating in a complex environment. It performed difficult
work under trying conditions. Given the nature of the product—
policy reports that could have considerable impact—it is obvious
that management was under pressure to pay close attention to
performance. The question is, could the first manager have done
better? Did the second manager improve on the first? We will
return to these issues later. But, for the moment, suffice it to
say that the rhetoric of increased professionalization was just
that—rhetoric. Other forces were at work that favor bureaucratization.

The Growing Importance of Bureaucracy

A bureaucracy is a large organization where rules, regulations, and routines are used extensively. There is a hierarchy,
people are assigned to specific tasks, and the organization is
subdivided into smaller units, each headed by line managers
with limited authority delegated by top management.

When the task is predictive and the technology is well
understood, routines work well. Let us be reminded that bureaucracy prevails, first and foremost, because it works.

I served in the early 1950s in what can be considered a
"successful" bureaucracy employing many professionals. This
was a large private electric utility. At the time there were no
problems with environmental groups, no controversy over
nuclear power, and the rise in demand for electric service appeared to be fairly constant and predictable. There were many
political uncertainties and the political environment was complex. The company was registered in Canada, but it was controlled by a Belgian holding company and operated in the
central plateau of Mexico. It was unclear how long the Mexican government would allow it to continue to operate or when
it might be nationalized, since electricity is so important for
economic development. Ultimately, the government bought
the company, but at the time we did not know that would
happen.

The company prided itself on efficient performance.
Much of the technical activity was highly routinized, and man-

agement kept the difficult political problems for itself: What mix of hydro and fossil fuel generating capacity was desirable? Where should new facilities be built? How would new rates be justified? These and many other questions were handled competently by a centralized formal hierarchy with well-defined responsibilities.

In this firm, routines worked well. The design and supervision of routines was one of management's tasks, in cooperation with the professional staff. For example, maintenance crews were told precisely when and how to perform their tasks. Operations personnel in the areas of generation, transmission, and distribution followed careful routines. The only department with greater discretion was construction, for there was far more technical uncertainty about drilling tunnels for hydro plants or building steam plants using new and unknown equipment.

But even in generation, there were moments when the unpredictable would take place. An accident would happen—a piece of equipment would not respond properly, a large perturbation on the electric system would result in load imbalance, the careful routines assigned to the steam-generating plants would suddenly become irrelevant as generators responded to too-rapid load fluctuations. Boilers would go beyond safety limits, the noise level in the steam plant would go up, and emergency lights would be flickering all over the place. Routines would no longer apply. In those instances, we would see the plant engineers drop whatever they were doing and rush out of their cubicles to attempt to control the situation. In those days, the steam plant had to be handled manually and orders to open or close valves, to release steam or increase pressure, would be shouted as engineers and technicians attempted to keep the plant on line without failing the remaining electric system.

This is common-sense organizational control: What can be routinized is routinized. What cannot be routinized is handled by specialized workers and professionals. In our case, most of the activities of the organization could be and were routinized, but professional discretion was used when necessary. Operations engineers were on hand to cope with emergencies. Their broad knowledge of power-plant operation gave them a repertoire of ways to think about the problem. Management trusted them to attempt to find solutions.

This was, to my knowledge, a healthy organization in the sense that routines did not seem to encroach on professional discretion. My fellow engineers did not feel hampered in their tasks. They believed in the routines and understood them. When routines had to be modified, they were instrumental in the changes.

Applied Research was a very different professional organization. Here the routines hampered the professional staff. The first manager's controls affected the quality of the product; the reports were not improved by excessive tampering. There were many conflicts between professionals and management and, in the last analysis, the staff was demoralized. "What's the use of working on this," staff members would say, "since they will change everything we write?"

Excessive bureaucratization is the encroachment of routinization and control on professional discretion to the detriment of the task.

Mosher and Stillman have documented, in a series of edited articles (1977, 1978), the extent to which the professions are dominated by bureaucracy. For example, lawyers are increasingly working for large organizations instead of in private practice; as a result, their independence tends to be eroded (1978). Other professions suffer similar fates. Today, many social services are deeply affected by external controls that have been imposed to ensure the protection of clients and the general public. For example, medicine is highly affected, on one hand, by regulatory attempts to control medical expenditures through standardization (and therefore routinization) of treatment, and, on the other hand, by the fear of malpractice suits that cause doctors to follow well-accepted (and therefore routinized) procedures to the letter. But, as Rahman (1983, p. 23) points out, even increased regulation and routinization conducted by peers are fraught with ambiguity:

> While peer review panels advocate cost containment, they give only lip service to quality care. The public urges doctors to give empathetic medi-

cal care, but the system is encouraging us to be impersonal.

Even if I follow the guidelines set out by the peer review panels and admit a patient, the panel can disagree with me later and, months after the patient has been discharged, disallow the admission and reimbursement. Technically, I can be labeled a "Medicare abuser."

Despite its name, a peer review organization's primary mandate is to slash expenses. In a given region, the panel that promises the highest cuts gets the Medicare contract.

Similarly, teachers are increasingly controlled by statewide accountability schemes designed to ensure that state monies are properly spent in local school districts. American experience with statewide accountability is in many ways unique because American education used to be highly decentralized and it is now centralizing (Benveniste, 1985). These accountability systems result in lowered teacher discretion and increased routinization. Similar accounts can be made about social workers, police officers, engineers, accountants, economists, military officers, and other professionals employed in large organizations. The problem is quite real and relevant.

As we shall see, external forces are not the only cause of excessive bureaucratization. There are also internal forces at work. But the fact is that at a time when one might expect organizations to become more adaptive because change is accelerating, at a time when there is considerable emphasis on adaptability, it appears that the trend is the other way—that there is less discretion and more rigidity. We tend to want to take refuge in formulas, in set ways of behaving. Is this an inevitable characteristic of large organizations? Is bureaucracy inevitably rigid?

A Linguistic Digression

Let me digress for a while and deal with the roots of the word *bureaucracy*. When we think of a bureaucracy, we first think of rigidity, of unwillingness to respond, red tape, paperwork, inability to be flexible. Actually, the word comes from the French word for desk: *bureau*. In time, the word for desk was extended to encompass the room in which the desk sat, then the set of activities taking place in the room, and later to a component of and, ultimately, the entire organization.

If we go back in time, we find that the French word for desk has roots that come from a flexible object, namely from a cloth. The French word *bureau* comes originally from *bure, burette,* and *bureau,* names given in the thirteenth century to rough woven cloths worn by peasants and used for other purposes. When writing on parchment, it was common practice to cover a table with a rough blue cloth, called a *bureau,* to protect the parchment. Around 1400, the table covered by the cloth began to be called the *bureau,* and the benches on which to sit were called *tabouret à bureau.*

This may not be sufficient proof that bureaucracy can be flexible. But I am always encouraged when studying large organizations to remember the blue cloth.

When Excessive Bureaucratization Is Undesirable

Excessive bureaucratization is the use of routinization where discretion is needed. Rules and regulations provide a means of controlling behavior without having to be on the spot to give instructions. But rules can be used for other purposes or have other functions, some of which may be quite important. For example, rules can be used to justify action or to depoliticize difficult allocative choices. These additional functions go a long way in explaining the phenomenon of excessive bureaucratization.

Before we discuss the various functions of rules, it is useful to clarify three kinds of situations where discretion is important but routinization is often imposed: (1) situations where we do not really know what the problem is, situations of "goal vacuum"; (2) situations where we know what is to be achieved but we are not sure how to proceed—that is, the technology is unclear; (3) situations where we know what our goals are, we know much about the ways to achieve desirable outcomes, but the tasks are so varied and changing that constant adaptation is needed.

1. The Problem Is Undefined. Not knowing how to proceed, or facing a wide range of opportunities, is common. For example, legislators appropriate funds and write language to the effect that something will be done about crime, or street people, or abandoned children, or some other social issue. Yet when it comes down to figuring out exactly what to do, the agency has no real understanding of the problem. There may be many reasons for this. The problem is new and came up so fast that no one has had time to really study it. Or the problem has been around for a long time, but it was not important and no one paid attention to it. Or it may simply be that the organization suddenly finds itself in a situation where there is considerable choice, where uncharted   courses of action are there for the taking.

These situations always call for a significant diagnostic effort, where professionals and other informed people spell out in greater detail what the problem consists of and how it might be remedied. These diagnostic efforts take time, something that the legislature and top agency management usually understand. But there is the issue of trust.

If trust prevailed, if the legislature was quite convinced that the agency would do its best, or if top agency management had faith in its professionals, considerable discretion might be given for a sufficient period of time to allow the staff to map the terrain and provide definitions of the issue. But if trust is not there, controls will be established immediately. The legislature will be sorely tempted to ask for results and top management will want early definitions of achievement to report back at the next budget hearings. Once this control process is initiated, tasks will be assigned, objectives will be set, and the agency will not only give every appearance of knowing what it is about, it will also reduce the alternatives. An informed observer may be aware that those who are close to the action have not been given the opportunity to figure out what to do, but meanwhile the agency pursues a predetermined course of action. In these situations, many mistakes are usually made be-

fore the organization finally realizes that it used the wrong set
of assumptions and did not sufficiently define the problem before acting.

2. *The Technology Is Not Well Understood.* Sometimes
the problem is well understood but the means to solutions are
not. This may be because the field is new; namely, new scientific and technological advances allow us to contemplate problems we could not address beforehand. Or it may be a new
problem; while we can define it, we do not really know what
works best to solve it.

When scientific and technological advances are recent—
say, in medicine or engineering—it is not uncommon for the applied technology to lag considerably. Various schools of thought
on how to proceed tend to exist. People working in these new
fields may have strong disagreements among themselves, which
will not make management feel comfortable. There will be
strong inclinations to want to keep the conflicts under control.

The same situation may arise when a new problem is addressed and not enough time is given to develop workable ways
to handle it. These situations also tend to generate various
schools of thought concerning how to proceed and, if the conflict involves not only professionals but also clients and the general public, the inclination to control will be very strong indeed.

Bilingual education is a typical example of this kind of
situation. When Congress initiated bilingual programs under
Title VII of the Elementary and Secondary Education Act of
1968, these programs were experimental. It was well understood that no one knew exactly how to run such programs. But,
after the 1974 Supreme Court decision in *Lau* v. *Nichols,* the
San Francisco school district was ordered to remedy the fact
that Chinese-speaking children could not follow English language classes. At that point bilingual programs simply had to
become operational whether anyone knew how to run them or
not (Sumner, 1977). Obviously, this kind of external intervention was designed to break new ground by forcing a response.
No one could readily predict that it would also result in what
we call excessive bureaucratization.

Once the Office of Civil Rights had issued the 1975 findings specifying remedies available for eliminating past educational practices that had been ruled unlawful under *Lau* v. *Nichols,* school districts had to comply. These findings were written by lawyers; they assumed the technology was in place when it was not. Very few districts knew how to handle the vast diversity of children coming from many different linguistic backgrounds. There were not enough trained teachers and curricular materials. For a long while, bilingual programs suffered from the fact that totally insufficient numbers of trained professionals had to work in a highly bureaucratized setting. Even today, shortages still exist. What was needed was technical assistance and professional experimentation. What took place instead was bureaucratic compliance paperwork.

These problems were the result of larger external factors. One could argue that once the Supreme Court decision was made, what happened was history and inevitable. If excessive bureaucratization took place, this is too bad, but could not be avoided. On the other hand, one could also argue that if the Supreme Court had had a clearer understanding of the professional problems involved or if the Office of Civil Rights had been instructed to pay more attention to nonlegal professional issues, the worst of these problems might have been avoided.

3. The Tasks Are Varied and Complex. Routines do not have desired consequences when tasks are varied, nonpredictive, and complex. For example, all patients do not come with the same ailment, the same attitude, the same experience, and the same fortitude. Considerable discretion is needed to handle these differences. To be sure, much of health care can be, and is, routinized. But there remain gray areas of uncertainty where discretion or interpretation of rules is required. Any professional working in an organization will be subject to some routines. The important question is whether this professional also has sufficient discretion.

In a more perfect world, the task would define how much professional discretion is used. If the task were too varied and cost containment were required, the task definition might be altered to fit managerial needs. Management might decide not to handle certain kinds of cases or to limit the discretion of professionals in certain areas. But management would not routinize tasks that are not predictive, and the task itself would define how much discretion is given.

However, we do not live in this more perfect world. There are many reasons why inappropriate routines are established. Some have to do with the growing importance of controls imposed by organizations on other organizations. Government regulation, court intervention, and legislative oversight generate external controls. We discuss this at greater length in Chapter Eight. Many internal factors are also at work. These have to do with the realities of organizational life, with the ways individuals and groups defend themselves in an uncertain bureaucratic environment. Bureaucratization is also a defensive tool that can be used to legitimize action. This can best be understood by describing the various functions of rules.

Seven Reasons Why Rules Are Overemphasized in Organizations

Rules as Protective Strategies. Rules and regulations have a most important function: they can be used to justify action, to explain why what was done was done. They can also be used as a benchmark to evaluate behavior. One can ask, "Did you follow the rules?" If the rules were followed, the outcome is justified. If the rules were not followed, one has a basis for assessing blame. This is one of the paradoxes of management, a paradox that may explain many of our bureaucratic problems (Crozier, 1964).

If the task is difficult and the outcome uncertain, there is an advantage in following the rule to the letter to justify a possible bad outcome. For example, take the case of a doctor who does not know for sure whether the patient can be helped, whether the operation will succeed. This doctor happens to be concerned with malpractice suits. If the outcome of the operation is bad, there is a real danger of a malpractice suit, which will mean time lost in court and increased malpractice insurance rates. Our doctor is therefore very concerned with the issue of negligence. Generally, negligence is defined in terms of not following an accepted standard practice. Our doctor will be very aware that there might be far less danger of a malpractice suit if medical texts are followed to the letter. But the medical text may not exactly fit the patient. The doctor may have far better intuitions about the specific ailment at hand. Yet the routine is a protective strategy. Our doctor adheres to the text, even if it is inappropriate, to avoid the danger of a lost court battle.

Medicine is a profession where clients have acquired considerable clout, through the use of the courts, but the example applies to other professions in other organizational settings.

Most organizations do not handle risk very well. They commonly espouse a rhetoric that strongly encourages professional workers to innovate, to be inventive, and therefore to take some risks. However, most organizations, with some exceptions, do not make it too clear that they actually encourage making errors. The general feeling among the staff is that management wants you to take risks, but they want you to succeed. Failures are not appreciated and are to be avoided.

Other professionals in different settings may not be concerned with malpractice suits, but they can easily be concerned with their promotion, their career, their status; with their not being fired or transferred; or simply with not having to endure harsh criticism. In any case, they have concerns that make them want to protect themselves.

This is where rules come in. Rules provide admirable justifications for failures: "We knew there might be problems, but never expected this explosion. We do not know how the accident happened. We followed all the accepted practices to the letter." Or, "This outcome is unfortunate. The patient simply did not respond. Our operating team did what was prudent and expected. Our log shows each of our interventions and they correspond to the routine established for this kind of case."

The beauty of routines is that they provide the basis for documented histories of what was done. Blame can be allocated on the basis of documents. The procedure was followed or not followed. Since the routine is predictable, documenting it is possible. Forms can be prepared ahead of time and provided after the task is accomplished.

The paradox here is that the greater the uncertainty and the risk of failure, the greater the tendency in most organizations to create routines as protective strategies. In task situations where management should be urging more field discretion and more on-the-spot problem solving, rules and regulations are instituted to protect the members of the organization. Management and professionals are both responsible for this. Very often it is the professionals themselves who have instituted the rules so that they can limit the consequences of errors.

Excessive bureaucratization is the widespread use of rules and regulations for the purpose of legitimizing errors in situations where the organization is not well equipped to handle risk and failure.

Rules to Depoliticize Decisions. Another important use of rules is to standardize complex decisions, to depoliticize them to reduce potential conflict. If there is no rule and you happen to want service from my organization, I may be at a loss to deny you. We may be involved in a political process. You may be a vocal, local political actor, an important influential person that I may fear or that my organization may wish to treat very delicately indeed. But the rule is there, and I can say, "I am so sorry, so sorry, but there is no way for me to break the rule. I cannot possibly comply." You may be very indignant and very powerful, you may even be able to go higher up and obtain a variance of the rule, but meanwhile our potential conflict was avoided and my action was justified.

For example, rules are used to depoliticize difficult allocative decisions where there is no easy consensus on how resources should be spent. This is often the case when budgets are allocated to social services. The politics of giving money to competing educational institutions, or the politics of controlling public health expenditures, are greatly simplified if relatively simple rules can be used. Formulas avoid the messy complexities of having to decide budgets on the basis of need or merit. The politics of these decisions are bureaucratized, and in these cases, this means less time reaching decisions and the advantage of an impersonal, egalitarian rule to justify the decisions.

Many rules inside the organization are intended to reduce

potential conflicts. Rules about office allocations and furnishings are probably the best illustration of this principle. Many organizations specify the size, number of windows, and furnishings that come with levels of the hierarchy.

In some cases, these rules are entirely justified; in others, they may be imperfect substitutes for decisions that would be better made in the political arena, but that is not the issue here. The interesting consequence is that these rules take on an importance of their own, which rapidly goes far beyond their utility in making allocative decisions. Management assumes that the rule is important and all sorts of internal professional decisions begin to be affected by it. If we take the case of universities where budget allocations are made on the basis of enrollment, it follows that money tends to echo student numbers. This has all sorts of consequences for the way resources are allocated internally. The rule tends to reduce professional discretion. But large enrollments do not mean that we have academic excellence. Here we have another paradox: decisions that require professional judgment are instead made on the basis of arbitrary rules that are irrelevant to the issue at hand.

Rules and Centralization. As uncertainty increases, there is a tendency toward centralization. The argument is simple. If things are stable, the organization can cope and maintain access to resources. As markets and technologies become more competitive, the stronger organizations know that they can handle the situation but the weaker ones cannot; their access to resources is tenuous. How can the weaker organizations improve their tenuous position? By uniting with other organizations. If they are government, they reorganize and consolidate under the banner of greater efficiency. If they are private, they acquire other firms, merge, or consolidate. To be sure, moves toward centralization are usually followed by moves toward decentralization, but generally speaking, one can assert that in rising uncertainty, centralization dominates (Benveniste, 1983; Jacoby, 1973).

The twin processes of centralization and decentralization, particularly when they take place rapidly, require routinization to be carried out. A second argument is made: If you centralize or decentralize slowly, you have time to establish trust relationships with your new partners and delegation is facilitated. If you centralize rapidly, these trust relationships are not yet there and routinization is the only practical control strategy to start with. If you decentralize rapidly, you still wish to maintain some controls and you institute reporting controls for that purpose.

Rules are also kept when no longer needed. The kind of debureaucratization we discuss in this book departs sometimes from early stages of routinization that are no longer needed. When we think about the phenomenon of repetitive centralization and decentralization, we realize that routinization, which may have been instituted for good reasons at earlier times, may no longer be appropriate later on. We stress this function of rules because excessive bureaucratization happens when trust could be substituted for control but management assumes that control is still needed.

Rules and Administrative Reform. Rules are the basis of administration reforms based on egalitarian treatment and the concept of the meritocracy. Rules are used to protect the rights of employees and clients. Discretion is associated with arbitrariness, capriciousness, and unfairness; lack of discretion ensures that all citizens are treated equally. Similarly, rules are used to avoid patronage. Discretion is associated with favoritism and despotism; lack of discretion ensures that merit prevails.

It is no surprise that rules prevail in all forms of administration, public and private. From the Civil Service Act of 1883 to the civil service reform of 1978, the trend in public administration has been toward the depoliticization of government service, egalitarian treatment, and the use of merit in appointments. People are not appointed to government jobs because of their friends or relatives, or because they were able to buy the appointment. They are appointed because they are qualified. How does one know they are qualified? Through standard examinations, which all applicants have equal opportunity to take. This goes hand in hand with careful classification and specification of jobs. A similar phenomenon takes place in the private sector where the independent, self-made entrepreneurs of the past are gradually replaced by trained graduates of business schools, and where the rights of workers are protected by collective contracts and by work legislation.

Egalitarian ideals permeate many other reforms, all the way from affirmative action to protect women and minorities to the protection of human subjects or animals involved in research.

This does not mean that meritocracy or egalitarian goals run contrary to professionalization. In fact, appointing individuals for merit is the underpinning of professionalization. It does mean that professionalization and egalitarian values can affect each other. This suggests that the implementation of reforms has to take into account the value of protecting professional discretion whenever possible. For example, compliance may be assessed in different ways, some of which limit professional discretion more than others, and choices that favor professional discretion can be taken.

Rules and Professional Responsibility. Rules are used to control professionals when they do not police themselves sufficiently. Excessive bureaucratization can be directly attributable to inadequate professional self-regulation. For example, the rise in medical malpractice suits can be attributed to the willingness of another profession, that of lawyers, to participate in lucrative activities. Or it can be attributed to the generosity of juries who have tended to provide large financial remedies to claimants. But it must also be attributed to inadequate self-policing by the medical profession.

Any attempt to reduce bureaucratization by increasing professionalization has to take into account the ethical posture of the profession. We will return to this issue in subsequent chapters. The important point to be made here is that achieving higher levels of professionalization and reducing inappropriate controls is not only a management task. It is also a professional task. It requires the interest, energy, and commitment of professional workers and professional organizations.

When the professions fail to take responsibility for policing themselves, others inevitably step in to control them. These controls tend to be dysfunctional, are resented by the professions, and may result in some dissatisfaction, alienation, and even burnout. This does not mean that professional discretion must prevail at all costs. It does mean that it is management's task to recognize that this alienated professional body needs assistance even if it is partly responsible for its predicament. The question then becomes, what can management do to enhance greater professional responsibility and reduce external controls?

Rules as a Source of Power. Rules are a source of management power. Excessive bureaucratization can be attributed to management's need for power, but a need for power that is dysfunctional to the task. Why would managers want to have more power than is useful for the work at hand?

First, excessive bureaucratization can be attributed to the fact that power is pleasurable. Those who set rules are also those who can provide dispensations. This means that those who need the rule to be relaxed will have to curry the favor of those who control it. Visit any government ministry in a Latin American country and watch people milling around offices as they seek favors from government officials. This happens also in the United States, except that the transactions are less visible and frequent. A considerable amount of stroking, cajoling, and corruption has to do with relaxing rules that may not be necessary in the first place.

Second, rules are used to assert authority when this authority is precarious. The first manager of Applied Research who read every report and changed the commas had strict rules about hiring outside consultants. He explained these rules as his attempt to hire the best people, but in fact, he was the final decision maker who approved the choice of consultants. This gave him additional power over the permanent staff. He could agree or disagree with their choices, although they tended to have far more information about the proposed consultants since they interviewed them or had worked with them previously. He seemed to use the rule to exercise pressure on the staff, showing them that he was someone to reckon with and to remind them they could not do without him.

Rules as a Substitute for Trust. Rules are used because

there is insufficient trust. The first manager of Applied Research did not really trust his staff, and said so. He said that he could not afford political mistakes and constantly kept an eagle eye to protect himself and the organization from potential bungling. In general, management's distrust of professionals has several distinct aspects. First, as was the case with the manager of Applied Research, there will be situations where managers simply do not think that their professionals understand the larger picture, or where they think that existing professional expertise is irrelevant to the management task at hand. Second, there will be circumstances where management believes that professional interests, goals, or values do not coincide with the organizational goals they pursue. Third and last, management may be threatened by professionals and be in direct conflict with them in terms of control or of long-term career objectives. There may be turf disputes over what is management terrain and what is professional responsibility.

These conflicts and this distrust result directly from role confusion. What is management responsibility and what is professional responsibility? (We discuss this at greater length in Chapter Three.) These conflicts also result from intellectual diversity. Managers are taught to have an overall view of problems. Most professionals use a narrower definition of the problem where their specialized skills are useful. Managers quite legitimately distrust narrow perspectives: the intellectual blinders of professions, their ignorance of other ways to consider problems, and their ignorance of larger contextual issues including their inadequate sense of the social, economic, financial, or political dimensions of problems. Managers often feel that professionals in organizations do not want to understand the stark realities of keeping on budget and are far too provincial and naive about the motives of their adversaries. The manager of Applied Research was not a rare case.

Managers may also distrust professionals who appear overtrained or who have acquired far more academic degrees than seem necessary for the task. There may be an anti-intellectual bias associated with professionalization. A suspicion is that young recruits fresh from the university with an advanced degree will come with pedantic theoretical ideas about what to do, but with little practical experience. These arrogant young upstarts need to be kept under control and reminded who is in charge.

The issue of professional self-interest is somewhat different. Managers control professionals because they distrust their motives—and for good reasons. Professionals are humans with the usual appetites, and they undoubtedly pay attention to their own personal or professional goals. This very human characteristic becomes of more than passing interest when the goals of organizations are subverted and displaced by the interests and needs of professionals. For example, managers may be suspicious when professionals happen to be both the prescribers of remedies and the furnishers of the services they prescribe. This happens quite often and not always visibly. For example, say federal or state programs have to be evaluated. The evaluators may operate in a tight circle of professionals who know each other. They may prescribe remedies and, at the same time, award each other lucrative technical assistance contracts. Managers may also be suspicious of professionals whose own research interest may dictate the choice of equipment or the direction of agency research priority without necessarily reflecting the goals of the organization.

Lastly, managers mistrust professionals when they happen to be perceived as a direct threat. The reasons may be valid or invalid, but this does not alter the problem. Managers may be threatened by the potential errors professionals can make but for which managers will be blamed. They may be threatened by professional challenges to their authority that will hamper their ability to function. They may be threatened by professional values that do not coincide with theirs or those of the organization.

Be that as it may, there is ample reason for management caution about ideas of increased professionalization and the notion of giving professionals in organizations greater autonomy. This explains, in part, why so much is said about the utility of greater levels of professionalization in government and why not too much is done about it. It also explains why some authors are quite opposed to the notion, arguing that no one has demonstrated that increased levels of professionalization result in higher productivity in government service (Ammons and King, 1984; Rabin, 1985).

Input, Process, and Output Controls

Professionalization, it bears repeating, is the substitution of discretionary roles for routinized roles. Professional roles rely on a knowledge base and discretion within the limited domain of that base. Professional roles also provide an ethical stance and assume a calling, a commitment, that goes beyond strict economic incentives. These roles depend more on peer evaluation than on line-management evaluation, at least in the more well-established professions. They also imply greater interaction with other professionals and greater discretion in designing and carrying out tasks (see Chapter Two).

But even when considerable discretion is left to professionals, management still needs to exercise some control. Managers can use input, process, or output controls; each of these has different implications for professional workers.

What are input, process, and output controls? Input controls are of this variety: "Here is a definition of the task, here are resources. Go to it and get things done." Input controls are very important in management. Line-item budgeting is the best-known input control. Personnel policies, purchasing, and facility management can all be interpreted as input controls. We do not always think this way, but the training and attitudes of management, professionals, and workers are a very significant input control. If individuals can be induced beforehand to behave in desirable ways, it follows that there is less need to supervise them and evaluate their work. Professionalization is an input control, in the sense that professionals acquire through their professional socialization selected desirable and predictable patterns of behavior.

Process controls are of this variety: "Here is the task. We want you to do it this way." Process controls are by definition routines, and their implementation calls for close supervision.

Output controls are of this variety: "Here is the task. We want you to achieve the following outputs, and we will evaluate you on this basis." Output controls are usually used when goals are precise and outputs can be readily measured.

Good management is the judicious use of these three kinds of control. We will discuss them at greater length in Chapter Six. For the moment, it suffices to emphasize that increased professionalization is a shift toward greater use of input controls. Why do we say this? Because professionals happen to be highly socialized workers who come to the task with a repertoire of behavior that implies they do not need to be constantly supervised. A strategy that emphasizes input controls instead of process or output controls is one that relies less on routines and evaluations and far more on the spirit, attitude, socialization, and technical knowledge and responsibility of the staff. This strategy has to rely on trust to succeed.

Why do we emphasize input controls? Because they fit situations where uncertainty is high and adaptive behavior is at a premium. What is wrong with process controls? Process controls work best when the task can be routinized. Therefore they tend to be effective in situations that are predictive and well understood. There is nothing wrong with process controls in these situations, but they are not suited to situations of high uncertainty requiring adaptive behavior. What about output controls? As we said, they are useful when goals are precise and outputs easily measured. However, they can be counterproductive in situations where an organization pursues several goals and where measuring outputs is not easy. In these situations, output controls tend to result in what is called goal displacement, substitution of a desirable goal by some operational measurement that does not really approximate the goal. For example, if you measure good education by the ability to score high on a skill test, sooner or later the ability to score high on this test will become more important than generating enthusiasm for learning. You cannot easily measure enthusiasm for learning, but you can measure ability to answer a set of true-false questions.

Many management practices seem to depart from the assumption that the more control, the better. But, as we see, controls have to be designed to fit the task. It is unfortunate that not enough attention is given to the impact of undesirable controls on those who implement them.

It is generally assumed in government that accountability is a very important function. Obviously, accountability is important, but not all forms of accountability are desirable. Certain accountability schemes emphasize output controls; they may work well in some situations and not in others. Similarly, one can design accountability schemes that emphasize process or input controls and, again, these will work in some situations and not in others. The point is that increased professionalization tends to depend on a greater emphasis on input controls.

Conclusion

Professionalization may seem desirable, but it is obvious that many factors hamper its flourishing in full. Relinquishing control requires trust, and sufficient trust may not be available. External forces may oblige management to adopt internal or external controls that hamper professionals. Even when there are trust and few external obligations, there may still be other internal paradoxes that drive management into excessive routinization.

One conclusion is that increased professionalization requires a commitment from management, that it is a management responsibility. If unsuitable controls are imposed from outside, what can management do to protect professionals? Can management argue for better controls and take a stance on the matter? Can management shield the professional staff from the more inept requirements that come from other organizations? If unsuitable controls are imposed because of insufficient trust, what can be done to increase trust? If unsuitable controls are imposed to provide protection or for other purposes, how can the factors causing this be corrected or modified enough to allow for greater professional responsibility?

A second conclusion is that professionalization is a professional responsibility. Professionals working in an organization are responsible for increasing the level of professional roles.

They are responsible for wanting to bring about change and for
helping management in all the tasks listed above. It is a common
enterprise and requires cooperation. It may take time because
accepted role definitions, customs, and assumptions about what
is right or wrong have to be modified. There are sensitive subjects to discuss, and matters of status, privilege, and turf protection to settle before minor improvement can be achieved.

A third conclusion is that the long-term success of serious
attempts to increase professionalization in bureaucracies has a
lot to do with basic assumptions about what are desirable levels
of professional education. Professionalization inevitably requires
greater attention to preparation and socialization for work.
Since professionalization relies on input controls, it has to depend on highly skilled and motivated people. This is a task that
requires leadership and vision and will take time to accomplish,
but it implies a wider net of responsibilities and commitment.

A fourth and last conclusion is that more professionalization is not always desirable. Professionalization is an alternative
to excessive bureaucratization. Professionals are valued workers,
and there is considerable social pressure to make work more
attractive and therefore more professional. However, it is inevitable that in many circumstances more professionalization does
not make any sense, either because of the nature of the task,
because of other more important goals, or because of the lack
of preparation of the professions themselves.

Our problem is to understand when to attempt to increase the professional role, when not to, and how to do it.

2

How Professionals
Differ From
Conventional Workers

I find it amusing, actually, when Jerome, our
lab technician, takes his uppish stance. "What do
you mean, I have to water the plants too?" he says,
looking like a tired sheep. "You know what I
mean," I tell him. "But it's not my job," he continues. "How do you know it's not your job?" I
ask him. "I am a professional," he answers, "I
work in this lab, I help you with the experiments,
but I should not have to water plants." "Jerome,"
I tell him, "why do you breathe air? Is it professional to breathe air? OK, it's part of living. Well,
it's the same with these here plants. We have to
water plants for them to live, and since I am your
boss, I tell you that is what you have to do."

Jerome is not really a full-fledged professional yet. He is
still a graduate student employed in a university laboratory. He
has a bachelor's degree in biology and is completing a doctorate.
Meanwhile, he has been hired as a lab technician. His task, at
this time, consists of administering different chemicals in the
diet of sets of rats and recording certain patterns of behavior.

Watering two green plants in plastic containers is obviously not part of his contract. But Jerome has not mentioned his contract, nor the national labor union the technicians joined some years back. He mentions his profession.

Jerome is a lab technician who aspires to become a biochemist and a researcher. He has a great interest in understanding about living organisms. He also happens to be a good student, a hard worker, and someone who does not like small talk and trivia. He objects to the many informal transactions that go on normally in work environments and in research laboratories. He does not think he should be asked to perform extra duties like running out to get sandwiches for the rest of the team, or the ultimate indignity, having to water the two green plants by the window. Jerome has a vocation, a commitment to the research enterprise, and he is always anxious to be around when future experiments are discussed. The work he performs requires some dexterity and attention. A good deal of the work is routinized, but he plans on getting ahead and becoming a full-fledged researcher with the title of doctor in front of his name. Meanwhile, he is internalizing the values of the profession, and this is why he always argues when asked to do nonprofessional chores. He wants to learn to behave like the senior members of the team, some of whom he admires greatly.

Characteristics of Professions

Jerome aspires to a profession, but what is a profession? When Carr-Saunders and Wilson wrote their pioneering work on the professions (1933), they were careful to point to the great diversity of vocations that could fall into a definition. At first they avoided any definition. They listed certain significant characteristics. They decided to study certain vocations of ancient lineage that by common consent are called professions, law and medicine among the foremost. In other words, they defined as professions those vocations that were already called professions. They then added other vocations that, though more recent and therefore less firmly established, are nevertheless usually granted professional rank—architecture, engineering, chemistry, accountancy, and surveying.

As their work proceeded, they became more analytical and decided to add selected characteristics. For example, they thought that vocations controlled by the state and therefore obliged to organize like other professions should be included. Here they listed midwives as an example. Finally, they also included vocations that had voluntarily organized, such as brokers. They rejected vocations that claimed to be professions but did not have these attributes. By the time they had completed their survey, they had listed two principal attributes of professions: knowledge base and organization.

Knowledge Base

The professional has techniques and performs specialized tasks that require training or formal education. Historically, the training may have been acquired in apprenticeship schemes. For example, before the creation of law schools, aspiring young lawyers apprenticed themselves with a practitioner who taught them the trade. Law schools came later. Other professions use both formal education and apprenticeship, as is the case in medicine.

The knowledge base may be extant or limited. Medicine or engineering rely heavily on scientific advances, and the education of a doctor or engineer requires considerable time. Law relies on various skills and knowledge: analytical skills, such as the capacities to distinguish some facts from other facts, to separate the relevant from the irrelevant, to sort out a tangle into manageable subcomponents, to examine a problem from close range or from a wider perspective, or to turn around a problem, surveying it from many perspectives; knowledge, such as significant aspects of the law; writing and research skills; familiarity with the institutional and nonlegal environment; and good judgment (Packer and Ehrlich, 1972).

The duration of training reveals the complexity of the field. Most doctors take at least six years to train after college, lawyers three, social workers or teachers at most one or two.

Professionals acquire a responsibility for their knowledge and technique. Their training instills a sense of responsibility for the competent performance of all other professionals. This they manifest in a concern for the honor of all other practitioners

(Carr-Saunders and Wilson, 1933). The term *honor* already suggests a set of values where devotion to the pursuit of the truth
as revealed by professional knowledge is more important, or
should be, than mere pecuniary gain or organizational advancement.

Professional Association

Carr-Saunders and Wilson emphasize the organizational
dimension of professions. The professions are organized, and
they are able to express responsibility for knowledge and technique collectively. The professions—alone or with the assistance
of the state—are able to erect machinery to determine whether
would-be practitioners are competent to practice. They police
access to the profession. It is not sufficient to be able to convince clients that one can perform services. It is necessary to
convince an organization that represents all or most practitioners that one has acquired the necessary skills.

In that perspective, the vocation sometimes labeled "the
oldest profession in the world" is not a profession. Male or female prostitutes do not pass examinations to demonstrate their
skills. They may be organized to defend their economic and
legal interests, they may even train in apprenticeships, but for
the moment at least, and in our Western culture, they do not
transmit to new members specific knowledge and skills that are
then tested. In contrast, the Japanese geisha should be considered a profession since these entertainers demonstrate well-
established sets of skills acquired through a long education.
They are examined by members of the profession who are able
to certify to their competence.

Concern for Clients. Carr-Saunders and Wilson pay special attention to professional concerns for clients. The fact that
clients are dependent on the services of professionals, as in the
case of patients or mothers-to-be for the services of nurses or
midwives, gives these vocations an important professional dimension. The relevant issue here is responsibility. Nurses and
midwives might not have as complex knowledge as doctors, but
they have knowledge or skills clients need but cannot neces-

sarily assess or control. The fact that clients cannot readily recognize charlatans and are, to some extent, at the mercy of the professionals, defines the need for a professional organization, one of whose missions will be to protect clients from potential abuses.

Most professions (with some interesting exceptions, such as policy analyst) have developed codes of conduct and ethics. The primary purpose of these codes is to spell out acceptable or unacceptable behaviors in the client-professional relationship. Again, some professions may have very detailed codes—for example, doctors and particularly psychiatrists—while others may simply have sketchy statements of purpose—for example, teachers.

Control on Accepted Practice. In her study of the rise of professionalism, Magali Sarfatti Larson (1977) emphasizes another aspect of the organizational dimension of professions. She discusses in some detail the way professions come to define what is acceptable knowledge and what is not, and how each profession creates a monopoly that controls what is good practice. Yet the professions are still able to accept new and reject old knowledge, taking into account the client, the public, and, we need also remind ourselves, their own interest.

She describes the case of a well-trained, talented Viennese doctor who, in the 1850s, came up with a speculative theory of humoral pathology based on humors, which had been discredited previously. The theory did not fit the accepted professional knowledge paradigm of the time. Thus, while the theory might have led to the creation of a new school of medicine fifty years earlier, by the mid-1850s the accepted knowledge base made it unacceptable. A young pathologist attacked it publicly, declaring it a "monstrous anachronism" and "it was abandoned, even by the author himself" (p. 33). The profession was strong enough to be able to adopt or reject theories and practices. Doctors who might attempt to stick to unaccepted beliefs would be excluded from the profession.

In some professions, this control may be more relevant than in others, but it is important in all professions because the organization becomes the source of professional legitimacy.

Doctors or lawyers or others act according to accepted precepts about what is good or bad practice. They obtain knowledge, ideas, and examples from their peers, and they also obtain from them definitions of what is acceptable and what is not. When they take risks, they do so in accordance with professional definitions of good or bad risks.

Jerome, if we may come back to him for a brief instance, is a novice entering the profession. However, Jerome is already socialized; he knows what is acceptable behavior and what is not. His main concern is to understand the paradigms of his profession, to internalize the assumptions, concepts, and current practice of scientific inquiry. He is not particularly interested in management issues or in concepts of professionalization. He probably has no intention of reading this book. He is a novice in the job and is insecure about his status. He balks at watering the plants because he feels he has to limit the power of his mentor and employer. In fact, had he acquired self-confidence, had he been fully incorporated in the professional role, he would probably have determined that watering the plants took little time and would have volunteered to do it as long as others cooperated and took on this minor chore also. Jerome is not really very important, although we shall discuss his case again. What is relevant here is that Jerome reveals some of the elements of professionalization, and he also reminds us that professionals espouse values that affect the way they perform in organizations.

Six Elements of a Profession

Since Carr-Saunders and Wilson published their book, much has been written about the professions (Blankenship, 1977; Burke, 1983; Dingwall and Lewis, 1981; Freidson, 1970, 1971; Moore, 1970; Vollmer and Mills, 1966). All these works use definitions of professions that are not too different from those of Carr-Saunders and Wilson. Generally, the definitions include either structural or attitudinal elements, with some overlap. We shall first discuss structural elements, such as knowledge base and association, and then move to attitudinal characteristics such as the common desire of professionals to have discretion in their work.

A compilation of twenty different definitions of professions undertaken by Millerson (quoted in Hickson and Thomas, 1969) provides six basic structural elements: (1) application of skills based on technical knowledge; (2) requirements for advanced education and training; (3) some formal testing of competence and control on admission to profession; (4) existence of professional associations; (5) the existence of codes of conducts or ethics; and (6) the existence of an accepted commitment or calling, or sense of responsibility for serving the public.

Application of Skills Based on Special Knowledge. The professional has special skills and knowledge. Today, the younger and most of the not-so-young managers are usually professionals, and if they have been trained in management, they use theories and concepts derived from several social sciences: decision theory, organization theory, industrial psychology, and so on. Some managers are not trained in management. They may be trained in other professions and later become managers. They learned by doing and they may not feel any need for more advanced managerial training.

The knowledge base provides the basis for professional authority. This means that professionals can exercise power that is considered to be legitimate because they have access to knowledge and skills others do not have *and* because this knowledge is needed in the task situation. Managers also have organizational authority, but this authority derives from their position in the organization. Professional and organizational authority derive from different sources. For example, I may obey you because I know that the board of directors has given you the authority to run the place, or I may obey you because I believe in your management skills and I trust you will make the right decisions. Similarly, I accept the doctor's advice because I know he or she is well trained and knowledgeable and it is for my benefit. But, if I am the hospital manager, I have to exercise my authority, and I sometimes have conflicts with doctors who expect me to provide them with scarce resources.

The professional acquires authority from the knowledge

base, and this professional authority is used in dealing with clients and with the organization. However, some professions have weak knowledge bases—these are often referred to as semiprofessions (Etzioni, 1969)—and the professional authority of these professions is much weaker.

The doctor's authority on the patient may go unchallenged; at most, the patient will seek a second opinion. In any case, the profession will be careful to close rank. In the United States, it is not common for doctors to criticize other doctors in front of patients. They do so among themselves. In other cultures, doctors may more freely talk to patients and more openly disagree among themselves, thus possibly losing and also gaining legitimacy in their eyes.

The semiprofessions have much greater problems maintaining their authority with clients and the organizations in which they serve. They tend to be under constant pressure because their knowledge base is not perceived to be as significantly differentiated. The managerial problems are therefore quite different and the issue of protecting the professions from external pressure may be more important.

Teaching is a good example. As educators are prone to mention, anyone who has gone to school or has children can have strong opinions about education. Teachers have to defend themselves against excessive parent pressures. Becker (1953, p. 129) quotes one such teacher: "One thing, I don't think a parent should try and tell you what to do in your classroom, or interfere in any way with your teaching. I don't think that's right, and I would never permit it. After all, I've a special education to fit me to do what I'm doing, and a great many of them have never had any education at all, to speak of, and even if they did, they certainly haven't had my experience. So, I would never let a parent interfere with my teaching."

This teacher spoke in the early 1950s; today the language would probably be more accommodating. Today's teacher might mention the need to have parents involved, the diversity of cultures, and the responsibility of the school to all communities. But the lack of authority is still present. Here is a teacher I interviewed in the mid-1980s in a small private school attended by the children of upper-middle-class professional parents:

In this town, you have all sorts of professional parents with bright kids and they want all of them to succeed. Practically every parent wants their kid to go to college. They also have very strong opinions about the way I teach. They want me to do all sorts of things. Many of them make sense, but I cannot do everything. They call me on the telephone, they send me written notes, they come to see me—not all of them, thank God, but there are at least five or six very active parents and a few more that have "ideas" to help me or maybe to reform me. I try to channel their interest. Sometimes they help, but more often they are a real pain, a real source of trouble. When they do not get what they want, they complain to the principal, they call some of the school directors, and I spend more time dealing with them than is really worth it. In our school, teachers have to stick together to survive and where you would think having all sorts of bright parents around would be an asset, it turns out it is also a real loss of time. Maybe it is because I am still new here. Some of the older teachers seem to manage better, but I do not know that this is the reason because all the teachers complain about the parents.

By virtue of both the knowledge base and their professional expertise, professionals are endowed with some kind of authority. Some professions have more authority, others have less. This differentiated professional authority across professions has various consequences:

- Some professions need managerial support to maintain their authority with clients and other external forces.
- Some professions are authoritative and challenge the organizational authority of managers, thus creating potential conflict.
- Professional authority derives from the knowledge base. The more the knowledge base is relevant to the task, the greater the professional authority.

Requirements for Advanced Education and Training. Today, most of the more developed professions require formal graduate education beyond college. The semiprofessions require less education, sometimes only a few years in college. There is considerable variety among professions concerning institutional setting, the extent to which knowledge and skills are acquired through academic work or through directed practice, and the length of time required for training. The level of professionalism in an organization is sometimes defined as the extent to which education and training are required for work in that organization. Professionalism is generally measured as the average number of years of education of all employees in the organization. This average may be as high as twenty years in medical and academic organizations, and less than ten in organizations employing fewer professionals (Daft, 1986).

Professionals may be trained in graduate-level professional schools, at colleges or community colleges, in specialized schools, through intensive training schemes, in government or private agencies, and on the job. In general, professionals have to keep up with advances in their profession through in-service or advanced training.

The characteristics of the knowledge base also help distinguish professionals from technical workers. Knowledge that can be used for problem solving tends to be used by professions. Technicians, in contrast, also use specialized knowledge, but it may not be sufficient to allow much discretion. Therefore, their work tends to be more routinized. As we saw, Jerome is still employed as a technician when his longer-term career objective is to become a professional.

Yet managerial approach to technicians and professionals need not depend on the nature of the training, or even on the circumstances of the tasks to be performed. Managers may treat technicians like professionals, and they may also treat professionals like technicians. For example, in some laboratories, technicians are encouraged to identify with professionals, to take responsibilities they might not otherwise take. We always need to keep in mind the characteristics of the task. However, there are also the characteristics of the staff. A well-educated staff will tend to prefer less routinization. When the organization shows overprofessionalism—when the staff is more educated than really required for routinized tasks—management would do better to pay attention to opportunities for increased discretion.

Testing and Control on Admission. Most professions control admission to their ranks. These controls may be incorporated into state requirements for certification and licensing. State or association *certification* usually refers to guarantees of the education and training of professionals, but no more. The word *licensure* usually refers to laws that both regulate the training and also define the scope of activities that constitute the professional practice. Licensure is the most stringent collective control, since it not only regulates who can claim a title, but it also regulates what professionals can and cannot practice. The term *credentialing* is used more generally to refer to all forms of control. The terms *listing* and *registration* refer to less stringent procedures whereby professionals can apply and demonstrate competence for certain practices. For example, the National Register for Health Service Providers in Psychology registers licensed psychologists who meet additional requirements so that they can be identified as providers and be reimbursed by insurers and health programs for mental health services. However, the register does not evaluate their competence for these services; it only lists them (Fretz and Mills, 1980).

Guarantees of education and training are usually based on completion of programs in accredited schools and universities. For example, the American Psychological Association designates the term *psychologist* only for individuals who have completed a doctoral training program in psychology in an accredited institution. For some professions, state certification or licensure requires passage of state examinations, such as the state bar examinations for lawyers.

Professions that have strong collective controls on membership and practice also have strong ties with the centers of learning where professional knowledge is developed and transmitted. The professions influence what happens in the schools and the schools influence what happens in the profession (Houle, 1980; Orlans, 1975; Roemer, 1974; Selden, 1960,

1976, 1979). Ever since the American Medical Association published the first list of classified, and therefore acceptable, schools in 1906, educators have paid closer attention to the professions they serve. Many undesirable medical degree mills closed their doors after the AMA intervened. Today all professions keep close contact with the professional schools that serve them.

All professions define the acceptable paradigm of their practice. The schools are integral participants in this process. Sometimes the schools move the profession ahead and sometimes the profession redirects the schools. When the schools go too far ahead or afield, the professions retract their support. It is no accident that the School of Criminology at the University of California at Berkeley closed in 1976. Professional law enforcement groups believed it had left mainstream American thinking about law enforcement. Some members of the faculty had become visible critics of current law enforcement practices, calling for large-scale social reforms. Some professionals in the field found their criticisms to be too close to revolutionary rhetoric. External support for the school dwindled, and it was abolished without much fuss. Professional schools on the campuses of state universities always have a responsibility to their field constituency. They cannot move too far ahead of prevalent thought within the profession. And, even when they innovate in desired directions, they cannot move too fast.

While some professions closely control who can practice, others do not. They are not regulated by the state, and market mechanisms operate freely. These professions are usually in sectors where client protection is far less important. For example, the artistic professions such as photography, commercial art, and interior designing do not commonly entail state certification. Anyone can practice photography professionally or become an interior designer or work as a commercial artist. Yet professional training may be extensive and time-consuming.

Market-controlled professions can be highly competitive, particularly if the work is attractive, as in the artistic professions. Highly competitive professions tend to have special problems of their own. Competition for jobs and advancement generates considerable intraprofessional conflict. Managing these professionals requires far greater attention to the possibilities of conflict, to professionals' aspirations, and to the need for visibility and credit. It also requires care not to downgrade professional identity and dignity and to foster teamwork.

Professional Associations. As Carr-Saunders emphasized, professions are organized into associations that represent, control, and set policies for the entire profession. These associations are supported by their membership, and they are therefore oriented to the needs of their members. They pursue objectives designed to enhance the well-being, status, recognition, and quality of the profession. The associations play a central role in government regulation of the professions. They are the principal proponents for certification or licensure from the state. This leads to interprofessional conflicts that can be bitterly fought. For example, the American Association of Marriage and Family Therapists, the American Association of Sex Educators, Counselors and Therapists, and the American Mental Health Counselors Association have all had problems defining and defending their turf and protecting themselves from complaints or encroachments from these and from other professions. These battles can be protracted. And while they take place in legislatures or in the courts, they can spill into the daily life of organizations employing contending professionals.

Conflicts between associations are often the result of past conflicts within associations. When different schools of thought emerge, it is not uncommon for professions to split and divide, creating various independent associations that inevitably overlap in practice, clients, or tasks. In any case, the trend is toward increasing numbers of associations, reaching into the thousands (Gruber and Cloyd, 1986).

The bureaucratization of professional work conditions is resulting in widespread unionization of professional workers. Professionals have turned to unions, just like other workers, to negotiate working conditions. At times, the unionization of professional workers runs contrary to professional values espoused by associations. For example, budget constraints have led many salaried doctors and lawyers to join unions. The AFL-CIO has a department actively organizing these professionals. The American Bar Association stipulates that an attorney cannot "abandon" a client. But with overcrowded courts, Legal Aid lawyers, public defenders, and district attorneys find themselves overburdened with more cases than they can handle. This is an instance where professional associations have not been helpful and unions stepped in. Unionized lawyers in some courts have staged small strikes to demand lighter case loads (Waldman, 1986). Unionization of professional workers does not reduce their importance, but it can complicate management's relationship with them.

Codes of Ethics. All professions define or are concerned with the ethics of their role, with what is proper and what is not. The stronger professions that are well organized have adopted codes of conduct and ethics that define desirable patterns of behavior intended to protect the public, the clients, and the profession (Barber, 1978; Bayle, 1981; Camenish, 1983; Goldman, 1980; Rohr, 1978). These codes are necessarily limited to well-defined practices. More importantly, they are not always easily enforced (Abel, 1981; Rhode, 1981). Yet we do know that the stronger professional associations police and reprimand the more obvious and visible challenges to their codes. For example, several lawyers involved in the Watergate scandal of the Nixon administration were reprimanded or disbarred by the American Bar Association.

Codes of ethics are designed to protect both the professions and their clients or the public. Most codes of conduct or ethics tend to be written from the client-practitioner perspective. From management's point of view, problems may arise when the ethics of the profession clash with organizational interests.

Organizational codes of conduct tend to define the general do's and don't's of professional service in specific organizations. For example, we may have codes of conduct for the Foreign Service, the Forest Service, the Teacher Corps, and the like, but these codes are not always operational, and they rarely address issues of potential conflict between organizational mandates and perceived professional responsibility. These issues are becoming more important in an age of increasing technological complexity where decisions made in the context of single organizations can have very significant repercussions for the general public or for nonmembers of the organization who may be affected. Problems of pollution, land poisoning, chemical dumps, or the risk of grave accidents, for instance, have sharpened professional concerns that go beyond the organizations involved (Martin and Schinzinger, 1983; Schaub and Pavlovic, 1983; Unger, 1982).

The problem has two distinct dimensions. First, we can discuss professional commitment and definition of client. The issue centers around assumptions of responsibility. Are professionals exclusively at the service of the organizational employer? Or are they responsible to a larger public? We will discuss this last issue at greater length later in this chapter when we address the value attitudes of professionals, but it is obvious that management is centrally concerned with understanding how professionals perceive the issue. Do professionals place the values of the organization above those of the clients or of the general public?

The second dimension of the problem is the potential impact of ethical or nonethical acts on the perceived legitimacy of the profession. If professionals are perceived to act as mere employees, do they reduce their legitimacy and therefore the authority of the profession? Their issues are quite important to professions involved in advocacy. If expert economists can testify to any side of a policy, or if various expert psychiatrists can be employed both by the prosecution and the defense and disagree, does this, in the long run, erode the credibility of the professions? Several professional associations, including the American Economic Association, have begun discussing this issue. They urge less militancy and advocacy and more objectivity from their members (Evangelauf, 1986).

One good illustration is provided by policy analysts. This profession is relatively new; it is organized and has its own association. Since policy analysts work for very sophisticated clients —large corporations or nonprofit or government agencies—there is not much need for client protection. There has been no effort to regulate the profession, and it is obvious that enforcement of regulations, particularly a code of ethics, would not be easy. And yet, one should be concerned about the way policy analysts define their role. Whom should they work for? Whose interests do they pursue? Are they to work exclusively for their employers or are they responsible to a larger constituency? Do they have a public trust responsibility? A code would not alter individual commitment, but it could alter public perceptions of the legitimacy of the profession. One can certainly imagine that policy analysts might have to disclose who pays for studies or in whose employ they work.

When all is said and done, professionals in public and private service must be able to convince the general public that they are able to render difficult moral judgments and that they are not using their professional prestige to favor narrow interests (Benveniste, 1984; Fleishman and Payne, 1980; Foster, 1981; Varga, 1980).

This does not mean that it is easy to upgrade the apparent morality of professionals. But it does suggest that management cannot be indifferent to what happens to the legitimacy of the professions, and that management needs to be prepared for situations where professional dissent within the organization challenges management authority.

Altruistic Responsibility: A Calling. Many professions instill a sense of duty, a love of the work, and a commitment to humanity that has nothing to do with pecuniary rewards. The notion that professionals do good to individuals and society differentiates these vocations from other work. It gives the professions an appeal of a quasireligious character that has much to do with making some of the professions far more attractive than they might be otherwise.

American teachers are rarely attracted to their profession by high salaries, prestigious career prospects, or high status in the local community. Generally, teachers enter teaching because they enjoy children and because they believe it to be an important societal function (Lortie, 1975). We interviewed teachers in a recent study on the professionalization of teaching. Most stressed their commitment to teaching; 92 percent indicated that teaching was most important to the long-term interests of society and 60 percent still thought that teaching was characterized by a high degree of idealism and devotion (Losk, 1986).

Some professions institutionalize this commitment by asking their members to devote time to meritorious causes. Thus, the American Bar Association model code of professional responsibility includes language about lawyers having a responsibility for *pro bono* work. The code suggests they perform at least forty hours a year for zero or much-reduced fee. Even if the idealized vision of a calling is not always implemented or even practical, it still highlights the potential importance of this sense of responsibility in many professions, particularly in the helping professions such as health care, teaching, and social work.

The notion of a calling affects the orientation of professionals to the organizational work situation because it affects their motivation for work, and management must pay attention. In the absence of strong extrinsic economic rewards, strong intrinsic rewards about the importance of work matter more. If teachers come to teaching because they love to work with children and are committed to contributing to the general well-being of the community, or if health and social workers are committed to alleviating suffering, it behooves management to give these workers a sense of efficacy, a sense that their devotion is not in vain. This is doubly important when work conditions are difficult, career opportunities are limited, and economic rewards unattractive. Much of the mismanagement of these professions results from the erosion of their sense of commitment—either because they are asked to perform tasks they cannot accomplish, or, as in many social delivery services, because they are also evaluated negatively by the public when they fail to achieve what cannot be achieved.

Policies to enhance professional commitment will be more important in professions that have difficulty attracting or retaining new recruits. Professions such as teaching, nursing, and social work used to rely on female recruits because employment in other sectors was not then readily available to women. With the advent of affirmative action and the emancipation of women in the labor force, these professions can no longer rely on a guaranteed labor pool. This is another reason why management has to be concerned with the professional attitudes and values of these professions.

Professional Attitudes and Values

We turn now to the attitudes and values of professionals, which are significant because they shape the way professionals adapt in the organization.

A classic paper on professional values was written by Hall in the late 1960s. He focused on five principal attitudes (as distinguished from the characteristics of professions, which we have just covered, although some overlap): (1) the belief that the profession is a significant reference group and the source of major ideas and judgments; (2) a belief in service to the public; the idea that the profession is indispensable and that professional work benefits public and practitioners; (3) a desire for autonomy in work situations; (4) preference for self-regulation, particularly for peer control and review; and (5) the notion of a calling, of a devotion to the work even if less extrinsic rewards are provided.

Hall used these attitudes to develop a scale of professionalization. He was careful to point out that professions vary among themselves and that, even within well-established professions, members would vary in their conformity to such values. Nevertheless, these are the delicate values managers have to take into account when dealing with professionals (Hall, 1968; Snizek, 1972).

Professionals Want Their Profession as a Significant Reference Group. Hall was interested in the way professionals pay attention to their peers. These are the people who will have ideas that may be useful in the work. These peers may be inside or outside the organization. The links may be formal or informal.

The main reason Hall thought peers to be relevant is that they enable professionals to keep in touch with new advances in the field. A second factor is related to professional careers. Hall did not discuss this in his paper, but it is clear that professionals pursue careers where professional visibility and status are important. Professional evaluators, either internal or external, may be more important to career advancement than the evaluations of immediate supervisors. Informal linkages and recognition may be more important than formal job relations. I once interviewed an economist then on the staff of an international agency we were considering for employment at Stanford Research Institute. She told me:

> The men who run this place are not going anywhere. They have reached the peak of their careers. Unfortunately, they do not seem to care about ours. They seem to think that working for [the agency] is sufficient and good enough or should be enough for all of us. All of our work has to be anonymous. None of our reports are ever published under our own names. It is always an anonymous product. They say this gives more authority to our pronouncements and more legitimacy to the agency. Presumably, it is also for our own good. They say it protects us, but I do not need that kind of protection—it sure does not help with my career. I do not get much visibility here. Some people know what I do, but who are they? I can name most of them. I tell you, there is no way I can stay here too long. I would become like them —ossified, like these old men.

Professionals in organizations usually occupy successive positions and, therefore, pursue organizational careers (Glazer, 1968). These careers can involve more than one organization, but even when the entire career takes place in a single organization, professional workers look to other professionals to evaluate their work. Some pursue "open sector" careers, in the sense that their career is professional skill-oriented—what matters is not knowledge of any specific sector, such as banking, education, or transportation, but a set of professional skills they can use anywhere. Many lawyers, engineers, computer specialists, system analysts, or economists use their professional knowledge in many different organizational settings. Engineers and lawyers often move from firm to firm or even from government to the private sector. Few lawyers pursue careers in the Department of Justice, but many young lawyers start there and after several years move on to more lucrative private employment or to other positions in the administration. This results in high turnover and relative youth of the professional staff (Horowitz, 1977b). For these professionals, the career requires visibility quite independently from the success of the organization. They need to be able to point to their own contribution as professionals. For them, colleagues outside their organizations and sector are most relevant.

In contrast, other professionals pursue closed-sector careers. Doctors and allied health workers have careers in health, teachers and professors work in education, and so on. These professionals tend to be judged, at least in part, by the success of their organizations. Yet, even in the case of closed-sector careers, professional evaluators are important. Doctors rely heavily on referrals by colleagues, professors who transfer university are often invited by colleagues, even teachers who are formally evaluated by administrators pay attention to colleagues. For example, as Becker (1952) pointed out, teachers pursue careers by moving from less desirable to more desirable schools, and they tend to keep moving until they find a school that they like and that is convenient for them.

The young economist I interviewed is no different from the young lawyers at the Justice Department or from teachers seeking a better school. The relevant evaluators for their careers are other colleagues who will notice their professional work, who may be instrumental in their progress. They probably do not even know who these people might be, but that does not make them less important. Their career and status as professionals depend on their professional visibility. The fact that they may be invited to address their professional society, or publish professional works, or receive professional prizes and recognition is very relevant to them.

The young economist was quite unhappy because her agency did not allow authors to use their name on the reports they produced (Stanford Research Institute did at that time). While she was known in inner circles working close to her field, she knew that her longer-term career had to take place in a much broader arena. She left a good position in an important international agency located in Paris to come to the West Coast. Salary was not the issue, professional visibility was what mattered to her. The international agency lost talent because of a policy that did not pay attention to this professional value. In many situations managers can easily provide visibility to their professionals and, in so doing, increase their commitment to the organization.

Professionals identify both with the organization they work for and with the profession. Organizational loyalty is not enhanced by downgrading the values of professionals. The "old men" who ran the international agency were not obtaining greater loyalty by keeping reports anonymous, nor were they enhancing the legitimacy of the reports. Stanford Research Institute was able to keep very good talent for the opposite reason, namely, that it provided a very visible niche from which one could move anywhere.

Alvin Gouldner (1957) alluded to all this some time ago in his seminal article about cosmopolitans and locals. He pointed out that cosmopolitans in organizations share their loyalty between the employing organization and their commitment to specialized role skills. These experts are never committed to a single organization even if they spend their entire working life in one. They are understood to be committed to professional values, values that are also important to the organization. This is in contrast to locals, who are only committed to the organization but may have less to contribute to it.

The second manager of Applied Research (see Chapter One) came into a situation where the senior professional staff was quite dispirited. As you will recall, the first manager controlled the professional staff closely, even changed every comma of the reports they wrote. The second manager was subtly concerned with the issue of professional cosmopolitanism:

When I came, I knew [her predecessor] had
not treated the staff properly. He had an autocratic
way to run things. He never, or nearly never, consulted the senior staff. Project managers were given
tasks, and when the pressure went up, he would
suddenly call someone and say, "Look Joe, drop
what you are doing on that comparative cost study
and get into this one. They need an answer in two
weeks." No discussion, no assessment of where the
staff was, what they were doing. I allowed the
senior staff to sit with me and understand the pressures we were under. It did not completely relieve
the complaining, but it made me aware of their
problems and they knew what I was doing. Looking back on those years, I guess I did give them
much more information—some of which they never
really could handle, but some of which they could
deal with. In any case, they knew I treated them as
equals. I also wanted them to feel good about their
work and to look good to the professional community in town. They knew I had to make difficult
decisions, but they also knew I paid attention to
the way projects were run. I was not like [the first
manager], arbitrarily cutting off some interviewers
in the field without batting an eye about how long
it would take to get that job back on track. I knew
his reputation and the reasons he had acquired it.
I also knew our outfit was not considered a good
place to work in. I wanted none of that for my
own reputation and for our shop. It did no good to
our image in the profession, and it did no good to
the image of the profession.

Professionals Believe in Public Service. Hall paid attention
to the orientation of professionals toward larger problems that
transcend organizational boundaries. He was interested in the
way professionals legitimize their role, what gives them a right
to feel that they could look beyond organizational mandates,

what gives them a right to be cosmopolitans instead of locals. He focused on the way professionals perceive the indispensability of their profession, on their belief that their work benefits the public and the practitioners. These attitudes are related to seeing the profession as a "calling," which we discussed and will discuss later, but they are also related to the universalistic values of science and progress that underpin most professional training. Professionals are not trained to espouse a narrow organizational perspective. They look at problems in a context that goes beyond the boundaries of the organization. They take a universalistic perspective. If they are not locals, committed to the organization, they are cosmopolitans, committed to a larger good.

Managers have problems with this. Organizational values and realities are tangible, whereas the "public good" or "doing the right thing" are not easily defined. When should management recognize a bona fide professional concern? How can this concern be recognized as such when it has immediate negative consequences on organizational performance? Can any engineer who expresses qualms about company products stop the production line? Much has recently been written about professional ethics versus organizational goals, particularly for the engineering profession (Kohn and Hughson, 1980; Luegenbiehl, 1983; Martin and Schinzinger, 1983; Schaub and Pavlovic, 1983; Unger, 1982). Similarly, there has been a lot said and written about managing professional dissent in organizations and, more specifically, the problem—or opportunities—provided by professional whistleblowers (Anderson, 1980; Bowman, Elliston, and Lockhart, 1984; Elliston, Keenan, Lockhart, and Schaick, 1985; James, 1980; Perrucci, 1980; Westin, 1981).

The question is how to enhance the sense of professional responsibility and reach professional consensus and decisions without having to suffer the costs of professional alienation and dissent. The point of departure is not whether alienation is inevitable and professional dissent has to be tolerated. Management's problem consists in recognizing that professional dissent is natural and that it is management's task to understand it and use it beneficially. Professional values need not hamper organizational objectives.

Professional management takes these values for granted. Organizational strategy considers the costs of going with or against these values. There may exist situations where professional values are not useful, when organizational imperatives have to prevail. But management's choice takes into account the consequences: misunderstanding and potential alienation of valued workers. It is not feasible to manage professionals and to systematically oppose their values.

Professionals Desire Autonomy. Professionals prefer work situations where they are able to organize themselves and determine how they will perform the task. This does not mean that they prefer solitude. It is often said that teachers have considerable autonomy since they can close the door of their classroom and be left alone with their pupils, but that is solitude, not autonomy. Teachers work alone, but they are not autonomous. They are rarely given collective opportunities to run things, to decide what they should teach, how to teach it, and how they might organize themselves.

Concern for autonomy, self-organization, and increased discretion and responsibility has been the hallmark of the quality of work life (QWL) movement. While QWL people are concerned with workers in general, they reflect deeply ingrained professional values. Ever since the first international conference on quality of work life in 1972, the QWL movement has been encouraging greater autonomy and self-regulation and has been decrying such things as excessive surveillance and discipline, regimentation, routinization, and the resulting alienation of the workforce (Goodman, 1979; Herrick, 1983; Meltzer and Nord, 1981; Toch and Grant, 1984). However, the major QWL experiment at the Rushton coal mine in western Pennsylvania lasted only from 1973 to 1979. It came to an end for many reasons, the principal one being that all the changes in work organization were never really institutionalized. While workers were expected to have greater responsibilities, management rarely expected their own roles to change. Gradually, the entire effort came to very little and the project was abandoned.

We are not reviewing QWL here, but its lessons are relevant to professional management because the same problems exist. Efforts to increase professional responsibility inevitably imply modifications of professional and managerial roles. For example, one cannot create totally different career roles for teachers without paying attention to the way these changes affect and therefore modify the principal's role.

The relevant issue is that professionals aspire to greater autonomy. Whether greater autonomy makes sense depends first on task circumstances and conditions and, second, on staff capability and aspirations. It does not depend on management's need to maintain its authority. Organizational authority is different from professional authority (see Chapter Three), and it is not a zero-sum game. The common managerial mistake is to assume that any authority given to professionals is authority taken away from management, but this is unrealistic. Authority or power does not evaporate when the task benefits from shared responsibility—it increases. It does evaporate when the task does not benefit. If a manager gives responsibilities to professionals that they cannot handle, both their professional and managerial authority will suffer.

It is an understanding of the task and of professional capability that determines how much autonomy professionals should have. Good examples are planners and policy analysts. These experts tend to prefer to work with their colleagues and to have as little contact as possible with politicians, the public, or some of the clients they serve. Here autonomy can be dysfunctional. This happens when planners disregard the realities of the field, the desires of clients, or the implementing capability of the agencies they serve. In these instances, managers have to encourage these professionals to plunge into reality and get their hands dirty.

Professionals Prefer Self-Regulation and Peer Review. Since professionals use knowledge and skills that are not readily accessible to the nonprofessional, it is reasonable for professionals to expect that peers should evaluate them. Thus, professors in research universities are evaluated by other professors who read their work, assess their teaching performance, and evaluate them on other criteria. The final responsibility for retaining, promoting, or terminating faculty is usually shared between the university administration and the various faculty groups performing these evaluations, but the administrators do not conduct the evaluation. These are undertaken by colleagues. In most American universities these processes are confidential, to provide frank assessments. However, secrecy is not always the norm in peer evaluation. Some research organizations, particularly in Europe, use open processes to select candidates for promotions.

The university peer model is not followed in most other organizational settings. The common situation is that performance evaluations are a managerial responsibility, a difficult task that has to be undertaken periodically, probably far too often. Why is it difficult?

First, because professional work is difficult to evaluate. Desirable criteria for evaluation are not always available or agreed upon and appropriate measurements not easily obtained. Organizations often employ individuals from various professions doing different work. The conventional wisdom in personnel evaluation is to develop clear and well-understood objective criteria that can be routinely administered. Subjective criteria are suspect because no one knows exactly what they are.

Therefore, does the manager evaluate everyone using a standard set of objective criteria based on outputs? On client assessments? On personality traits? Or does the manager devise separate assessments for each professional? Is output the desirable measure or is the effort put into the task more significant? Suppose you decide to evaluate teachers on the basis of the success of their pupils; are you evaluating the teacher or are you evaluating the distribution of bright children in the class? And if you decide to look at effort, how do you measure it? By the number of hours spent on the task? We all know that number of hours on task does not necessarily reflect effort. What time perspective should be used? Does the manager focus on short-term or long-term achievement?

We will discuss these issues at greater length in Chapter Five, but the point is that the use of objective criteria in professional evaluation is fraught with problems and usually results in professional or management dissatisfaction. For example, a recently published discussion by managers of investment analysts and portfolio managers highlights the advantages and disadvantages of objective and subjective criteria in profession-oriented firms. As the manager of an investment firm points out, formulas are easier to understand, but they can also lead to undesirable manipulation. These managers seem to prefer, or more exactly recognize, that sooner or later subjective criteria dominate and the manager and professional had better be aware of this (Vertin, 1984).

Objective criteria work well in routinized and predictive tasks and are ill suited to discretionary tasks. This is to be expected since objective criteria are themselves routines. What is left? The subjective assessments of the managers or of others. To be sure, objective criteria may be used to justify decisions, and rating scales, checklists, or other techniques may be useful in shaping subjective assessment, but in the final analysis, managers will be stuck with having to make subjective judgments. The real question becomes, are such judgments better made by managers, by professionals, or by both?

The second problem with evaluation is that it can affect learning on the job, either enhancing or deterring. To learn, one needs to make mistakes. Work that requires adaptation or problem solving is learning work. One does not learn that fire is hot and painful without a slight burn. Evaluation can be a learning experience, a way to find out what others think of one's work, what might be continued, what might be changed, what mistakes are being made. But when evaluation is tied to reward and punishment so that professionals perceive that evaluations will be used to judge whether they will be promoted, the learning process is affected. Unless management has made it clear that it expects mistakes, even wants them, professionals will want to look good and everybody will attempt to look as if they knew what they were doing, even if they have no idea how to proceed.

Conventional wisdom about evaluation is not necessarily useful in the management of professionals; the problem requires much consideration and thought. We will discuss this at greater length in Chapter Seven.

Professionals See Their Work as a Calling. Hall noted that
the strength of professional commitment is not always related
to how established or powerful the profession might be. He
found that some well-established professions showed less commitment than newly emerging professions with fewer extrinsic
rewards for their members (Hall, 1968). One can surmise that
professions that require difficult or less pleasant work, or that
offer few economic incentives, attract individuals with greater
commitment. Or turning the argument around, that individuals
with greater commitment do not need as many economic incentives to perform difficult but important tasks.

The notion of a calling means that those professions
where work conditions are difficult or economic incentives are
insufficient tend to rely more on the self-motivation of their
members. Managing these professionals can be compared to
managing volunteers. Most nurses, allied health workers, teachers, librarians, editors, social workers, doctors, and psychiatrists
fall in this category. Even among other professions—engineering,
architecture, law, accounting, pharmacy, real estate, planning,
and so on—one will find strong pockets of committed professionals who are working at tasks they know are very difficult,
dangerous, or poorly paid, that do not necessarily provide much
status or other extrinsic rewards, but are nevertheless important
to them.

These professionals are motivated, but their motivation is
centered on ways to perform the task they believe in. They
come to the organization with their own sets of values and goals
and, in the absence of sufficient extrinsic rewards, want to
experience the good days, when the work goes well, when their
commitment is fulfilled. Some sense of success is important to
maintain their commitment. We already pointed out that managerial practices that emphasize the negative do not encourage
these quasi-volunteer workers. Management has to be able to
nurture and defend the commitment of professionals. This is
why positive rewards and feedback are so much more important
to this kind of committed professional than they are to ordinary
workers. The comparison with volunteer work explains why:
one does not manage a volunteer organization by constant pun-

ishing, making volunteers feel unwanted, or providing excessive criticism.

Similarly, managers who disregard the professional goals of workers downgrade their commitment. The successful manager of the volunteer organization knows that the volunteers have to feel they are getting something for their contribution. These managers pay attention to the goals of the various groups who are willing to work for them. At times it may mean that the organization changes its own goals or adopts successive goals to reflect the pleasures of the membership. Since people are attracted for their own individual reasons, the working volunteers have many different agendas and do not easily reach a consensus about priorities for action. The dilemma of all volunteer organizations resides just there: how to build consensus and commitment among the membership without fragmenting in several directions at once (Benveniste, 1981). The dilemma is no less important in most professional organizations, and the manager must know how to maintain commitment and devotion while keeping the organization on line.

Conclusion

Professions differ markedly. Some professions are well established with long historical traditions; others are recent and emerging, which means that role definitions are not always well understood.

Some professions rely on a substantive body of knowledge that make them quite impervious to nonprofessional pressures on how they perform most of their professional work. Other professions rely on a less substantive body of knowledge and are therefore far more subject to pressures from external forces: their clients, lay managers, or the general public.

Some professions rely heavily on the commitment of their members and have few extrinsic rewards to offer; other professions offer considerable extrinsic rewards. But all professions rely in one way or another on the commitment of their members. The management of professionals has many similarities with the management of volunteers.

　　　We examined what makes a profession what it is, the importance of the knowledge base and of professional organizations. From the manager's point of view, there is an important difference between professional and nonprofessional workers. Professional workers are motivated by professional goals, pursue professional careers, and respond to professional controls. They are cosmopolitans within the organization. Managing professionals requires paying attention to their dual allegiances. In practice, this means the manager must be sensitive to the nature and realities of the career objectives of professionals, a recognition that the commitment of a calling has to be reinforced by the requirements of a potential career. The successful professional organization is one where professionals can pursue successful professional careers.

　　　We paid attention to areas of potential conflict between line management and professionals. Professionals' greater commitment to the public and management's greater commitment to the organization can be a source of conflict. Whistleblowing, a common practice these days, illustrates one well-known managerial problem. Professionals' concern with peer evaluation and control emerges from the complexity of evaluating professional work. The issue of managerial versus peer evaluation is another source of potential conflict. Professional desire for autonomy in work situations may be the most complex issue facing management. We suggested that implementing greater professional autonomy inevitably requires altering management roles and that such changes may create conflicts. Conflicts between professional and organizational goals can also tax management. We suggested that managers had to find ways to seek professional consensus so as to channel professional energy in directions beneficial to the organization.

　　　Professional management is inevitably messy. It is not as amenable to rationality, precise ordering, and ends/means calculation as some textbooks on administration would like us to believe. Creativity takes place in learning situations. Learning situations require autonomy, discretion, and motivation. They require also the possibility of making mistakes and learning from them. But autonomy and discretion engender ambiguity, so the organization can go in any direction. Resolving ambiguity is management's task. The management of professionals requires an understanding of the professions. This is why many line managers may also be professionals. It also requires a willingness to deal with intuitive subjective judgments, not to expect that rational objective tools are sufficient, even if they are helpful.

Remember Jerome, whom we left watering plants at the beginning of this chapter? Jerome is an aspiring professional, learning the culture of professionalism. He has a boss who happens not to have too much regard for students or technicians. His boss, Frank, is both a professional (a very distinguished professor of biology, at that) and a line administrator. He manages, with the help of an administrative assistant and another colleague, various grants and contracts from the National Institute of Health.

Frank never reads textbooks on management. He was never trained in management. He learned the skill by doing, by having to manage the long succession of grants and contracts he has obtained from the government. He did a stint at Dow Chemical for one year and was a noncommissioned officer in the army during World War II. He knows biology, and he also knows the perfidies, jealousies, and endless battles of academia. He has become a respected member of the faculty, someone who understands power and can deal effectively with his colleagues. He has recently served as chairman of his department and is under consideration for appointment as dean.

He is somewhat abrasive and not everyone enjoys working in his laboratory. He is definitely autocratic. His technicians are mostly graduate students. His management style consists of giving orders, and he expects a lot of work from them. He rarely has close contacts with his workers, although he keeps a sharp eye on their performance and is quick to catch mistakes. Some of his colleagues who dislike him suggest that his students really have the ideas and that he simply uses them and exploits them. The young technicians fear him, but Frank knows that in science, like in everything else, there is no place for sentimentality. "They might as well learn what life is about," he sometimes says. Jerome does not like him. "I do not give a damn about the project," he says. "I only care about getting my dissertation out of the way. Much of that work is wasted motion anyhow."

Yet Frank is very successful. He has run many projects, completed much work, published widely, and considers himself a successful research laboratory manager. He is not much concerned with any of the issues raised here. We need to be reminded that there are many ways to manage. Frank is probably successful because he is a top-notch biologist, and the commitment and allegiance of his workers is not that important to his success. He must also get strong support from some students and co-workers who admire his work and want to be associated with him. His operation is small. His laboratory is not a bureaucracy even if the university in which it is located is. Maybe Frank does not have to concern himself with motivation and participation. Maybe he should. Maybe he would be more successful if he did. He has not asked my advice.

3

Improving
the Relationship Between
Managers and Professionals

The relationship between managers and professionals differs from that between managers and other workers. One reason is that their mutual power and authority are different. To understand why this is so, we first discuss the concepts of power and authority, and then contrast professional with managerial authority. This allows us to examine the concepts of envelope supervision and of joint managerial-professional tasks. With these tools in hand, we proceed to discuss various governance structures.

Power

Power is the ability to get things done, to surmount resistances. Max Weber, the German sociologist, defined power (*Macht*) as "the probability that one actor within a social relationship will be in a position to carry out his own will despite resistance, regardless of the basis on which this probability rests" ([1922] 1964, p. 152). The notion of resistance need not bring to mind the exercise of coercive power. There may be different kinds of resistances: things fail to happen because no one was instructed, or because no one knows how to perform, or because we are in conflict and do not agree how to proceed.

The concept of power is much more than just pushing people around or even, God forbid, using physical violence. It is the ability to get results where these results would not happen otherwise, results that everyone may seek to achieve. Some authors like to distinguish between "getting things done" and "hierarchical domination," to point out that empowering others, namely giving everyone some control over the way they work, is a way to get more done (Kanter, 1977). But, strictly speaking, the concept of power includes both notions.

It is conventional wisdom in organizations to assume that power is a finite attribute of relationships, that there is just so much power around and no more. If I have some power, then I must hold on to it. If I let others have their way, I will lose my power as they gain theirs. This may be good for them, but not for me. This imagery deters one from delegating or granting discretionary rights, since such action is weakening, but it disregards where power comes from.

Power is not a finite attribute of relationships because power comes out of needs. If I need you and you do not need me, you will acquire some power over me. I will be asking favors from you, but there is nothing I can give you in exchange since you do not need me. You will then have power over me because I will readily respond to any demand you make. If I do not need you but you need me, then I acquire power over you. Emerson (1962) has pointed out that power relationships are the inverse of these needs, or dependencies, as he called them. In other words, if we both need each other, but I need you more, then you will have some power over me. Our mutual dependencies are unequal. When mutual dependencies are unequal, power emerges in the relationship. But when you need me as much as I need you, our power relationship is balanced.

The classical example is the triad love relationship. Mary and Peter, high school sweethearts, have some disagreements, but they also have many good times. They seem to love each other equally; they both contribute to each other's happiness. They need each other and their relationship is more or less stable because neither can really contemplate life without the other. The day Mary meets John, things change radically. Mary discovers she likes John very much and finds him very attractive. She still has Peter in tow because she still loves him. Now both young men phone her for dates. She finds she has to make choices but each of them does not have the same opportunity —at least not yet. The dependencies have shifted. In her relationship with Peter, Mary needs Peter much less since John is now available and inviting her. Yet, with John, Mary has considerable leeway since she can still turn back to Peter and accept his earlier invitation. Thus, Mary acquires some power over both her suitors. The day either Peter or John gets tired of the situation or meets someone else, Mary's power evaporates. Meanwhile, she can tease each of them and drive them frantic. As Emerson suggested, power emerges out of unequal dependencies.

Authority in Organizations

How does this apply to organizational life? Where do organizational power and authority come from? First, let us define the term *authority:* the legitimate use of power. The supervisor gives orders and they are believed to be proper, part of his job. Authority rights come with positions in organizations: "He is the supervisor. His role is to assess work conditions, make task assignments, and evaluate performance." In other words, the organization invents authority. When we design the organization and we say that there will be three managers reporting to the assistant director and that the managers will each be responsible for X, Y, and Z, we are inventing authority rights. Later, the managers are hired and they exercise the authority vested in them.

The reason we invented these authority rights has to do with the task. When we sat around discussing how to run things, we had ideas about what had to be done. We said someone has to assign tasks, otherwise they will not get done. Someone has to process patients and schedule appointments, someone has to handle complaints, someone has to deal with the press. Then we thought that someone should supervise the work and see how well it is performed, and someone should take a broader look and make sure the way we are organized makes sense, and last-ly, taking the broadest look, someone should think about why we are doing what we are doing and ask whether we should do something else. All these organizational tasks create needs and dependencies. Line authority is invented to meet them.

We can observe this by studying what people do. How does this assistant director spend her time? She spends it re-solving conflicts between the production and marketing people. Where does her authority come from? At one level, we answer, "Her authority comes from the fact the board and the managing director created the job and gave it these responsibilities." At another level, we say, "Her authority comes from the fact that she solves problems. If she did not intervene, there would be much more friction. Production and marketing people would be at each other's throat. They need her and this is why they re-spect her." Getting things done gives her authority, not the title on the door, although the title on the door permits her to do things. Therefore, authority and power come from being able to meet needs and simultaneously from being asked to meet these needs.

The classic study of this phenomenon was reported by Crozier (1964), who studied the operations of a government monopoly producing cigarettes in France. He observed a typi-cal cigarette factory with production workers whose task was to operate cigarette-making machines. These workers were on piece rate, that is, paid in proportion to their output. They were controlled by supervisors who were their hierarchical superiors. But Crozier noticed that the production workers were far more influenced by the maintenance workers than by their super-visors. More power, in that task situation, was held by mainte-nance workers than by supervisors. Why? Crozier explained that the production workers were anxious to reduce machine stop-pages to maximize pay. They were highly dependent on the good will and responsiveness of the maintenance workers. The maintenance men could help them where their supervisors could not: they were the only ones who could maintain and repair equipment when needed. Thus, the production workers were consistently trying to please and cajole the maintenance workers to ensure prompt service. They needed the maintenance workers but the maintenance crew did not need them. Out of this state of affairs a power relationship developed.

The point was that the line supervisors who were given authority over the production workers had less real authority than the maintenance workers who could meet their dependencies. This led to instability when maintenance workers did not reinforce the directives of the supervisors.

Professional Versus Managerial Authority: Common Problems

In the mid-1970s, Florence, an experienced nurse, and two friends initiated an important citywide program for battered women. At the time, federal and state monies were more readily available and community funding permitted the program to grow rapidly, and the issue of battered women attracted considerable attention. Florence's small program, called the Refuge, grew rapidly. She easily found volunteers to work with her and, in due time, hired a small group of devoted and committed people: two other nurses, one medical doctor, a psychiatrist, three social workers, someone with experience in counseling, and four women who had experienced difficult marital relationships and were, as I recall, trained in law and other professions. They were supplemented by a group about twice their numbers working on a part-time volunteer basis.

Florence had no managerial training, although she had had considerable experience in hospital work situations. When the three of them started, they did all the work together. They found a very suitable location in town, which they were able to obtain at very low rent from a philanthropist. They initiated a telephone emergency line and began covering it on a twenty-four-hour basis, wrote grant proposals, found a number of interested men and women to serve on the Board, and began handling their first cases. The three of them would usually work together, talking to women who might call or come to see them. When they obtained more money and had to deal with funding agencies, they hired an accountant and expanded the volunteer and permanent staff. Some of the paid people started as volunteers and in time were hired, but the three of them remained the original founding group with Florence as head. The new staff members and the volunteers were integrated gradually as they joined the group, but Florence and her two friends never quite came to grips with the fact they were no longer a very small ad hoc task group and were, in fact, a medium-size professional organization.

Conflicts Between Professionals and Managers. By the time I, and several others, were invited to discuss problems with her, Florence was having many difficulties with both the professional and volunteer staff. She complained particularly about the professional staff. They did not perform as well as she thought they might. There seemed to be considerable friction among staffers and some dissatisfaction with the program, although turnover remained nonexistent. Florence found that the two males on the staff (the doctor and the psychiatrist) were not cooperative, that the four professional women, particularly the lawyers, were trying to run things. In fact, she felt quite threatened by everyone in the group, believing they were continually challenging her. She put it this way:

> At first they come and want to help. We usually work very well together. They get interested in a case and are very involved with it. But those who stay on gradually become more difficult. It is always as if they do not want to cooperate any more. They promise to do things, but do not do them. The three of us have to do everything and, frankly, we are running exhausted, continually dealing with problems that no one handled. The phone central is not covered. No one thought of the heat in the building. Someone turned in time sheets all wrong. But, meanwhile, they all have big ideas as to what should be done. Whatever needs doing, they miss doing it and we have to do it ourselves. They only want to run things.

When we interviewed the staff, both the professionals and volunteers, we heard two different accounts. Some volunteers felt quite isolated. They were assigned to work on cases and had little contact with other workers. Few of the volunteers seemed to know much about the organization and particularly about the qualifications of the professionals who could help them. They had little in-house training although, at a minimum, Florence tried to introduce new workers around.

The professionals gave other accounts. They did not think Florence managed the organization properly. They felt she did not involve them sufficiently in decisions where they happened to have expertise. They thought she was insecure about her own managerial abilities and went out of her way to keep all of them at arm's length. The only people she seemed to trust were her two co-founders, but they were not able to bring a core group together to plan a strategy for the Refuge and to deal effectively with task assignments. They described Florence as a crisis manager, always trying to extinguish fires.

We found that their descriptions were quite accurate. Florence had always run the operation single-handedly, but as the program expanded, size meant that many managerial tasks were left undone. When we queried Florence about this, she said she was responsible and had to be. "The board appointed me [in fact, she appointed the board], and I am responsible for the Refuge. I have to be and no one else can be."

Excessive Centralization. The rapid growth of the organization made it impossible for Florence to handle everything. She could not be on top of each case and all the external problems and still determine how volunteers and professionals could help each other. It was difficult to deal routinely with the cases because of the various emotional content of each situation and the vast differences among cases, their management, and disposition. More important, as the Refuge grew and became known, many unforeseen problems were emerging, which required considerable thought. Some of these problems had to do with other agencies, with how to deal with the courts, with the police, with community groups, and so on. All these issues affected the staff and required their help and participation.

Florence attempted to centralize decision making. She failed to delegate responsibilities for these managerial tasks. Thus, she would continue to write grant proposals, hire more staff, deal with the agencies, and attempt to decide all task assignments.

We explained about organizing for a much larger staff and suggested to her delegating managerial responsibilities so that someone would be responsible for assigning new cases, someone would be responsible for new volunteers, someone would take responsibility for grant preparation, and someone would run the business end of things. We urged her to establish an executive committee composed of many key members of the professional staff to deal with these and all the complex external issues.

Our suggestions were common sense, and we assumed Florence would change her ways. In fact, she did not invite us back. We only continued to hear about the clinic because one of her volunteers was enrolled in our graduate program. In the ensuing months, problems at the Refuge did not improve. We heard that the psychiatrist had left and, later still, that there were fiscal accounting problems. Within eighteen months, the Refuge was absorbed by another organization, and we heard that Florence had retired.

Confusion Between Managerial and Professional Authority. This is not an uncommon case. Many professional organizations are created by professionals. As these organizations grow in size, managerial skills are found lacking. Interestingly, it is often the case that the untrained managers who happen to run these organizations are confused about the concept and the reality of their authority. They do not see or understand the distinction between professional authority and managerial authority. They often attempt to exercise both. Thus, Florence was still the professional she had been at the beginning, even handling individual cases and expecting others to somehow pitch in. She was imbued with her managerial responsibilities but was quite unwilling to delegate to anyone. At the same time, she perceived suggestions or participatory efforts of her colleagues as threats to her own managerial authority.

Professional authority emerges from dependencies, just

the same way managerial authority does, but the dependencies are different. The group may need the manager to resolve conflicts among themselves, and this may be one of the underlying dependencies that makes the group pay attention to the manager. Some of the battered women who came to the clinic need medical care, which is why the doctor is there and why his professional authority is exercised when he deals with a patient. But professional and managerial authority overlap any time managerial decisions have to take into account professional knowledge, or vice versa.

Case assignments at the Refuge were still handled by Florence. That solution had worked relatively well as long as she could play both professional and managerial roles—that is, as long as she knew the characteristics of most of the cases and had time to assign some to herself and to others. As the victim load and the staff grew, Florence was faced by the classic dilemma of centralized control. Given that she opted not to delegate, she could either routinize or continually enlarge her span of control. Since case load assignments required individualized knowledge of needs and capabilities, she could not routinize. She enlarged her span of control to the point that she could no longer handle both her managerial and professional roles.

Overlap Between Managerial and Professional Authority. When professional knowledge is needed in managerial decisions, some form of professional participation or delegation of managerial authority takes place. What Florence really needed was the help of a professional task group charged with external policy and case assignments. This group would need to know about victim needs and number of cases and about professional and volunteer capabilities. The task is not simple: victim information is sometimes fragmentary, patient crises difficult to predict, and even patient cooperation not always assured. Moreover, since assistance from outside agencies is often needed, obtaining their cooperation and support is quite important, but such support, the Refuge found, was not always there and had to be nurtured. Sometimes the police or child protection services had to be called in or employers approached, and friends of the victim might participate in counseling activities. Managing the Refuge required setting priorities and deciding among complex courses of action where the involved professionals and volunteers had much to contribute. Florence was able to move quickly and, at times, response speed was an important asset, but she could never duplicate or replace the knowledge and experience of the other members of the professional staff.

Managing professionals requires more than giving professionals sufficient discretion to carry out professional tasks. It also requires sharing managerial tasks where professional values, knowledge, and skills are relevant. These are two distinct dimensions. Florence thought she was a good manager because she did give considerable discretion to her caseworkers, but that was not enough. She did not realize that while there were several managerial tasks she alone could handle, there were many others that could best be handled jointly, by involving far greater professional participation.

A Typology of Management-Professional Problems

Florence's case is not unique, but there exist many variations on the theme. She represents the case of the entrepreneurial professional who happens to become a somewhat domineering manager. Let us list a few other specimens of this fauna. But let me assure you, dear reader, that you are not included in the list. Anyone who reads this book already knows enough not to fall into these stereotypes.

The Political Manager. The manager of the service is a political appointee, a good friend of the governor or of someone high up in his political campaign. The professional staff finds that the manager understands politics inside out, but is totally unaware of professional values, practices, and expectations. Yet, when these are brought to his attention, he disregards them or treats the professionals as one more pressure group that has to be cajoled. He wants to negotiate about professional issues where there is little to negotiate. He will not stay in the position for long since he has ambitions elsewhere. Is it worth it to attempt to educate him?

The Efficiency Expert. The manager is a well-trained efficiency expert. He understands all about the new management techniques: management information systems, strategic planning, model building, cost-effective analysis, and many more. The management language of the organization is dominated by his own professional language. The other professionals in the organization espouse somewhat different values and concerns. Their language does not always lend itself to measurements and quantifications. The efficiency expert distrusts these different professionals and prefers to surround himself with bright young policy analysts who can help him to decide how to proceed.

The Incompetent Manager. The manager is a chemist and just does not understand about management. He has not integrated the various dimensions of the role and continually fails to act or to assume his duties. Many managerial responsibilities drop between the cracks. The poorly qualified manager often blames the rest of the professional staff for operational errors he should have foreseen and acted upon. He knows his weaknesses, but is too pleased with the status of the position to discuss problems. He cannot afford to trust his professional staff since they might be able to get the goods on him. He works alone and secretly.

The Conventional Manager. The manager has been in charge of factory production for ten years before this appointment in the research department. He came with his management team. He expects to master the problems and issues facing the research department in six weeks. He will run a tight, no-nonsense operation. He expects to receive cost-effectiveness reports on all operations each week. At staff meetings, he instructs and directs. He is a leader.

The Manager Caught in Conflict. The manager is a physician in an organization where several allied health professions are in constant conflict among themselves. Since he belongs to one of the professional factions, he is distrusted by the other factions. His ability to resolve conflicts is hampered. Moreover, he avoids the professional staff because he fears the conflict and fears that he will be caught in it. He maintains an aloof and unseeing position.

The Committee Manager. Twelve professionals created

the organization several years ago. They are all equal partners, but none of them is a competent manager. Managerial responsibilities are rarely assigned. The managing committee is not particularly efficient or quick on its feet. Each member tends to blame others for failure. Intracommittee conflict leads to many wasted motions. Most partners prefer to keep away and not get involved.

The Manager with Different Values. The manager has been appointed to make certain that the service organization will keep within budget cuts and will not engender political scandals that could be inconvenient during the mayor's reelection campaign. Most of the professional staff happen to belong to a different political party and are incensed by the constant budget cuts. They distrust the manager, and he distrusts all of them. They keep away from each other and take great pain to blame each other.

The "Old Man." The manager has had an extensive career in the civil service. He is close to retirement age. He perceives his role as that of the cautious old bureaucratic infighter who has seen all the tricks of the trade. The professional staff is young, dedicated, and committed to action. The old man wants to take time, to be careful. They want to push ahead and do things. They see him as old, senile, and lacking the energy to move. He sees them as immature, unaware of the bureaucratic traps ahead, and in dire need of his wisdom. He cannot entrust anything to them: "They are so young, the poor things."

The Ambitious Manager. The manager is the shining young protégé who has been making television news. Success is his onion. His greatest concern is to show results, to be visible. His time dimension is now, not tomorrow. The federal agency deals with long-term problems where patience and repetitive efforts may pay off. The professional staff distrusts his public relations orientation. They would gladly sabotage him if they could do so without endangering their clients. He has little use for them. They rarely get together, and staff meetings are devoted to trivia.

The Invisible Manager. If there is a manager, it is in name only. The manager tells everyone how good his professional staff is. They know what they are doing. He sleeps most of the day in his office and avoids making any decisions. In fact, he avoids doing anything. If there is trouble, it must be because of the clients. One cannot be too careful these days. Surely it cannot be his fault if the program experiences difficulties. One cannot really blame him, given the scope of his inactivity. Good management, he likes to say, is total delegation. The place runs on wheels. When he wakes up, he reads the paper and orders a coffee.

The Lord Manager. The manager enjoys every morsel of power that comes his way. What joy to know that senior professionals have to wait in his antechamber while he is so busy doing nothing at his desk. When tempers rise in the professional staff, he calls them in and shows them the poor performance records of the last six months: "No point having more conflict when we are already in trouble," he says. "Be careful," he admonishes, "or we will all finish by losing our jobs." But he also likes to make speeches and be applauded. From time to time, he gathers the professional staff and gives them a pep talk. When someone suggests he delegate, he answers: "I don't want decisions being made at that level."

The Hard-Working Manager. The professional staff does not understand how much external pressure the manager is diverting away from them. They see him rush out, meeting all sorts of people, handling endless telephone conversations, and writing long reports. They are unaware that he manages a threatening external environment and keeps it under control. He has no time to explain what he is doing, and they have no opportunity to appreciate or help him.

The Good Manager. Finally, we have a very good manager, a manager with a good sense of the long-term strengths and weaknesses of the organization. A manager who has established good working relations with the professional staff. She is quick to move in areas of opportunity and avoid pitfalls. She handles external pressures, maintains staff morale, and establishes task orientation. The professional staff does not understand what good management is all about. They take what she does for granted. They will tell you that she does not earn her salary. They tell you they would abolish the position if they could.

Delegating Authority: Envelope Supervision

Managing the professional organization involves two distinct operations. The first consists of establishing a process that gives sufficient discretion to professionals. This we call the concept of envelope supervision. At this level, we are exclusively concerned with professional tasks. The second consists of setting an authority structure that allows management to share some managerial responsibilities and tasks with the professional staff. This we label the concept of joint managerial-professional tasks (Antonio, 1979; Felsenthal, 1980; Landau and Stout, 1979; Lehman and Waters, 1979; Meadows, 1980; Ouchi, 1977).

Florence never designed an effective monitoring system for the Refuge. In fact, she gave too much discretion to her caseworkers. She never really had the time to keep up with all the activities of her staff once case responsibilities were assigned. Her supervision was inadequate. In addition, she never allowed the professional staff to help her with the various important managerial tasks she performed. She neither used envelope supervision nor did her staff participate in joint tasks with her.

Monitoring and Controlling

Envelope supervision implies providing discretion. The supervisor envelopes but does not control every aspect of the work. Envelope supervision has two aspects: (1) agreeing with the relevant professional staff about desirable monitoring controls that will not erode professional discretion where needed, while still providing management with the feedback it needs, and (2) establishing control limits or parameters within which professional discretion can be exercised.

The purpose of envelope supervision is to provide sufficient discretion to the professional worker while providing necessary management information for supervision and feedback. Since tasks are varied, envelope supervision is designed to fit each assignment. The design involves both professionals and management.

What might Florence want to know about each case? How they were progressing? What help might be given? When to intervene? When to seek external help? Obviously, she had to delegate responsibility for answering most of these questions to her caseworkers, but she needed to know how the cases were evolving so she could use the Refuge resources effectively.

Envelope supervision leaves considerable procedural discretion to professionals. Control tends to be oriented toward input resources and task achievement. Since professional tasks are, by definition, those that cannot be easily routinized, envelope supervision avoids day-to-day process controls. Presumably, Florence should not direct every intervention of her staff. The first manager of Applied Research should not change the commas in the reports of his staff.

Important inputs may be controlled. Had envelope supervision been used at Applied Research, the work of the research teams would have taken much less day-to-day management control. Aggregate controls would be mostly in the form of input and output controls: "This is your team's budget. We expect your report in six months. Go to it and good luck." One question, of course, would still be what process controls to use. Would the manager simply wait for six months and call on the due date to find out if the report was finally ready? How would the manager handle the budget? Would it be rigid or flexible? What about overruns? How would these be handled? Would a contract be written? Would he detail the specifications for the expected report? Would the manager attempt ahead of time to decide how the work would be carried out or would the professional team decide? How would professional appointments on each team be determined? How much discretion is good discretion?

Past practice may give us a sense of what works and what does not. In professional research organizations, a great deal of day-to-day discretion is necessary and yet considerable monitoring is also exercised by managers. Detailed specifications of the objectives of the research, of the work to be performed, of the expected costs of every aspect of the research, and of the talent

to be employed may be required. These specifications are reviewed both by professionals and managers. Once the work is
underway, it is closely monitored. Major deviations in the research are cleared with the management team and close watch
on costs and on expected expenditures is maintained. Lead-time
analysis and other management techniques may be used to ensure completion of the work on schedule.

Participation in Establishing Procedures

However, past practice is not always a good guide. The
bureaucratization of many professional organizations may already result in far too many controls. The notion of envelope
supervision starts with a joint attempt to redefine what kind of
control and monitoring will enhance performance. Participation
of professionals is essential since they can assess the consequences of controls.

What topics might be discussed?

Access to Resources—Input Controls. The team has options regarding inputs; choices are possible. Management and
professionals have formally agreed to define all the input
choices professionals consider important in the task situation.
This may require interventions fairly high up in the hierarchy
because organizational rules or legal constraints impede professional discretion. Can the professional team make low-level personnel appointments or does it have to go through the personnel department? How about short-term consultants? What
salary scales have to be used? Can the professional team bypass
central purchasing? When? How often? These and other questions are discussed. Management sits with the professional team
and an agreement is reached on every area where discretion is
suggested. What about flex-time? What about work sharing?
Can the professional team commandeer space? Obviously, even
if the task is top priority, space will always be a delicate matter
and management may still be involved.

Monitoring and Feedback. Process supervision is also detailed and agreed to beforehand. The needs of management and
of the professional team are taken into account. What decisions

have to be cleared with management? What decisions do not need to be cleared? A purpose of envelope supervision is to provide agreements about the scope of responsibility so that neither management nor the professionals need be in doubt about their areas of competence. Another purpose is to have the decision-making responsibility as close to field operation as possible.

How often should the team report to management? What kind of reporting information is needed and for what purpose? How will management act on this reporting information? What kind of reporting information is needed by the professional team, and how will it use it? When is management expected to leave the professional team alone, and when will it provide feedback? What kind of feedback will management provide? What kind of feedback do the professionals need? What kind of feedback enhances professional values (Yeager, Rabin, and Vocino, 1985)?

Output Agreement. Outputs have been spelled out. Management and the professional team know what is to be achieved, but the level and type of specification are suited to the task. Management has been attentive to professional descriptions of output and to professional concerns with unsuitable output measures. Professional consensus is obtained on the choice of output measures. If quantitative measures are inappropriate, a consensus has been reached on the use of qualitative measures.

Incentive Agreement. How will the professional staff be rewarded if they succeed at the task? If economic incentives are used, are they considered fair? Will they be the same for all professionals, or will the different needs of professions and individuals be taken into account? Is the incentive scheme revealed to all the professionals or are salary differentials kept secret to avoid jealous comparisons? These issues are discussed and cleared up beforehand.

Contrast with Other Techniques

Envelope supervision differs from conventional rationalistic controls such as PPBS (planning, programming, and budgeting systems) or MBO (management by objectives) on several counts:

1. Goals or objectives are not assumed to be known. In some situations, the overall goals of the organization may be clear but the task to be performed may not be clear at all. The usual MBO call for setting "clear" objectives may be quite inappropriate. Envelope supervision would simply call to "find out what should be done in this case and do it."

2. A first concern is to protect professional discretion. The amount and extent of supervision are set so as to enhance professional work. The amount of supervision is chosen to fit needs of both management and the professional staff. For instance, can decisions be made at lower levels? How much management feedback would help?

3. Envelope supervision is a participatory process involving both management and members of the professional staff.

4. Once agreement is reached, envelope supervision is supportive. Well-understood areas of discretion exist where management is not attempting to second-guess professional judgment. More important still, professional errors are not jumped upon in an attempt to rapidly blame those who perpetrate them. Discretion is not used to find fault nor is it allowed to provide for competition between managers and professional teams. Discretion is not used to threaten, as in: "We give you discretion, but at the first mistake, we will be there to catch you and make sure you are blamed and not us." When discretion is given, management remains responsible. If discretion is not working properly, it means that too much or too little discretion has been given. Nothing more.

5. The ability to exercise discretion requires the ability to anticipate the sequence of events that will follow from any particular action. As Jaques (1956) puts it, the ability to anticipate may be conscious, or intuitive, or a mixture of consciousness, imagination, and intuition. He goes on to say that perception will become cloudier the farther into the future the chain of events is traced in one's mind. It may, therefore, be that the length of time into the future that an individual can likely trace consequences is related to a mental capacity to organize previous experience. He goes on to suggest that individual ability to exercise discretion is related to the ability to use past experi-

ence to recognize organized continuous sequences of events or to have theories about those events that allow one to make judgments about the future.

Therefore, the ability of professional teams to exercise discretion is different from the ability of management. As we saw in the preceding chapter, they have different kinds of theories, knowledge, and experiences. Professional discretion will be essential as long as the task remains within the confines of the professional domain. A professional may answer whether an experiment has a chance of success and how to maximize these chances of success. This professional will not necessarily be able to judge whether the organization will benefit from the experiment.

Adaptive Authority Structures

Envelope supervision is a process for implementing necessary professional discretion in task situations. It requires considerable discussion between managers and professionals, to clarify which tasks are purely managerial and which tasks may be preferable to handle jointly.

Managerial Tasks

To be sure, some organizational models, such as the professional partnerships, vest all managerial responsibilities into the professional staff. That does not alter the fact that some managerial tasks can only be handled by management. What are these few tasks?

Official Representation. First, the legal or official representation of the organization. Management speaks for the organization and signs legal documents. Professional participation may be needed to set policy or to decide to sign, but not for the act of signing. The manager remains the official mouthpiece of the organization.

Adjudication of Conflicts. The manager is the adjudicator of conflicts. Can professional conflicts be adjudicated without professional knowledge? Sometimes, not always. Depending on their content, the adjudication of conflicts is either exclusively a managerial task or a joint task.

Negotiation. The manager is the negotiator. If she represents the organization, she will still need to be advised. Joint decisions may be taken, but in the end, she may well have to act singly.

Delegation of Authority. The manager is the only one who can legitimately delegate authority. Therefore, the organization of joint managerial and professional decision-making bodies always requires managerial intervention. The definition of scope of responsibility in envelope supervision is arrived at jointly, but management makes the final decision.

Responsibility. Lastly, the manager—whatever authority model is used—is responsible for results. Management can always delegate authority, but it cannot delegate responsibility.

It is obvious that this list is very short indeed. Many significant managerial tasks are not included. These may require joint managerial-professional cooperation and participation.

Joint Managerial-Professional Tasks

The characteristics of the organizational mission, the environment in which it operates, the complexity of the technology, and the nature and relevance of professional tasks within the organization determine the extent to which management retains or shares many of its functions. Setting goals, specifying objectives, planning, organizing work, assigning responsibilities, supervising, evaluating, hiring, firing, managing the organizational environment, coordinating, and communicating may all be carried out either by management or by some form of professional-management participation.

How much participation depends on organizational imperatives and on professional values. Designing an adaptive authority structure requires some attention to the way the authority structure affects the professionals in the organization: do they want to participate *and* can they contribute?

We will discuss participatory governance structures later on. But first we should note that *participation* is a word that provides for many different levels of involvement. Its meaning can move along a continuum from simple acts such as notifying professionals of one's intent, on to seeking their advice, to consulting them and obtaining their support, to having them participate and vote in decision. Even voting can give different weight to their opinions and judgments. Who votes? Does the majority control or are decisions taken only when unanimous votes are obtained?

Similarly, the scope of the participatory membership can vary. As we shall see, some authority models create a status ladder within the professional staff and give managerial responsibility only to those professionals who have achieved high levels of performance and recognition. Other models involve practically every professional in the organization. Some models create permanent structures, others do not. Some managers do not use formal participatory schemes and prefer to keep responsibilities to themselves and to consult as need be.

The following considerations come into play:

Impact on Professional Motivation. How are cooperation and participation perceived by the professional staff? Do formal structures—for example, the fact that there is a senior professional staff with considerable managerial responsibility—enhance the perceived quality of work life in the organization? Or does participation in management take too much time away from valued professional work?

Legitimation. How are cooperation and participation legitimized? How do management and the professional staff come to define and accept overlapping roles? Is this made possible only by formal appointments (for example, when a professional is appointed to a managerial position), or can the authority structure be modified to encompass shared roles?

Adaptive Structure. How can the authority structure remain adaptive? That is, how can changes in the authority structure take place fairly automatically when external or internal situations require these modifications without causing major staff conflicts within the organization? Are some models more rigid than others in this respect?

Importance of Professional Knowledge. How essential is

professional knowledge to managerial decisions? Can managers really understand the professional issues under consideration? Can strictly managerial tasks be separated from joint tasks? Can management retain final authority where it has to do so for legal or other reasons?

Importance of Traditional Managerial Responsibilities. How do managerial tasks affect the choice of authority model? In some organizations, coordination of different subsets or units is extremely important to the mission of the entire organization. In other organizations, many different subsets, or semi-independent units, exist together but are very loosely linked. What happens to one, does not affect the other. The internal managerial problems of these different kinds of organizations differ. Do some authority models fit some better than others?

Matrix Management

We may choose to organize by functions; we will have a budget department, a marketing department, and a production department. We may organize along services; we will have a cardiac unit, a children's department, and a maternity ward. We may organize around areas and have a San Francisco campus and a Berkeley campus. We may organize around products and have financial analysts working on banking and finance, stocks, public utilities, electrical equipment, and so on. These conventional hierarchies and structures do not allow for extensive lateral communications and coordination. Basically, information and instructions flow up and down lines. Integration is achieved at higher levels of command.

In bureaucratic organizations the problem of lateral communication is accentuated because individuals identify with their departments and units. There is suspicion of the motives and the self-interest of other units. Since control, resources, and evaluation come through a vertical chain of command, lateral horizontal cooperation across units is less important than pleasing or responding to vertical instructions. The dilemma of most organizations is that whatever organizational arrangements are made, the vertical slicing of the organization tends to reduce or impair horizontal linkages.

Yet tasks often cut across units and departments. If my research unit wants to bid for a complex research project on education and rural development in Latin America, we will have to cooperate with researchers from the Center for Latin American Studies, the Department of Agricultural and Resource Economics housed in a different professional school, the Department of City and Regional Planning, in a third professional school, and so on.

Organizations that employ many professionals tend to have considerable lateral interdependencies and the need for horizontal linkage. One reason is that these organizations deal with information and knowledge and all the information and knowledge is dispersed across units.

Vertical communication and decision making are far slower and more expensive than simultaneous vertical and horizontal linkage. For example, the portfolio managers in the financial management firm need to have close links with security analysts in the research department. Vertical integration is complemented by horizontal linkages. There will be many contacts between the two even if they belong to different units in the organization.

Another reason is that these organizations require greater integration of resources than can be handled effectively through vertical communications, decisions, and controls. In engineering or scientific research, the ability to create project teams out of existing departments leads to a different managerial approach.

Matrix management is the extension of the concept of the project approach. In fact, the concept came out of project management in the aerospace industry (Davis and Lawrence, 1977). Basically, it replaces a single hierarchical line of command with only one person responsible, with a team or project approach, where individuals may have two bosses instead of one. If I am assigned to the major research project on Latin America, I will still be supervised by the dean of my professional school, I will still be reviewed by my peers in my department, but I will also be supervised by the project director in charge of our work in Latin America, and this person may participate in the evaluation of my work.

Task forces, projects, and permanent structures are the

three most common forms of matrix management used in professional organizations.

Task Forces. Task forces are short-term and task-oriented groups. A good many joint managerial-professional tasks may be entrusted to task forces. They provide flexible mechanisms to bring people together from different units to tackle new problems and to discuss new approaches. They provide lateral communication across units and vertical integration across managerial and professional staff. As a rule, task forces are advisory and report through conventional lines of command.

Projects. Projects are longer term and operational. Individuals assigned to projects may remain under dual supervision and serve to link departmental and project activities. In general, projects have greater access to resources and operational responsibilities than task forces. Projects are used because they vary, they have definite beginnings and ends, and each of them requires different configurations of resources and manpower.

Permanent Structures. Permanent structures across departments are used when lateral integration is a vital long-term necessity that requires formal channels of communication or commitment of resources. For example, we may decide that a permanent group staffed from many departments should be entrusted with the professional development function.

Participation: Myth or Reality?

The concept of participatory management conjures many images.

Participatory management is sometimes associated with concepts of client or public participation in management. Ever since the 1960s programs such as the War on Poverty or Model Cities, client or public participation has been mandated or adopted in many sectors of government and in government-funded programs (Barber, 1984; Krislov, 1981; Mazmanian and Nienaber, 1979; Riedel, 1972; Stenberg, 1972; and Susskind, 1983). The experience with citizen participation is varied. It is of concern to us later in this book when we discuss accountability at greater length (see Chapter Eight).

Worker Participation. Professionals are workers and worker participation in management has a long history. For example, the Scanlon plan, conceived in the 1940s, consisted of increasing workers' participation in management, particularly by having workers use greater discretion in production processes while sharing in productivity gains (Scanlon, 1948). During the 1960s, there was considerable interest in worker participation as a means of increasing productivity. A classic case experiment was that of the Weldon Company, a pajama manufacturer in trouble that was acquired by a competitor, the Harwood Company. Harwood instituted participatory schemes, and the success story was widely reported (Marrow, Bowers, and Seashore, 1967; Seashore and Bowers, 1970). The participatory movement in the United States was partly influenced by developments abroad, including the experience of Western European countries where, after World War II, much legislation was passed mandating worker participation in management (Duffy, 1975).

More importantly, interest in worker participation and more generally in participatory management and industrial democracy came out of the thinking of organization development theorists, particularly the ideas of McGregor (1960), which have now become part of the jargon: Theory X and Theory Y. McGregor pointed out that conventional management wisdom assumed that workers dislike work, that they have to be coerced to work, that they prefer to be directed, that they wish to avoid responsibility, that they have little ambition and want security above all. With this set of assumptions, McGregor pointed out, one inevitably designs organizations that cope with these characteristics. Theory X fits this description. These organizations control workers closely and give them as little discretion as possible.

But, McGregor argued, workers are not that way. They happen to like and need work for their own self-actualization. They do not respond well to fear, but exercise self-direction and self-control if they are personally motivated. Moreover, they can pursue this need for self-actualization at the same time they pursue organizational goals, particularly if they identify with and internalize them. They like responsibility and there usually is—

in any worker—considerable untapped creativity and talent that can be mobilized by Theory Y managers.

Participatory management espouses Theory Y assumptions and has had a permanent impact on American management practice (Argyris, 1964; Blumberg, 1969; Katz and Kahn, 1978). In terms of morale and job satisfaction, the evidence is relatively clear—participatory schemes seem to lead to greater worker satisfaction (Blumberg, 1969). However, regarding efficiency, the data is far less conclusive (Duffy, 1975). In any case, it is difficult to generalize about a multitude of different cases where the term *participation* is used to describe rather different situations and different levels of discretion. The overlap between some worker participation in decisions and the level of organizational routinization is not always clear, yet this overlap is significant to professional participation models. It is no surprise that some authors are not particularly oriented toward worker participation or organizational democracy (Mintzberg, 1983). On the other hand, it should be clear from our previous discussion of professional values that some form of participation is usually desired by professionals and that there is a direct link between their participation and their motivation.

Worker Participation Versus Joint Tasks. There is an important distinction to be made between the concept of participatory management and our discussion of joint managerial-professional task groups.

Participatory management starts only from assumptions about worker motivation. The question being asked is whether greater worker participation in management, which results in increased motivation, can enhance worker effectiveness. It may also be hoped in passing that such participation might enhance management knowledge and effectiveness, but that is still a secondary concern. In contrast, the concept of joint managerial-professional task groups derives from considerations of professional values and expectations *and* from task realities. The more important question here is whether professional participation is essential to enhance management performance, that is, whether professional knowledge is essential. The secondary question is whether professional participation in management enhances motivation and professional effectiveness. The emphasis is quite different (Blau and Alba, 1982; Ewing, 1983; Hopkins, 1983; Toch and Grant, 1984; Pelz and Andrews, 1976; Pinder, 1984).

Governance Models

Partnership Model

The partners may select a chairperson, but they are collectively responsible for managing the organization. They may decide to assign specific responsibilities to some partners, they may hire professional managers to carry out some tasks, but by and large, they keep major policy making for themselves. In professional partnerships, it is not uncommon for some partners to acquire more influence, either because they happen to be among the original partners and have acquired rights and privileges over time, or because they own a larger portion of the equity, or because their professional contribution to the organization is more significant than most, or simply because they happen to be skilled in group leadership.

In the partnership model, the professionals of the organization fall into three groups. First, there are the young professionals and the new-hires who aspire to a career. They expect to be recognized and hope to be invited to become full partners before too long. Second, there are those professionals who know their limitations, or have become aware of them, or whose professional specialization is such that their qualifications do not allow them to contemplate becoming full partners. Last, there are the full partners, some of whom may have been with the partnership for a very long time, and others may only have been appointed in the recent past.

The partnership model has distinct advantages and disadvantages. First, the advantages.

Control. It gives professionals full control of the organization. They are not subject to managerial direction. It allows highly talented individuals to work together without any lesser status. The partners own the organization, so they are highly motivated to perform.

Careers. It gives younger professionals in the organization a clear view of career opportunities facing them. The responsibilities and privileges of full partners are clearly different from those of the younger recruits. They play different roles, have greater status, and receive higher emoluments or a share of the profits. The career structure is, therefore, very real and tangible.

Selection. It provides a formal mechanism to separate out the members of the professional staff and to select those who participate in managerial tasks. The partners are the managers and the partners select, evaluate, and invite certain colleagues to join them in management. The decision to invite professionals to assume managerial responsibilities is, therefore, made by a selected group of professionals who have acquired some managerial experience.

Incentives. It provides strong incentives for professional roles, since (1) the career ladder structure is highly visible—namely, professionals know who the partners are, they know the significant evaluators within the organization, and (2) the partners provide role models where professional values and concerns dominate, given that the identity of the partners remains professional. The professional who becomes a full partner remains a professional and usually carries on professional work together with new managerial responsibilities.

The major deficiencies of partnerships are:

Constrained Membership. The partnership creates a constrained professional career path. The size of the management group has to be limited. First, it cannot become so large as to be unwieldy. Second, in some partnerships total benefits or volume of work does not grow in proportion to the number of partners. Adding partners requires redistribution of assets. Third, adding partners always redistributes influence and control. As a result, there are managerial constraints on the number of professionals who can be promoted to the full partnership, which means that the career ladder may be more restrictive than is desirable in some cases. Some good people may be lost if they perceive that opportunities for promotion are limited.

Ineffective Management. Group decision making can be preferable for certain kinds of decisions, but, in general, it is slower, more cumbersome, and less effective. Since most partners are often professionals with little if any managerial training, it follows that partnership management may easily be in the hands of fairly mediocre managers who happen to be excellent professionals—whether they be lawyers, engineers, scientists, accountants, or financial analysts. Specific managerial tasks may not be assigned and may fall in between chairs. Jealousies or conflicts between partners may result in odd behavior patterns.

Conflicts. Conflicts between partners are not easily resolved, either because partners are presumably equal or because partners compete among themselves for greater shares of control. The managerial role of conflict adjudicator and resolver is missing. To be sure, some partners will come to assume the role and exercise greater influence on the group. However, the absence of a formal hierarchy constrains the legitimacy of such acts: older members of the partnership may assume this role, because they happen to have the legitimacy provided by their longer association with the partnership, yet they may not have the qualifications or the ability to maintain consensus and resolve conflicts.

The partnership model does not readily provide means to resolve conflicts. As Auletta shows in his account of the fall of the house of Lehman on Wall Street (1966), conflicts between partners lasted for years and had devastating consequences on the firm. Managerial talent per se is less relevant in the selection of partners than professional qualifications and potential contribution to the collective good of the group. Thus, a colleague is invited to become a partner because he or she can bring to the partnership many new contracts and clients. Yet, this individual happens to be a very poor manager and will not enhance the overall managerial performance of the partnership.

Many professional organizations are organized on the partnership model—law firms, accounting firms, financial management firms, management consultants, and many other professional service firms. In general, these tend to be organizations where:

• The professional content of the work is central to the mission of the organization.

- One profession within the organization is central to the mission of the organization. If various professions work together, there is a common specialization binding them together.
- The organization benefits from size, but does not depend as much on internal integration. Each partner may run his or her share of the work relatively independently from other partners. Managerial tasks of coordination and integration are less significant. Major collective managerial tasks can be handled by the partners, and they are inclined to put in the time and energy because their own practice benefits from it.
- In the case of private firms, ownership of a share of the firm is an important motivator of individual and group performance.

Senior Staff Model

In the senior staff model, managerial responsibility is vested into a single manager, but this person shares managerial responsibilities with senior professional staff members. The senior staff, like the partners, have been selected and are only a portion of the entire professional staff. As in the partnership model, the professional staff plays a managerial role, but under the supervision of the manager. Individually or collectively, the senior staff may be involved in long-range planning, task assignments, personnel policy, hiring, promotions, firing, coordination, and evaluation. Since the single manager has ultimate responsibility, the degree of participation of the senior staff will depend on the various considerations discussed earlier in the chapter.

The senior staff model has the following advantages and disadvantages:

Single Manager. It vests managerial responsibility in a single individual. Therefore, the degree of actual senior staff participation in decisions is dependent in part on the experience, sophistication, and style of the manager. As you may recall from Chapter One, Applied Research was headed at first by a manager who simply did not believe in, or was not capable of, delegating managerial responsibilities to his senior staff. In fact, that manager intervened directly into areas where professional discretion would normally be expected.

Participation. If the manager is talented and is able to involve the senior staff in assuming professional responsibilities for joint tasks, the model has some advantage over a partnership since the organization benefits both from the advantages provided by a single manager (speed, leadership coordination, conflict arbitration) and the advantages of collective participation (professional inputs in relevant decisions, collective judgments).

Career Ladder. To the extent the senior staff actually assumes both professional and managerial responsibilities, to the extent these roles have status within the organization, and the senior staff receives greater economic incentives, the model provides for a differentiated career ladder structure and, therefore, a professional incentive structure within the organization. But, as we saw in the case of Applied Research, the incentive structure will be nonexistent if the senior staff is senior in name only and opportunities for managerial roles are nonexistent. This will be particularly damaging if there does not exist a strictly professional career ladder.

Authority Conflicts. Conflicts between managers and senior staffs will center around their respective responsibilities and extent of participation as long as the practices are not institutionalized. This means that there is a propensity in this situation to seek to set a pattern through repetitive practice that defines and establishes the legitimacy of each participant, in contrast to the partnership where the legitimacy of the participants is already institutionalized and depends much less on repetitive practice. Therefore, ability to experiment, modify, and alter the mix of professional-managerial joint tasks might be lower in this model or require more managerial sophistication to surmount than in the partnership model.

The senior staff model is more often used in government and in the not-for-profit sector where ownership, a characteristic of many on the partnership model, is less relevant. Research organizations, think tanks, museums, philanthropies, social service agencies, and other similar organizations often use this model. From our point of view in this book, the senior staff model is a most important alternative to the bureaucratic model. It is preferable to the bureaucratic model when

• Professional knowledge and experience are important to managerial decisions.
• Professional self-rule is important to professional motivation.
• Management requires greater centralization than is conveniently achieved under the partnership model.

Yet the career structure provided by the model is a motivator for performance.

The Dual Governance Model

In the dual governance model two distinct hierarchies have institutionalized and separate responsibilities for the running of the enterprise: management, on the one hand, and the professional body on the other. In these organizations, management has formally delegated selected managerial responsibilities to the professional body. Thus, in large research universities, or in community hospitals, it is common practice for boards to delegate responsibility for academic or medical matters to senates or medical staffs composed of some or many members of the professional staff. In the case of universities, these academic senates therefore exercise considerable influence on a wide scope of decisions ranging from student admissions, curriculum, requirements, to faculty selection and promotion. Since power relations determine the final outcome of many decisions, in practice, the administration maintains exclusive control on some managerial prerogatives and shares the rest of them with the senate. Thus, in some universities, the administration may have a minimal impact on faculty hiring and promotion, while in others it still plays an important role. Control of budgets often reveals the overall extent of relative administrative versus faculty control. When faculty has considerable control over internal budget allocative decisions, the overall administrative control is weak. When faculty cannot reach a consensus on budgets and has to depend on the arbitration and decisions of the administration, the relative power of the administration is enhanced. Therefore, it is the relative facility with which professional groups can reach a consensus that determines the extent to which this model is more or less participatory.

The advantages and disadvantages of the dual governance model are:

Power Relations. Participation is institutionalized, but the exact definition of relative roles is determined by practice, where the ability of the professional group to reach consensual decisions determines its relative weight in the balance. This explains why this has sometimes been described as a political model of governance (Baldridge, Curtis, Ecker, and Riley, 1978).

Diffused Decision Making But More Consensus. Decision making is shared and, therefore, diffused. The manager and the management team do not have direct control on the professional body. It follows, therefore, that certain kinds of decisions may take an inordinate amount of time. Since professional consensus is important on certain issues, the search for this consensus may be time-consuming. Elaborate committee work has to precede decisions to assure that all professional views are expressed.

Greater Participation. The model usually involves a greater proportion of the professional staff in the managerial decision making. In contrast to the partnership or senior staff model, the dual governance model usually involves most professionals in some form of participation in managerial tasks. Thus, in some universities all the tenured professorial staff might exercise important professional-managerial tasks. In others, even some non-tenured professors may be included. Yet other members of the professional community might not be included—lecturers, part-time faculty, and teaching assistants. The selection procedures for these positions may also differ. Such levels of participation in managerial decision making are inevitably cumbersome and are, therefore, suitable only for professional institutions of great stability.

The dual governance model is used in organizations such as universities or hospitals where it is desirable to delegate selected managerial decisions to the entire professional staff and where other managerial responsibilities are best handled by management. The model tends to be used when:

- Professional participation in selected managerial decisions is crucial to the success of the enterprise.
- Greater levels of professional participation are important to professional motivation.
- Some managerial tasks do not benefit from considerable professional participation.
- Professional consensus building is important.
- The organization is relatively stable. It does not need to adapt too rapidly to the environment and can benefit from careful examination of alternatives in making professional choices.

The Collegial Model

In the collegial model, all professional participants are equals and participate fully in the collective managerial task. The collegial model extends the partnership model to include all professional participants. It is usually not practical for larger organizations, but is quite often used in small, intensive professional organizations where democratic participatory management is practiced. These organizations will often involve most of their entire staff in decision-making processes and seek to maintain internal cohesion and avoid the need for management conflict arbitration by reaching consensus on all or most decisions (Mansbridge, 1980). The advantages and disadvantages are:

High Motivation. In general, these organizations are able to maintain high levels of individual commitment as long as professional consensus is easily reached among all members of the organization. When conflict erupts, decision-making processes can become both time-consuming and erosive of professional values. This is particularly relevant when the organization seeks to achieve unanimous consensual decisions.

Lesser Career Structure. Since these organizations tend to promulgate democratic ideals of equality, status differentiation among members tends to be eliminated. This may be attractive to some professionals who espouse the same personal values, but fails to provide a visible career ladder.

High Trust. Given that professional-managerial role definition is institutionalized and that most relevant decisions require a consensus, experimentation with different work patterns is facilitated by the trust that prevails among members. These organizations can be highly adaptive and responsive to changes in the environment.

Instability. In due time, certain personalities and power relations inevitably emerge among the members. Sooner or later, an informal power structure is established, but since this is contrary to the ideology of these organizations, this tendency toward a managerial reality where unanimous consensus is no longer effective tends to create the seeds of destruction of these organizations.

The collegial model is often used in voluntary or similar organizations where commitment to the task and to participatory ideals is high and where trust is important to task performance. In general, this model is used when:

- The organizations are small and collective decision making is possible.
- The organizations perform complex tasks where high levels of trust have to exist among members of the staff.
- The organizations cannot offer many economic incentives and high motivational energy is obtained from commitment to egalitarian and participatory ideals.

The Bureaucratic Model

In the bureaucratic model, management controls professionals and routinizes participation. In contrast to the senior staff model, where the manager shares managerial responsibilities with a selected group of professionals, in the bureaucratic model ad hoc routines are established to elicit limited and routinized professional participation among any and all members of the staff.

Professional input into decision making is guaranteed by procedures whereby opinions are obtained and routinely processed. In this model, management determines the scope of professional participation in decisions. Routines provide the institutionalization of procedures. A bureaucratic model of a Mexican public utility where professional work is routinized is briefly described in Chapter One. Even unforeseen events can be categorized ahead of time and situations when more professional discretion is needed are predictable and therefore routinized. Thus, my engineer friends would jump out of their cubicles when the steam power plant was in an emergency. They would exercise greater levels of professional discretion during the length of an event that could have only two predictable outcomes: either the steam plant stabilized and remained on line, or it had to shut down. Their participation in higher levels of decision making was routinized.

As mentioned earlier, this model applies perfectly well to organizations in stable environments with well-understood technologies with little need for organizational adaptation and learning.

Few organizations fit such complacent realities. Therefore, one should expect few professional organizations to use this model. However, reality is otherwise. The bureaucratic model is widely used where it is not the correct model. We will explain why in the next chapters.

Conclusion

Managerial authority and professional authority inevitably overlap. We have discussed why authority is needed in organizations and showed that certain tasks are clearly managerial, others clearly professional, but that there exists a spectrum where joint managerial-professional responsibility and participation are required.

Two distinct perspectives can be adopted. One might think exclusively about the organization. One might focus on organizational goals, on the means needed to reach these goals, and spell out when and where management might seek out professional participation. Or, going a step further, one might conceptualize the professional organization as an aggregate where many talented individuals carry out professional careers to the benefit of the organization, the clients and public, and themselves. Again, one might spell out when and where management might seek to include professional values and knowledge in its decision process. The second approach might give somewhat different results. The terms of reference would be broader and the values of the professional staff would be taken into account. It is important to realize that there is no absolute rule as to how to conceptualize an organization. What I am suggesting is that successful professional organizations cannot disregard professional values.

A first objective is to clarify when professional discretion is needed for selected professional tasks and what professional participation is required in selected managerial tasks.

A second objective is to institutionalize management-professional relationships. As we saw, there are various institutional models. Some, such as the professional partnership or the collegial group, emphasize a professional orientation. Others blend managerial and professional influence in decision making. The choice of model depends on the characteristics of the organizational task, the environment the organization operates in, and the importance and relevance of professional knowledge to the organizational mission.

Basically, the underlying principle that determines how much influence is given to a professional voice in management is determined by organizational dependencies for professional knowledge and skills. Greater professional participation in managerial decisions may not always give the kind of answers management wants to hear. But we may want to remember the failure of the space vehicle *Challenger* on its launching on January 28, 1986. Low temperatures were experienced on the launching pad during the preceding days, and engineers at Morton Thiokol, the manufacturer of the booster rocket, had argued against the launch, fearing the effects of these low temperatures on the gas seals of the booster rocket. As the *New York Times* reported several weeks later, and as was confirmed in the subse-

quent official investigation, management overrode professional
advice:

> According to all accounts, Thiokol's first
> recommendation, based on the potential effects of
> the cold on synthetic rubber seals that keep hot
> gases from escaping from joints in the solid-fuel
> rocket booster, was not to attempt a launching be-
> low 53 degrees. The predicted temperature for the
> launching the next morning was in the mid-thirties,
> and the nighttime temperature was dropping well
> below the freezing mark at Cape Canaveral, Fla.,
> even as the conference wore on.
>
> "At some point after that recommendation,
> someone called a five-minute break," said the
> source, who insisted on anonymity. But the recess
> stretched more than half-an-hour, the source said,
> and when it resumed, top Thiokol managers re-
> versed themselves and gave approval for the launch-
> ing.
>
> Both investigators and engineers at the com-
> pany say they do not know what led to the reversal.
> A company spokesman has said that the reversal
> came "after considering some additional informa-
> tion," but the information itself has never been
> specified. One engineer, who insisted on anonym-
> ity, said today that it was clear the final decision
> to launch or not to launch the Challenger "was
> going to be a management decision, not an engi-
> neering decision, but no one said that explicitly"
> [*New York Times,* February 21, 1986, p. 9].

4

The Role of Planning
in Professionalized
Organizations

We are concerned with managing what the organization will become. In this chapter we focus first on goals. Our purpose is to clarify the important difference between professed and operational goals. Professed goals are the ones we like to talk about, those that are commonly taken for granted. Operational goals are the real goals we actually pursue. They may not be as popular or recognized. We stress this difference because managers of profession-oriented organizations have to pay far more attention to operational goals. Otherwise, valued professional and organizational activities may be jeopardized.

Having made this distinction, we then discuss ambiguity and the management of ambiguous situations where it is not clear what we might or should do. These kinds of situations often prevail in profession-oriented organizations.

Last, we spend considerable time discussing partial planning. Our purpose is to better understand and explain the process whereby management and professionals jointly define desirable operational goals. We discuss the potential utility of partial planning as a complementary managerial tool that helps specify operational goals and facilitates envelope supervision and the performance of joint managerial-professional tasks. We

97

stress the importance of partial planning as a means of facilitating a discourse between management and the professional staff.

Two Concepts of the Organization

When thinking of the future, we can use two concepts of the organization. The first is given by the conventional imagery of a goal-oriented organization. The organization employs professionals and other workers, many white-collar employees, and is no different conceptually from any other organization. Management is concerned with using the most effective and efficient means to reach organizational goals.

The second concept is more complex. The organization is understood to pursue goals, and the conventional imagery we used is still relevant. But superimposed on that image we add the organization as a location where many individuals pursue careers, where professionals perform tasks according to organizational and professional norms, and where the interests of the entire staff, the clients, and the general public are also pursued. Management in this more complex imagery is not just concerned with using the most effective and efficient means to reach organizational goals; it is also concerned with overlapping goals—those of the organization, those of the staff and the professions they comprise, and those of clients and of the general public to the extent they affect the organization. The bottom line may still be to use, or find, effective and efficient means to reach organizational goals, but new constraints have been added. The goals of the organization may not be the only relevant goals. Pursuing these other goals may be necessary to satisfy needs that cannot be disregarded. Even if management wants to be hard-nosed and organization-centered, paying attention to these constraints may make the difference between failure and success.

In this construct, the professional organization is far more than an aggregate of employees. It is imbued with values, with human capabilities that cannot be disregarded without making errors of judgment. The goals the organization pursues are many, and management needs to understand their elusive and transcendent quality.

Goals: Myth or Realities?

What is a goal? As Scott says, "Goals constitute a central reference point around which we can understand the organization" (1981, p. 16). They are also crucial to those who manage or work in the organization. Their daily language continually refers to organizational goals, and they use goals to define what they will do and how they will do it. As Simon (1976) has pointed out, goals are the value premises that guide managerial decision making. He views goals as the assumptions that lie behind management thinking. It is, therefore, possible to understand the goals of the organization by describing the structure of the organizational decision-making mechanism. For example, one can find out to what extent overall goals, like "profit" or "conserving forest resources," help to determine the actual choices and decisions of management.

A goal is a statement about the future. It is a desired condition to be achieved. Goals can be specific or vague, and they can be overarching or broken down into subgoals.

Professed Goals. Professed goals are statements, accepted dogma, or implicit assumptions behind what the organization says it is about. In contrast, operational goals are the actual purposes pursued as revealed by actual behavior, including the use of resources or the actual premises of managerial decisions.

Professed goals are important to the organization because they define what the organization claims to be about. Professed goals serve to motivate participation of the staff. Florence's battered-women refuge was able to attract resources and volunteers because she announced what she was attempting to accomplish. Her staff might have had different motivation in joining, but the general purpose was clear to them. The goals also served to mobilize resources. The funding agencies were suddenly concerned with a problem that had been disregarded until then and quite happy to find a group of professionals already in place and able to initiate programs.

A principal function of professed goals is to provide legitimacy for action. We can start with the division of labor. Once we state what we are doing, we can divide up the means to these ends, assign tasks, and rationalize our actions.

Professed goals are not always explicit or detailed. What exactly a mean is, and what exactly a goal is, are not always agreed to easily. When the organization is broken down into subunits charged with achieving means to broader organizational goals, these means become the goals of these subunits. Professed goals also serve to define what the organization does not do.

Florence's Refuge was dedicated to helping battered women. The goal statements did not provide specifically for marriage counseling, although the center did, in some cases, provide this service. The Refuge claimed that it was not interested in male rehabilitation, although it could have been. It just happened that most of the staff did not feel they could help both the women and the men in the same organization and at the same time. There were some disagreements about this, but by and large, the goal of the Refuge was to serve and help the battered women and to deal with the men only to the extent it helped the women. Thus, resource allocations, task assignments, and the whole ethos of the Refuge went into that direction. When the issue was raised, the professed goal was reaffirmed in meetings or in conversations: "We are not dealing with the men. We are helping battered women." But this did not stop staff members from attempting to guide disturbed males into therapy, and, operationally, the Refuge had considerable involvement with males.

Operational Goals. Our informant student was a volunteer at the Refuge. She used her work experience for a master's thesis, and she undertook an evaluation of the early years of the Refuge. The evaluation included an assessment of the goals and broad objectives of the Refuge as revealed by the professed goals, the grants and contracts the Refuge had received, and the programs that had been put in place. She paid attention to the difference between professed goals as enunciated in documents and to operational goals as revealed by the way the staff spent time and resources. She ended with an account of what seemed to have been achieved and what had not been achieved. She discussed some outcomes and made a few recommendations. But when she handed in her thesis, she said that she had had considerable difficulty. She had found that the Refuge staff was involved in many activities, and she was no longer quite certain which were means to goals, which were professed, and which were operational. She said that she was not so sure the concept of goals was very helpful to her. At that point, I encouraged her with some remark about wisdom residing in the awareness of ignorance.

When we look carefully at the Refuge or at any other organization, we rapidly notice that the organization undertakes many different transactions with its environment. Thus, in the case of Florence's Refuge, there were other purposes and functions underway.

A principal concern at the Refuge was to raise the levels of consciousness about the problem of battered women. Florence and many of the other staff members were active in the feminist movement. They knew that many women were subject to male abuse, but were not sufficiently aware of their own predicament and condition or were afraid to seek help at the Refuge. The Refuge organized conferences on the subject and called attention to its work. At one point, several anonymous case studies were published in newspapers, and some battered women spoke on the radio and took phone calls from listeners. Many members of the staff lectured to groups about their work and experience. These activities were not spelled out in the reports or official evaluations, but they took place and were considered quite important by most of the staff, both professionals and volunteers.

The Refuge was also concerned with getting other agencies to respond to the problem of battered women and more specifically battered wives. The staff of the Refuge had rapidly found out that there was considerable reluctance by many agencies—social work and church groups and, quite importantly, the courts and the police—to step into what was generally labeled as a family dispute. Cases would drag on and the home situation would reach very dangerous conditions before the court or the police seemed able to respond. In fact, as Florence pointed out in anger, it was as if "they want a dead body before they will do anything!" Thus, the Refuge staff, particularly the volunteers who were lawyers, were devoting some time to cultivating and establishing trust relations with other agencies. They wanted to be able to call on them when something serious was about to happen, and not have to wait until after it had happened. Other groups were important for other reasons. One repetitive problem the Refuge kept finding was that many a battered woman did not leave the relationship for lack of any plausible alternative. Family and friends might not be available. As a consequence, temporary housing, child care, and employment were relevant issues that had to be addressed. This required cooperation and support from a totally different set of agencies and organizations, many of which were not necessarily aware or even very interested in these problems.

The Refuge was also involved in political transactions with the city and with the mayor's office. The programs were given some publicity and were part of the mayor's attempt to build coalitions of support across many different emerging political groups. The mayor's office had been instrumental in getting the Refuge funded, but was concerned that the political benefits of the program might not also yield political costs. Some of the activities of the Refuge raised eyebrows. The mayor was quite concerned with the more flamboyant aspects of the feminist rhetoric sometimes heard from Refuge staffers, and the relationship was not always harmonious. From time to time, efforts were spent to clear up misunderstandings and keep channels of communication open.

The Refuge was involved in a growing network of similar groups. They kept informed and exchanged information within the United States and abroad. Time was also spent organizing the national network to spearhead a legislative agenda at state and federal levels.

All these activities might quite justifiably appear to be means or goals of the Refuge, but it is also obvious that they were not spelled out in the professed goal statement. Florence and her staff were feeling their way into a new situation with few precedents. It may be quite correct to say that they were working on the means toward goals, but there were no road maps to follow. Part of the reason Florence had trouble with the staff was that she assumed her vision of the Refuge, her definition of what needed to be done, was shared by everyone. In fact, there existed within the staff many different perspectives on what the Refuge was all about. There were differences of view about goals and about means to goals. There were also those who thought the Refuge should not be involved in politics, and they did not want to deal with the mayor, the police, or with other feminist organizations. There were different opinions on the attitude toward the men in the case load and on the ultimate Refuge orientation. Was the Refuge to be oriented toward counseling and improved marital relations, or was it to be used as a means of providing an alternative for women seeking to break away from unsuitable and violent partners? Was the Refuge a symbol of women's oppression to be used to foment an antimale stance within the women's movement? Some lesbian women activists saw it that way and wanted to use the Refuge as a visible clearing house for the worst of male oppression.

The professed goals of the Refuge were careful and benign statements written to elicit support from those that were expected to provide it. But its operational goals were far more complex. They arose from the large web of relationships in which the Refuge had to operate. Florence never confronted the lack of consensus within her professional staff and never attempted to establish such consensus. Yet the daily experiences each professional had were related to learning how such refuges operate. Knowledge was essential to deciding what external needs the Refuge would or would not meet and what techniques worked or did not work.

Florence's Refuge is useful to us because we do not have preconceived notions about how these new social institutions operate, and we do not assume we know what their goals are. But the same is not true of many older, larger, and institutionalized organizations. It is not uncommon for managers, the staff, or oversight functionaries to be overconcerned with professed goals. The reason is simple. Professed goals are the legitimate official goals of the organization. Control and evaluation center around goal specification and prioritization. Yet, all organizations use professed goals the way Florence's used hers. Professed

goals are the overt statements used to attract resources and provide legitimacy for the organization, but professed goals may be
only the tip of the iceberg of transactions that the organization
has with its environment.

Let us take another example—say, the public schools. If
we ask the school board member about the goals of the school
district, she or he will first answer that the goal is to provide the
best education possible for the children in the district. After
that, the board member may go into more detail, speak of raising students' scores on state tests, the need to provide job-ori-
ented education, or the need to provide better art and music
programs. But the discussion will center around professed goals
of the district. However, the schools fulfill many other transactions with the local community. They serve to store the children while the parents work. They serve to keep them out of
mischief. They serve to begin the arduous task of selecting those
children who will continue on to higher education and select
out those who will not. They serve to operationalize societal
objectives such as racial integration. They serve to provide non-
family role models. We could continue to list other functions
besides educating, transmitting the culture, or inculcating the
values of the society.

One might want to argue that every one of these other
transactions is a means necessary to reach the broader goals of
educating children. For example, one might argue that storing
children in the classroom is necessary so that the teacher can
impart instruction. Therefore, it is one of the means toward the
goal of educating these children. But, if this were the case, there
would be no parent objection to home-based school programs
using educational television and computer-assisted instruction.
Whether the school wants it or not, parents, and particularly
working parents, schedule their own time and life around the
expectation that children will be in school several hours a day.
This external need is not related to the goal of education unless
we agree that in this universe all things are related. This is a secondary function or transaction that the school undertakes with
parents. If we observe how school administrators spend the
school resources, we find that this activity is very much in their

minds. We find that they discuss it openly, and they may even establish after-school programs for children of working parents.

Operational Versus Professed Goals. Florence's Refuge and this public school case provide us with two dimensions of the difference between operational and professed goals:

1. Operational goals reflect all the transactions that have to take place as the organization discovers what needs it meets in the external environment that supports it. It may find conflicting needs. For example, the needs of battered women were not always coincidental with the needs of the mayor's office or of more militant feminist groups. The mix of transaction the organization meets depends on the ability of the organization to drop some needs and clients and still attract resources for survival. Thus, to the extent that the Refuge was in a crossfire between the mayor's office and some feminist groups, it attempted to deal with the ambiguity of the situation by having different relationships with these external forces and by keeping the transactions out of the floodlights of publicity. This was done at all levels, including that of individual professional workers.

2. Operational goals include transactions that cannot be explained in terms of the rhetoric of the professed goals. Yet the organization does not alter or drop these transactions if doing so would jeopardize its own survival. American public education has seen many programs designed to use technology that would dispense with the school "storage" function. These programs have tended to fail. On the other hand, other similar needs have been dispensed with in other social sectors. These tend to be situations where the affected citizens are not as numerous, as affected, or as vocal. For example, the reduction of funding in child care or in length of hospitalization illustrates this. One can also speak of the storage function in health care. Hospitals store the physically ill and mental institutions store the mentally ill. Given cost constraints, many more patients are discharged from health institutions sooner and certain kinds of cases are no longer treated permanently in mental institutions. Here the trend has been toward decentralizing, moving away from large mental institutions toward community facilities, and many slightly crazy people who might have been stored in the

past now roam the streets, possibly for their own good, possibly not.

Private Firms. We might assume that the distinction between professed and operational goals is more relevant to government and not-for-profit organizations than to profit-making firms. After all, profit-making firms have a simple goal, that of maximizing profit. But, while the concept of maximizing profit may seem simple, it does not tell us exactly what kinds of services we should or should not provide or products we should manufacture. It does not tell us which clients we should serve and which we should avoid. It provides very few guidelines about the future. We may select products and clients purely on profit considerations and be out of business in no time at all. Firms that employ many professionals, such as management consulting firms, investment managers, and research and engineering firms, intertwine relationships with their clients and the public and government. In the case of manufacturing firms, they may have intertwined relationships with their suppliers also.

When I was at Stanford Research Institute in the early 1950s, the best-known management consulting firm in the United States was Booz Allen & Hamilton. In those days, that firm was strongly oriented to professional values. It selected clients and the work it undertook with care. Later the firm was run more along profit-maximizing considerations. At that time it also converted from private to public ownership. The new management ran it more as a business than as a profession-oriented organization. The firm did not do well, and it is no longer a leader in the field although it has been brought back by a group keen on rebuilding it (Vertin, 1984). The point is that private firms that employ many professionals undertake complex tasks. These firms cannot be run on a simplistic notion of maximizing profit. They have to pay attention to the transactions they have with their environment.

Goal Displacement. The definition and the scope of the transactions the organization undertakes are obviously professional concerns where management and professional knowledge are relevant. It is also obvious that any management approach that overemphasizes professed goals and downgrades operational goals does not deal with the relevant reality. But, as we shall discuss in the next chapter, the bureaucratic organization uses professed goals to rationalize work. In our current administrative culture, it is normal for these controls to emphasize a rational approach where professed goals have a dominant place. The question is, are professed goals useful? Do they represent what is important? If they do not, overemphasis on professed goals can result in goal displacement.

Goal displacement is the substitution of narrower goals and specifications for more desirable, larger, and unspecified goals. This is often a situation where quantifiable specifications of professed goals are used to justify what is done, but if these specifications are carefully examined and discussed with the professional staff or with clients, they are not considered too important. For example, most teachers and parents would agree that test scores are not that important per se and do not represent what they mean by the word *education*. And yet, in the absence of better indicators, most parents will tell you that they prefer their children to do well on tests, and most teachers and school administrators become very aware of this desire. As we shall see in subsequent chapters, their response often overemphasizes tests to the detriment of their performance as educators.

The reason management has to be very concerned with the difference between professed and operational goals is that overemphasis on the wrong goals reduces professional discretion and can be dysfunctional to the organization. This, of course, is the problem in overbureaucratized organizations where professional values are downgraded but where service and products suffer because the wrong objectives are pursued.

In the next section, we will examine in greater detail how managers and professionals can jointly decide what useful goals are to be pursued. We will discuss situations of ambiguity such as Florence's Refuge to perceive the way transactions are discovered, met, kept, or rejected.

Managing Ambiguity

Every manager experiences situations where possible alternative courses of action emerge: new programs might be initiated, new pressure groups ask for services, but there is ambiguity as to how to proceed. Conflicting viewpoints are expressed, and it is not clear which course of action is preferable. These are situations where approaches are still tentative and the organization is experimenting with the environment. Florence's Refuge is a small organization in an ambiguous situation where different clienteles with different viewpoints exercise pressure on her and her staff. However, her experience is not so different from that of larger organizations in similar situations. As we examine the experience of the Refuge, we notice an eight-step repetitive pattern that is not uncommon in organizational life.

1. Trust. There is an attempt to establish trust relations within the staff. These trust relations revolve around what the group is about. In the case of the Refuge, trust relations were not achieved. It is useful to understand why.

2. Symbols. Next comes a search for a language and symbolism that represent what the organization is doing. These are both ideological and mythical. They are the kinds of statements that say "we stand for quality." In professional organizations, the search for and the meaning of this language are very important to the staff.

3. Experimentation. Then there is a phase of experimentation, of trying things out in the environment. This is a threatening period because some approaches work and others do not.

4. Stabilization. This is a time when the staff begins to define more exactly what they are doing and not doing. They begin to give names to activities. This may be labeled as the phase when environmental transactions and the use of relevant technology are defined.

5. Selection. The next phase consists of choosing among these activities, rejecting those that create too much conflict, absorb too many resources, or simply do not work.

6. Reaffirm Trust. At this point, the staff needs to reaffirm trust. So much change is taking place that it is important to know whether everyone is still satisfied, to resolve conflicts, and to reestablish trust.

7. *Modify Symbols.* Once trust is reestablished, the organization alters its ideological and symbolic representation. It talks differently about itself because it knows what it is no longer doing and what it will continue to do. If external pressures are exercised, internal trust will be important.

8. *Normalization.* In this last phase, the organization is no longer in an ambiguous situation. Transactions with the environment are normalized. This is the institutionalization phase.

Internal Trust

While it is true that Florence never achieved the kind of cohesion one might expect in a small task group of very dedicated people, it was obvious that she and her staff sought such relations from the start. Everyone sensed the importance of working closely together and many members realized they were involved in a complicated task. Why did she fail? What are the requirements for trust relations between managers and professionals (Deutsch, 1962; Zand, 1972; Barber, 1983)?

Acceptance of Rules of the Game. First, trust depends on a shared acceptance of the rules of the game. In any organization there exist both formal and informal rules as to what is done and not done. It may be paradoxical, but it is nevertheless true, that trust which allows us to let go of controls, to avoid routines, has to depend on shared acceptance of rules. We trust each other when we both accept and practice according to a well-understood code of behavior. This code may vary in different cultures and contexts, but it has to exist. I need to know how you will act if I give you secrets, how you define agreements, and so on.

A first problem Florence encountered was related to her lack of understanding of the role of management. Trust was difficult to establish with the professional staff although she had known many on the staff in previous social and work situations.

She had been friends with several of them, and they all shared a very strong concern for the battered-women issue. Clearly, these were dedicated people and every one of them expected close working relations with Florence. But Florence misread their genuine concerns for desires to impose their will upon her. She saw herself as the only person in charge. Conversely, they thought she was not a good manager and did not trust her at that level even if they liked her and supported her.

Predictability, Reliability. Trust requires predictability and reliability. We trust individuals when we can predict their behavior, and when they perform as we expect them to behave. From the start, Florence was taken aback by the behavior of many members of her staff. She expected them, somehow, to spontaneously gather around her and assist her. Since they did not seem to do what she thought they should do, she had trouble predicting what they were doing and they did not perform as she expected. Similar problems arose within the staff and trust was eroded further.

Integrity. Trust requires a belief in the integrity of all participants. We trust those we believe will respect the rules of the game even if it is not in their interest to do so. They fulfill promises and agreements. It seems that this was not the case at the Refuge. Did the staff overcommit itself to tasks it could never accomplish? Did Florence expect too much? Whatever the reason might be, Florence did not trust the promises of the staff. Some of these problems were a matter of capability, but as external pressures and internal conflicts grew, it became a question of integrity. In the end, Florence was no longer convinced of the purity of the acts of some staff members.

Shared Commitment. Trust requires a shared commitment. While the staff and Florence shared a very strong commitment to the cause, there were many divergent views as to how to proceed. Florence probably sensed this underlying unrest quite early in the activities of the Refuge. She realized that, left on its own, the staff might go in many directions at once. She was, in all probability, tempted to assert her vision to maintain the Refuge on a reasonable compromise between the many factions at work. But the fact that she asserted authority without attempting to work out internal conflicts tended to reduce internal trust.

Capability. Lastly, trust requires a recognition of mutual capability. We not only trust those who play by the same rules, are predictable and reliable, have integrity, and share a common interest, we trust those whom we know to be capable. We know they can perform. Unfortunately, at the Refuge, there was considerable doubt about the mutual capabilities of management and the staff. As a result, there was far less trust than was needed to deal with a very ambiguous situation.

Since trust was lacking, it was difficult for Florence to delegate. She centralized, but was rapidly overwhelmed by the amount of work she and her two co-founders were faced with.

Search for Ideological and Symbolic Myths

In all organizations there is a set of normative statements about the organization, statements that depict what the organization is about. They may include public relations–type language, but that is not all. They include all the assumed values and purposes that the members of the organization use both formally and informally to describe themselves: "Here, at the clinic, we are very concerned with doctor-patient relations. We want the patients to feel that we have a genuine concern for their health. Our staff goes out of its way to make patients feel that we really care."

In ambiguous situations, the ideological and symbolic language is used for several purposes. It is used to determine whether certain actions should proceed: "We do not do that kind of thing. It does not fit our image of our organization." It is used to legitimize action or to explain why action is to be undertaken: "It is our style. It is the kind of project we undertake." The language is important because it symbolizes positions in conflicts: "They want to go ahead, but we never undertake that kind of project. We cannot accept."

The Mexican electric utility had clear-cut goals. What was ambiguous in that situation was the long-term relationship with the government. Ideological and symbolic discourse was focused on these issues. The company attempted to present itself as an efficient producer of electricity. Some political factions depicted it as a foreign capitalist ogre. The reality was that the company was efficient, but since the government controlled the electric rates, the government could strangle the expansion of the private companies while fomenting that of the state electric enterprise. In due time, a compromise was reached and the company was purchased by the government. Meanwhile, the symbolic and ideological representations were very important to each side. They were tools in a value conflict.

In most professional organizations, external or internal myths are very important to the staff. They are part of the accepted culture of the organization. They are the myths of the organization (Bhagat and McQuaid, 1982; Dandridge, 1980; Meyer and Scott, 1983; Schein, 1985; Smircich, 1983; Wilkins and Ouchi, 1983). If various professions coexist within the organization, or if various schools of thought hold sway, these representations will be important to each of them. They legitimize ways of thinking and acting. As Argyris and Schon (1974) have shown, effective professional practice derives, in part, from intuitive knowledge and this intuitive knowledge is related to professional mystiques that are to be found in all professions. Similarly, the choice and affirmation of organizational representations is important to all professionals: "We like to work at the lab. We want it to be the best in the country. Management is dedicated to quality. We never accept contracts unless we know we have access to the best people." The language may be fought over because it symbolizes deeply felt values and commitments.

In Florence's Refuge, the staff was small enough to be able to discuss the definition of what the organization was about. Florence apparently never really discussed the topic officially, although in daily contacts, she must have stated beliefs and discussed them. There were ideological cleavages among staffers and arguments about what the Refuge was or was not. Florence probably saved time by avoiding formal participatory discussions. She may have fomented internal conflict in so doing.

The Experimental Phase: Testing the Environment

The organization invents representations of what it claims to be and do, and also tests out the environment. The professional staff enters into transactions. Reality begins to prevail. The clinic may be dedicated to having all its doctors show a genuine concern for each of the patients, but patient load and time demands result in impersonal, routinized relationships. Some of the early myths begin to be eroded by actual experience of repetitive transactions.

Attempts to maintain ideological or mythical purity may take place. We see all this in the Refuge. From the very beginning, Florence and the staff were experimenting with the environment and with the technology to be used: What kind of clients would the Refuge take on? What role would the Refuge play in the community of relevant agencies? Some staffers felt that the Refuge should spend much more time as an advocate of their clients *vis-à-vis* all other agencies. The male psychiatrist stressed rehabilitation and wanted the Refuge to take a greater role in marital counseling. Other staffers supported his stance. There were also considerable differences in interest and participation in the larger issues of the women's movement. Staffers were not always clear in their own minds how much of the Refuge effort should go into feminist work even if they were totally committed to the cause. Some argued that the success of the Refuge would be the best contribution they could make to the movement and that Refuge needs should take precedence. Others argued that movement needs should take precedence over Refuge activities, or they argued that movement needs coincided with Refuge needs. Symbolic and ideological representations were used to justify activities.

In the midst of these discussions, learning took place. In most instances, the staff learned from direct experience. They learned from the battered women who came to them with real problems and had no desire to wait for the enunciation of more perfect symbols and better ideological definitions. Reality asserted itself. Cases had to be handled and cases determined practice. Here, Florence lost out because she never involved the professional staff as much as she might have in experimenting with new approaches, creating different work teams, or exploring different alternatives to generate external support.

Stabilization, Selection, and Definition

As experience is acquired, the staff and management learn from errors and successes. Practice stabilizes as some activities are extinguished and others are initiated. This is an important period because the decisions made affect the future course of action. This is a time when management needs close contacts with the professional staff, when joint managerial-professional decision making is important. Florence and her professional staff did not achieve high levels of formal communication and did not reach a consensus. There was a lot of informal communication, but it tended to create factions and conflict. In any case, Florence and her staff were able to define what they thought the Refuge should and should not do. They established patterns of behavior that were responsive to the needs of most of the women who came to them. Without too much internal cohesion, they were able to meet client needs. But their experience was affected by the nature of their work, and, in any case, they had considerable conflict at the time of Florence's departure. However, they were a small group and they were highly committed. In most professional organizations, size and hierarchical structure impede close cooperation between management and professional staff. Formal attempts to link the two are necessary.

Reaffirmation of Trust

To summarize: At first, the organization faces considerable ambiguity. Many choices and courses of action are possible and open. There are supporters and detractors, advantages and disadvantages. Experimentation and learning take place. Ambiguity is reduced somewhat as some paths are revealed to be nonexistent or clearly unsuitable. Theories about how to manage are emerging, but internal management-professional trust is affected because the organization is shifting course and this is not readily understood by everyone concerned.

Trust has to be reaffirmed to allow all members to internalize the new set of priorities and values that emerge from experience. Now the external environment can be better understood and described. The political forces at work, their interests and motivations, are no longer mysteries. The rhetoric of outside factions is not taken at face value. At this point, management and staff need to express and discuss the recent learning experience—to share it, digest it, and reaffirm trust. Florence went through such a process personally and may have shared it with her two co-founders. She did not succeed in bringing the rest of the staff with her to share this new knowledge. To be sure, the organization was small enough to permit sufficient flow of information in spite of Florence's managerial deficiencies. In a larger organization, these problems would have been far more intense. At the Refuge, enough was said to sense how the Refuge could adapt and progress. But by then Florence was disliked by many. The psychiatrist remained alienated and ultimately left the staff. The seeds of discord were becoming more visible. Florence was not able to maintain trust. In due time, accounting irregularities were to result in her resignation.

Modification of Ideological and Symbolic Representations

Had trust been reaffirmed and prevailed, the lessons of experience would have resulted in a simplification of ideological and symbolic representations.

There is no need to repeat over and over again what we are doing when we do it all the time. Professional norms emerge from experience. The staff at the Refuge are no longer flustered when the police misbehave or a battered woman suddenly returns to live with a dangerous man. They have learned from experience how to deal with these eventualities and do so. They internalize procedures and experiences and develop an accepted practice. The conflict around ideology and symbolism becomes far less intense as practice is institutionalized.

But as soon as changes take place, as soon as existing practice reveals itself to be insufficient, new ways of doing are needed and the ability to deal with ambiguity is needed. Yet the external presentation and rhetoric of the organization may not be altered too much even if everyday internal symbolism is simplified. Professed goals that were used to initiate action will probably survive. They are probably sufficiently vague to allow for any reinterpretation.

Institutionalization of Process

By now, many transactions have become part of accepted professional practice. The problem will be that they have not become part of the rational constructs management is tempted to use. We will discuss problems of rationality at greater length in the next chapter, but for the moment we will understand the process. Many transactions have emerged; some have been selected out. These transactions bind the organization with its environment. It is the sum of these transactions that provides the flow of input resources the organization acquires. In time, these transactions will change as external values and needs change. New needs in the environment will generate new transactions. New values in the surrounding culture will also result in abandoning some patterns and accepting new ones. New technological innovations might be the underlying cause of many such changes. Meanwhile, the profession adapts as knowledge and values are modified in the environment.

Similarly, the profession will adopt selected practices because they have been discovered to work. For a time, there may not be any theory as to cause and effect. We may not know enough to elaborate what economists call a "production function," a theory that explains why input variables are associated with output results so that we can use the theory and manipulate inputs to achieve desirable outputs. Much less may be known about the practice, but the good professional is able to use existing knowledge to solve problems.

We have spent considerable time discussing Florence's problems because I wanted to emphasize management's responsibility to understand what it is that the organization does. We tend to take the goals of the organization for granted as if we knew what they were. But goals are a very complex concept. Good managers are aware of this. They understand the difference between professed and operational goals. They know that professional knowledge and experience help define operational goals. They avoid goal displacement. They are oriented to professional values and eschew bureaucratic solutions that deal with appearances but not with reality.

Planning

In the concluding pages of this chapter we discuss planning in some detail. Planning is important in adaptable and flexible organizations because it provides the necessary lead time for defining new goals and learning how to do. Planning has other functions in organizations with many professionals. It provides a vehicle for managerial-professional discourse. It helps dispel suspicions between the professional staff and management. It provides opportunities for creating trust relationships.

Some planning is useful and some is not. When planning is overemphasized, it is overambitious and unrealistic. Good examples of this include planning, programming, and budgeting systems (PPBS) and comprehensive strategic planning, two instances when planning became dysfunctional. Planning is important to managers of profession-oriented organizations because it substitutes for excessive routinization. But to be useful, planning has to be partial and incomplete. Otherwise, better forget about it. As a shrewd manager once told me when he heard I was writing a book about planners: "I don't mess with planners. It's a waste of time. They want to reinvent the wheel. I want to do things and that takes all my time."

Planning Defined. Planning is a process whereby an organization, or several, or a city, region, nation, or several nations agree on a set of specifications about the future. In contrast to goal statements that tend to be general in nature, more often vague than not, plans have a time dimension and an operational specificity. We may plan for several months ahead, a year, or several years. We may provide fairly detailed specifications of what we expect to accomplish in this period: "In five years, we expect to reduce the illiteracy rate by half" (Benveniste, 1977; Boguslaw, 1965; Gans, 1968; Harris, 1949; Krieger, 1981; Mannheim, 1965; Schaffir, 1976; Steiner, 1979).

Plans have a very different function from goals. Where goals serve to elicit external support and provide legitimacy for the organization, plans are far more important in reducing internal uncertainty and ambiguity about the future.

Plans can never cover all the operational goals or transactions of the organization, but plans operationalize *both* professed and operational goals. This is why planning can be so important. It allows management and the professional staff to pay attention to important operational goals and not get trapped in the limited and artificial discussion of professed goals.

Goals are usually purposefully vague so as to allow many different interpretations. With vague goals, support is obtained from many factions that might not readily agree if goals were specified in detail. But vague goals are also a source of uncertainty. Plans deal with this uncertainty by specifying actions to be undertaken.

Avoiding Errors, Buying Lead Time. Science and technology are continually contributing to massive reinvention of the culture, and as a result, interdependencies are multiplied. The organization cannot proceed without care. Experimentation and the search for accommodation with the environment are important. Some errors are desirable, but major errors have to be avoided, primarily articulation error where the organization fails completely to sense important changes in the environment or in the technology it uses. An articulation error results from the absence of coordination or mutual adjustment between needs and availability.

What is an articulation error? Suddenly the demand for widgets evaporates or the techniques used to deal with a social ill no longer work or one trains to become a scientist and research money is cut and opportunities for scientific careers are greatly reduced. An articulation error can be caused by external shifts in consumer demand or by technological change or a wide variety of factors that impinge on the organization. The ability of the organization to learn and to adapt to such changes depends very much on the time dimension involved. Hirschman (1970) describes consumer response to declining product quality. Faced with one supplier whose product quality deteriorates with no corresponding price change, consumers will simply shift supplier. If product quality goes down gradually and consumers begin to change supplier one by one, the supplier will note the problem but have time to learn and remedy the situation. With enough lead time, the recuperation process may take place. Hirschman then suggests that it is good for organizations to have both alert and inert consumers. The alert consumers provide the supplier with negative feedback, but the inert consumers remain unaware of product deterioration and continue to buy, thus giving the organization time to learn and adapt.

Planning for a single organization is buying lead time. A typical planning exercise consists of scanning the environment of the organization and matching internal capabilities to environmental change. The future is uncertain and considerable research has to be conducted to begin to have a perspective on changes taking place. The shrewd manager who did not waste time talking to planners did his own planning. He ran a very small firm, so this was possible. But he kept his ears to the ground; he watched the course of events. When he acted, he knew what he was going to do. As he would say simply, "I have it figured out."

Deterministic Planning. Certain probable changes in the environment, or in the organization, are determined by forces outside the control of the organization. For example, probable enrollment in the schools during the next few years is already partly determined by the number of children born in the last few years. The total age cohort that could be enrolling in kindergarten, high school, or college is already determined by many independent decision makers, namely by the new parents. For these children, there is no retroactive policy that will increase their total number. The planners will also have to pay attention to migrations into and out of the area and to expected death rates to determine the total age cohort that might enter the schools.

Policy Choice Planning. Other probable changes in the environment or in the organization are determined by factors that are amenable to policy action. In other words, actions of the organization may alter the way the future evolves. The proportion of the total age cohort of children who will go to public school instead of private school depends on many factors, some of which are controlled or influenced by the public school. Moreover, as we follow this age cohort as it proceeds year by year through the public school, we will find that the proportion of children who have to repeat classes or who drop out is partly affected by policies instituted by the school. Similarly, the proportion that continues from high school to college is also partly affected by the counseling provided in the school, the availability and quality of precollege programs, the availability of fellowships, information about college, and so on. All these factors are amenable to organizational policy.

The elaboration of a plan involves elements that have to be taken as given—namely, aspects of the future that can be predicted at some probability level but cannot be affected by policy, and elements that are amenable to policy choices. This second dimension of the planning process inevitably involves planners in managerial and professional dimensions of decision making.

Planning is future-oriented but relies on past and present data to forecast or estimate probable developments. Therefore, planning exercises are necessarily dependent on a relevant data base. This implies the creation, use, or design of management information systems (MIS) that are policy- and future-oriented. My friend, the shrewd manager, was keen on data. He obtained government reports and bought trade publications. But he always tried to make sense of the figures by talking to others in the field. "Got to interpret everything," he would say. "Got to know what's really happening to make my moves."

The Planner Is Not a Technician. For a while, during the early days of the planning movement in the 1950s and 1960s, it was common to describe planning as a technical nonpolitical activity. For example, Charles L. Schultze, who was the Director of the Budget under President Lyndon B. Johnson, was also an early advocate of planning, programming, and budgeting systems (PPBS). In 1961, PPBS was introduced in the Department of Defense after about a decade of research by the Rand Corporation and other think tanks that had been applying systematic analysis to defense problems. In August 1965, President Johnson directed the major civilian agencies of the federal government to install PPBS along the lines of the Department of Defense model.

Schultze delivered a major lecture at Berkeley in 1968 in which he described the role of PPBS. He was keenly aware that analytical techniques were imbued with value content and that introducing PPBS in a political and managerial context was bound to have effects, but the concept of planning was then seen as technical. Schultze argued that the nation was faced with many problems and needs and that the federal government had mounted a large number of programs addressed to these needs. But government has limited funds. Program objectives require the application of resources over time. To reach any given objective, some means are more effective than others. Therefore, long-term planning and careful systematic analysis are needed to assist in the choice of alternatives (Schultze, 1968).

Schultze went on to show that analysis is politically neutral since it provides facts on which political decisions are then made, but that PPBS could be used to control large organizations. For example, the fact that agency heads would have to use output-oriented program categories for making broad, strategic budget decisions would oblige them to cut across artificial internal boundary lines. PPBS required agencies to drop line-item budgeting (where resources are required on the basis of expenditure categories such as 10,000 pencils, 20,000 notebooks) and to substitute programming budgets where money is required on the basis of spelled-out objectives. (We want to eradicate illiteracy in this village in three years. For this we need 2,000 pencils, three teachers, and so on.) Obliging the agencies to spell out objectives would provide top management with greater control over the choice of activities to engage in.

Schultze also saw PPBS as a means of providing more centralized control by giving agency heads far more programmatic

information about what was going on within the various bureaucracies they were supposed to manage. More importantly still,
he saw PPBS as efficiency advocacy, a kind of partisan work
where planners would normally encourage the decision process
toward the more efficient choices (Schultze, 1968).

As everyone knows, PPBS did not survive beyond the
mid-1970s (Millward, 1968; Schick, 1973; Wildavsky, 1969;
Worthley, 1974). We will not examine the multitude of reasons
for its demise. There were many reasons, but it is interesting to
think that the demise of PPBS did alter completely the "technical" perceptions of planning or of other rationality approaches
to management. Many planners today are still perceived and still
perceive themselves as professionals requiring autonomy. The
persistent imagery is that of the specialist, the professional who
has acquired analytical skills. Planners perform analysis and give
their analysis to management for action. In a recent study,
Baum (1983) interviewed fifty planners; he found they still
want autonomy and are frustrated by the fact they rarely obtain it.

We might expect this, since planners are in a profession
among other professions. The fact that planning takes place,
that planners are trained in analytical techniques and acquire
specialized knowledge and skills, means that it is normal for
them to behave as professionals. They desire autonomy, peer review, and so on. The problem, of course, is that professions like
that of planner are not independent activities. They have to be
linked to the other professions in the organization. They have
to learn to work together. They have to be able to communicate with my old friend, the shrewd manager.

The Demise of Comprehensive Planning. At first, planning was conceived as an overarching enterprise. Given that organizations, cities, or nations pursued many objectives, it was
plain common sense to wish to put some order in a complex set
of decisions. If resources were to be allocated more reasonably,
it was necessary to have an overview of the sum of objectives to
be pursued. PPBS asked each agency to spell out and prioritize
objectives so that rational allocations might be made in light of
the relative importance of each objective. The comprehensive
overview had many advantages for management.

First, it gave agency management a privileged position *vis-à-vis* the competing demands of the various bureaus or subunits of the organization. With their staff planners, top managers were in the position to see a larger universe than the narrow views of the bureaus and of the professions that inhabited them.

Second, the comprehensive approach gave the planners and top management legitimacy to question the activities of all subunits, including those that might have powerful constituencies and be quite accustomed to protecting their turf. In most planning situations, the comprehensive planners serving top management were authorized to obtain data from subunits and to use this data in their analysis. Knowledge is power and could be used to control.

Third, the comprehensive approach served management well in the search for external support. Agency heads testifying at the time of budget appropriation could present a rational, integrated overview of agency purposes, which gave the impression, if not the reality, of effective, purposeful management.

Why did the comprehensive approach collapse also? Because planning happens to also be a political process of consensus building. The more comprehensive the plan, the harder it is to create a consensus among all those who are to be involved in its implementation. Their support is necessary to create a belief that the plan is indeed going to be implemented and is not going to end up on a shelf gathering dust. There exists a multiplier effect in the planning process, whereby a careful choice of technical data and analysis combined with political support come to create a generalized belief in the plan. Once this belief is generated, other relevant actors shift attitude and preferences to take into account the high probability the plan will be implemented (Benveniste, 1977). This imagery is quite different from the conventional role definition that asserts that planners serve management and that management has the authority to instruct implementation.

Of course, management has the authority to instruct implementation, but that authority is associated with the position. It is not authority emerging from felt needs coming up from the bottom ranks. Planners may write beautiful blueprints for the future that have no impact on organizational activity simply because the plans are opposed and sabotaged by the staff of the agency. Management may order but not be obeyed, and advise and the advice not be taken. Or, it may be obeyed or followed to the letter and we quickly discover that the plan does not work.

Comprehensive plans often bog down because the political process of interest aggregation and consensus building is too complex. Planners who are wise to the political dimensions of the planning process soon discover that it is not feasible to reach vast agreements involving thousands of people and dealing with the long-range future. Too many individual and group interests, or ideologies, are at stake. Turf protection becomes a central preoccupation of participants. In a way, planning is an open discussion of future arrangements and power relations. The moment the discussion is initiated, it is as if planners were attempting to resolve, in the present, all the potential future conflicts that can be expected over a long period of time.

Comprehensive planning received a *coup de grâce* from Caiden and Wildavsky (1974) in a study of planning in Third World countries. They demonstrated that comprehensive national economic plans undertaken at the behest of foreign aid agencies were not worth the paper they were written on. Caiden and Wildavsky chided Third World country leaders and all other managers and politicians still attempting to write comprehensive plans. They suggested it was not worth the effort. If people insist on comprehensive plans and one cannot change them, one has only to provide a glossy brochure. It would be just as useful.

From then on, comprehensive planning was discredited, but that did not mean that analysis was discredited or that planning was ended. It simply meant that the process of coalition building and the creation of a multiplier effect could be achieved only on a small scale where the time and resources available to the planners, combined with the participation of relevant implementers, result in an agreement about the future course of action.

Planning in the Profession-Oriented Organization. Here planning is a participatory process, preferably a continuous and permanently staffed process, involving small participatory teams.

Each of these teams is charged with a set of specific finite studies on policy topics amenable to forecasting, projections, or model building and charged with determining and shaping professional consensus on desirable courses of action. From time to time, these studies are aggregated, and the professional staff participates in a larger discussion of the broad alternatives facing the organization. Applied Research practiced this kind of planning under the second manager. She would meet with the senior staff in periodic planning exercises. Together they would take a retreat of several days, to assess their long-term position, achievements, and prospects and to assign specific planning studies and tasks to selected members of the staff. Once these studies were completed, they would meet again, discuss them, and make long-term decisions on space, hiring, equipment, and the pursuit of new clients.

Specifying future objectives in greater detail may not always be feasible or desirable. As we saw in some of our case studies, the organization may be involved in emerging transactions in a changing environment. The nature of external needs may not be well identified or may be changing. Planning in these situations does not consist in making detailed specifications of objectives, but instead in undertaking market-oriented research to sense and evaluate potential needs and clienteles.

If the environment is better known and transactions well established, the specification of objectives might take various aspects: It might be a search for a consensus when consensus is lacking. Or it might be an attempt to involve the profession in defining valid and reliable objectives when these do not exist but are desired. Or it might be an attempt to better understand the consequences of using selected target specifications on the way tasks are performed. For example, management and professionals may participate together in defining specifications that enhance performance (see Chapter Five).

The fact is that management can use planning to establish new linkages with the professional staff. Joint assignments on planning task forces of both management and professional personnel provide opportunities for profession-management discourse as well as new ideas and opportunities.

Planning Conceived as Incomplete or Partial. The mix of

transactions the professional staff has, or might have, with the environment might not be known ahead of time. As we saw, the professional staff espouses an ideology and uses symbolic representations of its activities that do not necessarily describe what is significant today and may be significant in the future. It is, therefore, necessary to establish trust relationships among management, planners, and professional staff to elicit accounts of these transactions. The design of a good plan for the future cannot be derived from an erroneous assessment of what is really taking place in the present. Therefore, planning in the profession-oriented organization has to be incomplete and partial. The planning exercise does not attempt to unravel every policy option. It is focused on discrete topics.

Since planning is a process of coalition building and consensus seeking, the role of planners is constrained by the knowledge they bring to the situation, that is, by the choice of analysis and data they can produce. Planners will have more influence than other professionals where they are able to quantify and project data about systemic changes in the environment or in the organization. This urge toward quantifiable data influences the content of planning exercises. It tends to create more interest in those aspects of the organization or of its environment that are both predictable and measurable and less interest in those aspects that are less well understood, less predictable, and less measurable and therefore require learning and adaptability. This is as it should be. Planning should be used to reduce uncertainty where possible. The wise manager, however, cannot allow this natural propensity toward quantification to downgrade those aspects of the organization that are not as easily understood, predicted, and analyzed. As long as planning is understood to be partial and incomplete, the problem can be avoided. In that perspective, planning is used only to settle courses of action that are clearly predictable and amenable to a rational calculus, thus leaving time and resources to attack those issues that are not well understood, where professional discretion is important, and where planning is not yet relevant.

Planning as a Management Tool. Planning can be used to define, within a future time horizon, the elements of envelope supervision that are predictable. Let us take an example, that of strategic planning in the public schools. Planning exercises might provide school managers with relevant data and projections of school-age population, student flows, revenue and expenditures, aggregate faculty recruitment needs, facilities inventories, and site planning. Other portions of the exercise might focus on assessing client preferences (parents, citizens, and students), assessing teacher and management opinions on selected policy options, analyzing student outcomes, examining the governance structure of the schools, mapping the significant political actors in the local community and surrounding environment, conducting analysis of plausible coalitions of support for various policy options, and so on.

All this might be amenable to policy research and to quantifiable results. Some issues might be left purposely unresolved. The planning exercise might discuss various concepts of educational goals, curriculum, and student performance indicators. It might identify data sources and indicate their strengths and weaknesses. It might provide preliminary analyses of relevant relationships, but restrain from going into areas where knowledge of the process is still limited.

Envelope supervision is the delegation of task authority to professionals within a parameter of controls that are selected because they are well understood. We may understand quite correctly how many pupils will probably attend school next year, how many will have preferences for certain kinds of program, what facilities might be used, and so on. This planning information provides the framework for shaping the definition of the tasks to be accomplished. What may still be left to the discretion of the professionals in the organization is the whole gamut of issues where knowledge of the process is not well understood and where task variability deters routinization. How the teachers organize themselves, what mix of programs are used, might still best be left to the discretion of site professionals who deal on a day-to-day basis with the clientele.

Planning as Efficient Professional Participation. Planning reduces the overall costs of professional participation. Planners are the staff of the organization. They provide the flow of information needed to keep all parties informed. In Chapter Three, we discussed the importance of professional participation in decision-making processes—when professional knowledge is needed in managerial decisions.

However, participation is time-consuming and expensive. It can also cause delays in the decision-making process. Professional workers are rarely inclined to want to spend many hours in policy-making meetings. While they may want to have an impact on decisions that affect their work, they are conscious of costs. Management has similar concerns. Planning is used to reduce these costs. Analysis of the options facing the organization can be undertaken in such a way that professionals can have input in the analysis without having to participate in every step of the process. Since planning has a future orientation, it is possible, ahead of time, to determine the content of professional inputs and to provide this participatory information at decision points without causing unnecessary delays. In this imagery, planning is the search for a consensus, but this search is carried out by a small permanent staff.

The organization may still use professional and managerial time to discuss how it will deal with environmental and internal changes. For example, the entire faculty of the college may be asked to join the administration in a three-day retreat to discuss a five-year plan to renovate its undergraduate programs and initiate a new extended professional graduate program in the city. This particular participatory effort comes in the course of an ongoing and continuous planning effort in which most of the faculty have participated in one way or another. The retreat is highly successful because all the groundwork has been completed and many sidetracks have already been eliminated. The two or three important decisions that remain can be handled by the large group without having to bog down in endless meetings. As one participant reports:

> Many in the faculty claim they wish to be
> more involved in policy, but that does not mean
> they are good at policy making. There needs to be

a strong guiding hand to keep the discussion on track. The propensity to act out, to assert one's pet theory about life, is always present. Faculty simply love to talk. They surely enjoy displaying their eloquence and influence. This planning effort proved very productive. There were much fewer wasted meetings, although we still have some people who cannot resist the opportunity to shine, and some of them can drag us into arcane discussions, but the work had been done. A number of the right people knew what was important. I believe we discussed the option of the extended program competently and thoroughly. This was a big step forward for our faculty.

Planning as a Troubleshooting Unit. Planning provides management with additional informal links with the professional staff. Planners emphasize their concern with the future and with policy choices. Specific issues place them in direct contact with relevant professionals, but they are not involved in a supervisory relationship. Planners are perceived as other professionals and not as significant supervisors and evaluators.

As long as planning is not perceived as a managerial technique of evaluation, it may, in fact, serve as an effective source of monitoring information. As we shall see in the next chapter, excessive evaluation can also hamper learning behavior. Faced by a problem, career-oriented professionals may not reveal their doubts and difficulties if they sense that their supervisors will also use this information when evaluating their performance.

An advantage of planning over direct supervision or even evaluation is that it tends to place today's issue in a time-future context. The time-future perspective of the plan makes current practice less relevant. The question is what to do next instead of asking what did we do right or wrong. To be sure, evaluation of the present is implicit in planning, but the problems of justification and blame are less salient. This is relevant in organizations that depend on the ability to recognize errors and learn from errors, a characteristic of most profession-oriented organizations. In this context, planning serves to protect management and allows it to give greater discretion to the professional staff. It protects management by providing necessary monitoring information.

Planning Contrasted to Regulation. Lastly, the reason the profession-oriented organization relies on planning is that planning—in contrast to regulation—emphasizes a system approach where inputs and outputs are relevant but procedural controls are not.

Current regulatory practice affects management in many ways. All organizations are regulated in one way or another by statutes or by specific government agencies. As a result, the style, culture, and language of regulatory practice tends to prevail in administration (Benveniste, 1981).

As we shall discuss at greater length in Chapter Eight, regulatory practice emerges from legal thinking and intervention. Regulation is centrally concerned with issues of fairness, consistency, and reasonableness. When statutes are enacted, the problem the statute addresses—say, affirmative action or collective bargaining—is defined in language that is defensible in the courts. The questions are formulated in procedural terms and use standards and rules. Is the standard fair, reasonable, and consistent? Can the procedures be detailed so that it can be determined whether or not compliance has been achieved? Can legal enforcement be obtained? These legal concerns drive administrative practice directly toward routinization and the reduction of discretion. To be sure, too much discretion can result in arbitrariness, unfairness, and inconsistency. But too little discretion can also be a problem. Good laws should enable action, not hamper it (Horowitz, 1977a; Nonet and Selnick, 1978; Shklar, 1964).

Planning is not dependent on rule setting and the reduction of discretion. Planning is far more suited to the concept of envelope supervision and, therefore, more appropriate to profession-oriented organizations. It is to be hoped that drafters of statutes and regulatory legislation will pay more attention to these issues in the future.

Conclusion

In the bureaucratic organization, goals are well understood because the future is predictive and repetitive. But in the kind of organizations that interest us here, the future is often highly uncertain, practice and products are changing, and management has to be keenly aware of the need to focus on what it is the organization does. We stressed the difference between professed goals and operational goals to point out that rhetoric can be confusing. Transactions are what matter. The profession-oriented organization engages in a multitude of purposeful transactions with the environment. In exchange, the environment provides the necessary resources for the survival of the organization. It behooves management to eschew rhetoric and pay attention to reality. These transactions are the iceberg of the purposes of the organization. The professed goals of the organization happen to be the visible tip of the iceberg. They may well be a very important part of the iceberg, but they never represent all the relevant transactions.

When the organization is new, it learns about its environment, about the needs that it can meet, about the purposeful transactions it engages in, and a selection process begins to take place. Management or the professional staff might decide that some transactions are undesirable, that some purposes are more valuable than others, either for the organization, the staff, the clients, or the public. In time, external intervenors or controllers might also impose controls and see to it that the organization responds to client or public needs.

Since many of these purposeful transactions are not part of the official rhetoric of the organization, management and professional staff have to become aware of their existence. I know of no better demonstration of the importance of this simple statement than the multitude of futile efforts to initiate home programs using new educational technologies such as television- or computer-assisted instruction that might eliminate, or significantly alter, the schools' child storage function. It is revealing that such technologies and programs are well accepted in higher education or in public schools in areas of the world where low population densities and great distances make this a necessity. Such programs do not prosper otherwise. I would argue that the managers who initiated these programs did not pay sufficient attention to the difference between professed and operational goals. They did not have close enough contacts with professionals in the field who might have told them why the projects would probably fail.

One conclusion is that trust is more important in professional than in routinized organizations. Trust is not only needed to allow for delegation of authority and discretion, it is needed to allow a flow of realistic information about the purposes and activities of the organization. Bureaucratic organizations that have simple goals, operate in stable environments, and use well-understood technologies, do not need to experiment with their environment or with their technology. In these simpler situations, the official rhetoric of the organization, including their goal statements, is probably a fairly good approximation of what they are about. The Mexican electric utility is much easier to study and understand than Florence's Refuge. A simple diagram and description tell us much about the roles and functions of the operation, maintenance, and construction departments. In contrast, Florence's Refuge is not so easily described, and many staff activities and purposes do not immediately appear so evident. Managers whose training or experience has not been in professional organizations tend to underestimate this need for close ties with their professional staff. This is not an issue of people-oriented versus task-oriented managerial style. It is the matter of communicating realistically instead of ritualistically.

Another conclusion is that management of profession-oriented organizations needs greater reliance on analysis because it cannot rely as much on routinization. As we explore the reality of professional organizations, we discover over and over again that their activities are not as easily routinized, that more judgment has to be exercised. The professional staff needs to learn when to act and when not to act, when individuals should clear decisions with others and when they should not. Rules may be established, but in the final analysis, it is not so much the rules that matter as the ability of task groups to know how to work together. This is not a simple matter, and there is no easy definition that tells us what is an appropriate level of discretion. Management in professional organizations needs more planning and analysis because such knowledge provides protection. Protection is essential to permit delegation and discretion. It is not useful to tell managers that they need to learn to delegate authority and, as we did in the preceding chapter, remind them they can never delegate the ultimate responsibility for outcomes. Planning and management information systems are used to monitor in a nonevaluative mode that allows both the flow of relevant information upward to management and still maintains staff ability to commit errors and learn from them.

Not all planning is desirable. As we saw, planning can be overambitious and unrealistic. The demise of PPBS, or of comprehensive planning, provides us with an approximation of what is meant by overemphasis on planning.

We stress again that the profession-oriented organization pursues both professional and organizational goals. This is another way of reminding us that the professions will have goals of their own that cannot be disregarded. As practice evolves, the many transactions the organization has with the environment will reflect subtle overlaps between what is purely organization purpose and what is organization and profession. If I can remind you again of Florence's Refuge, many of her activities and many activities of her staff had more to do with professional development in the emerging practice of these centers than in specific goals of the Refuge. The manager of professional organizations needs to keep these distinct dimensions in mind as he or she applies a rational calculus to determine the effective or efficient path into the future. If there is one lesson to conclude with, it is that simplistic rationality does not always work best. We discuss this at greater length in the following chapters.

5

Managerial Approaches
That Enhance
Professional Productivity

We have discussed the utility of partial planning as a management tool. In this chapter we explore other tools, including programming, management by objectives, management information
systems, cost-benefit analysis, and performance monitoring systems. All these tools are fairly conventional. Here we want to
understand their utility and also to stress their limitations, even
the danger they present in adaptive organizations.

To do this, we need to better understand our central purpose: to reduce bureaucracy and increase effectiveness. In the
first chapters, we emphasized what is wrong with bureaucracy.
The time has come to define what we mean by organizational
effectiveness. Then we will examine the relationship between
management tools and the system of rewards and punishment.
Why is this relevant? Because organizational ability to learn and
adapt depends on the correct linkage or lack of linkage between
management tools and motivators for professionals. We, therefore, spend some time explaining how the system of rewards
and punishments operates.

Having defined organizational effectiveness and having
understood how the system of rewards and punishment functions, we next describe management tools, their utility and lim-

its. We conclude by describing six dangers the manager of the profession-oriented organization needs to guard against.

Organizational Effectiveness

What is organizational effectiveness? Individuals evaluate the performance of organizations depending on their own experiences as clients, staffers, or plain observers. Barnard, in his classic book on the functions of the executive (1938), defined organizational effectiveness in terms of being able to attain specific desired ends. However, the question still remains, whose ends are sought and achieved? From a theoretical point of view, there are several ways of thinking about organizational effectiveness.

Professed Goals. The analysis can begin in terms of professed goals: Is the organization achieving what it claims to be doing? This raises the iceberg issue. Suppose the professed goals are only a small part of a larger set of transactions between the organization and the environment? Or suppose we stress profit maximization but we have a very select clientele and, in fact, if we pursued the notion of profit maximization and forgot about our select clientele we would be out of work. That is not effectiveness.

Transactions. The analysis can start with a list of many transactions. This involves a system view of the organization, and how effective it happens to be in a multitude of different exchanges with its environment. Now we are looking at what the organization actually does for its environment and whether it does it well.

Constituencies. From a political perspective, one could narrow the discussion to different constituencies. We could conceive of the organization as serving many different publics, including that of its own professional staff and of the public at large. The question then becomes, how is the organization serving the different demands of these constituencies? How is it serving the public good?

Meta-Values. One might initiate the analysis on the basis of meta-values criteria and ask how well the organization is performing on these criteria. For example, one might be concerned with organizational health (Kets de Vries and Miller, 1985) or with productivity and creativity (Nash, 1985) and ask about effectiveness in reaching criteria of health or creativity. Or we might be concerned with larger environmental and ecological issues or with how the organization contributes to world peace.

Goal-Free. Last, we might approach the problem with no preconceived notion. We might simply find out what the organization is doing both for the environment—that is, its clients and so on (the transactions)—and for itself (the staff, the stockholders), and then evaluate how effective it is, even if it is not pursuing its professed goals.

Given these different possible approaches, it is no surprise that the concept of organizational effectiveness acquires different meanings. The literature on organizational effectiveness provides many possible criteria that can be used. For example, Cunningham, in a paper on the selection of criteria to assess organizational effectiveness (1977), suggests various models: the rational goal model; the systems resource model (how does the organization allocate its own resources internally? is it using them optimally?); the organization development model (is the organization able to solve problems and renew itself?); the bargaining model (is the organization able to elicit support from the staff?); the structural model (how stable is the organization? are lines of command legitimate? is there continuity? is there homogeneity of outlook?); the functional model (how does the organization serve client groups or society?).

Steers (1975) reviewed many such models. Analyzing the most important evaluation criterion used in seventeen models of organizational effectiveness, he found considerable divergencies in point of view. Only one criteria was used in more than half the models: adaptability-flexibility. The other criteria used, in descending order of frequency, were: productivity, job satisfaction, profitability, acquisition of scarce and valued resources, absence of organizational strain, control over external environment, employee development, efficiency, employee retention, growth, integration of individual goals with organizational goals, open communication, and, last but not least, survival!

Since our focus is on reducing bureaucracy, we are especially concerned with adaptability and flexibility. This is an important criteria not only for achieving results, but also for motivating the professional staff. Job satisfaction, employee development, open communication, and employee retention mesh well with professional values and the importance of intrinsic work-related motivation. Effectiveness, efficiency, productivity, and the integration of individual and organizational goals are central concerns of the profession-oriented organization.

Effectiveness, in this context, is the ability to create an organizational structure that provides for sufficient professional discretion and yet maintains the organization on course. As we saw in the preceding chapters, the concepts of envelope supervision and of joint managerial-professional tasks provide both for professional autonomy and participation in decision making. Our concern now is to understand better how motivators are activated. How does the professional respond to the system of rewards and punishments? How is the system of rewards and punishments linked to management tools?

The System of Rewards and Punishments

I use this term to include the sum of organizational motivators that orient professional behavior. The system of rewards and punishment (R&P) includes both extrinsic and intrinsic motivators.

Extrinsic and Intrinsic Motivators. Extrinsic motivators are economic rewards such as salary bonuses, fringe benefits, expense accounts, paid vacations, and so on. Intrinsic motivators are rewards associated with the work itself, such as the quality of work, opportunities for exercising professional roles, the status associated with the job, the importance of the job to society, opportunities for self-actualization or self-improvement (Clark and Wilson, 1961; Hopkins, 1983; Pinder, 1984).

Herzberg (1966) claims that five intrinsic motivators—namely, achievement, recognition, the work itself, the level of responsibility, and opportunities for advancement—are satisfiers. By this he means that their presence is sufficient to motivate positive attitudes toward work. He then lists eleven other motivators that act as dissatisfiers. Their presence is not sufficient to motivate better performance or positive attitudes, but their absence causes unhappiness and negative attitudes. Among the eleven dissatisfiers, he lists salary, possibility for growth, relations with subordinates, status, relations with peers, supervision, and job security.

Herzberg's satisfiers are high in the set of professional values discussed in Chapter Two. These include the work itself and the opportunity to perform professional work, the level of responsibility and discretion that can be exercised, professional visibility, and opportunities for professional advancement. These satisfiers are particularly important to the overall system of reward and punishment. More recent research on professionals in organizations confirms the importance of these motivators, particularly career status within the organization (Guy, 1985).

The Danger of Goal Displacement. The system of R&P relies on the appeal of the organization's professed goals. Most professional organizations pursue goals that are strong motivators of behavior. As mentioned previously, the professional organization is similar in this respect to the volunteer organization, where the goals of the organization motivate participation. Therefore, goal displacement is a serious problem in professional organizations because it can result in reduced motivation for participation. Goal displacement is the substitution of desired goals by other, less desirable goals. It usually happens when goal specification requires use of proxy measurements and the proxy measurements come to displace the goals or when means to goals become overimportant and replace the goals themselves.

Any time management sets performance objectives and ties strong incentives or sanctions to achievement, it risks goal displacement if the specified objectives do not represent or include valued goals.

An illustrative and vivid example of goal displacement and its impact on professionals is provided by the history of the World Bank under Robert McNamara. Prior to McNamara's tenure as president of the bank, his predecessors had pursued complex objectives in using the resources of the bank to help developing countries. Without going into the ramifications of the development process in Third World countries, we can simply summarize their efforts: they used bank lending to transfer resources from the rich countries to the poorer countries and, at the same time, they used the leverage of the bank lending to promote more desirable internal economic policies. This leverage function was quite important to the professional staff of the bank, who were highly motivated to use their broad knowledge of economic development to help the borrowers improve their economic prospects.

When McNamara joined the bank in the late 1960s, he paid attention to quantifiable outputs and emphasized volume of lending. It became known in the bank that volume of lending was an important criterion. His first major policy objective was to double the average rate of lending during his first term. As Kamarck (1982, p. 952) tells the story, growth in the volume of loans continued to be his most important management goal throughout his administration:

> McNamara's emphasis on achieving quantitative loan targets had large repercussions within the Bank. Whatever the president's rhetoric in acknowledging other goals, every one of the staff knew that what counted was to fulfill the lending program. However, the staff had been trained under Black and Woods to regard a loan as a vehicle through which to secure better economic management in a project, sector or economy. What this means in some cases is that it is better to refuse than to make a loan. (For example, in 1957 when Spain joined the Bank, Black informed Generalissimo Franco that, on the recommendation of the Bank mission, the Bank would not consider lending until Spain had made drastic changes in its financial and economic policies. With a parallel position taken by the International Monetary Fund and OECD, the liberalizing group within the Spanish government won the day and Spain took off on a

sustained burst of growth.) Under McNamara, a
conscientious Bank staff trying to achieve "management" objectives at the cost of the lending program did so at some cost to themselves.

Putting the emphasis on the need to achieve
lending targets resulted in what some bitter Bank
staff called "reversal of roles." The loan officer's
career was dependent on the willingness of borrowers to accept loans. The official Bank line . . . was
that the quality of Bank projects was as high as
ever. But this is not to the point: a power project
during the McNamara years was undoubtedly a
good project but the real question is whether the
Bank negotiators were as successful as they would
have been earlier in getting improvements in rate
policy, for instance.

Organizational Transactions with Environment. Since the
organization may be involved in many other transactions with
the environment, these transactions also motivate participation.
Mercenaries join armies not because they believe in the cause,
but to make money and, more importantly, because they enjoy
the work. They enjoy the excitement, adventure, and risk. As
we saw in Florence's Refuge, some staff members were motivated not only by the work itself, but also by its contribution
to feminist causes. They saw the Refuge as a vehicle to carry
that cause forward and to participate in the movement. Overemphasis on objectives that do not include valued activities can
also reduce professional motivation.

Linkage Between Objectives and System of R&P

The operation of formal or informal links between targeted behaviors or objectives and the system of R&P involves a
four-step sequence: (1) criteria setting; (2) sampling performance; (3) comparing performance and criteria; and (4) applying rewards or punishments (Dornbusch and Scott, 1975).

Criteria Setting

Criteria setting and criteria perception are keys to understanding how the internal control system functions. At Applied Research, the professional staff knew, or thought they knew, what their manager wanted. As one staff member reported: "[The first manager] is a shrewd politician, but he worries much too much about the reports. He also pays too much attention to details like who works when. If he calls you at 8:15 A.M., he expects you to be at your desk. He is always visibly annoyed when he does not find you *in situ* grinding away. He expects everyone to work overtime. In fact, he expects everyone to work overtime every week of the year. That's what matters to him. Also, he does not want complications or trouble. He wants a simple report, lots of data, a few cautious assertions, and please, 'no waves.' "

Most of the staff knew that to stay in the manager's good graces they had to be available and on call, and had to produce reports on time that caused no embarrassment. It was well known that this manager liked those few staff members who were always willing to respond to his call. They formed a small group of intimates around their prince. They would work late at night and on weekends. He shared small talk with them, but even so, he rarely brought them into his confidence. Still, promotions and the more interesting assignments went to them.

At Applied Research, there were a variety of rewards including recommendations for better jobs elsewhere. It was generally assumed that to succeed with the first manager, one had to be around, be willing to spend the time on the job, and produce whatever he asked for. Staff members who balked at sudden changes of assignment, or had ideas or plans for new activities, or preferred to work on flex-time, or asked to be allowed to attend professional meetings, or departed in any way from the two valued criteria, seemed to be in trouble.

When we interviewed the staff, we were surprised by the extent to which the professional staff members seemed to be informed of this manager's predilections. There was a strong consensus about what were perceived to be the criteria he used to reward or punish the staff. These perceptions are what mattered. The staff responded accordingly. The internal system of control linked the various goodies the manager could distribute to what the staff thought he wanted. He was vocal enough and consistent enough to give clear messages.

Formal Criteria. In some organizations, criteria are formal. For example, one purpose of management by objectives (MBO) is to set individual criteria for performance evaluation. Where tasks can be routinized, performance evaluation can also be routinized. The conventional personnel department establishes criteria and formal procedures for this purpose. In professional organizations, even if formal procedures are used, informal perceptions and linkages remain important.

The main reason is that extrinsic rewards, such as salary raises, are usually linked to a formal system while intrinsic rewards like a good work assignment are linked to informal daily managerial practice. As a result, perceptions of what is important come from both formal and informal processes.

Even when criteria are formal, perception of their relative importance is affected by staff experience. If experience is fairly consistent and repetitive, as was the case at Applied Research, a consensus emerges. Perceived criteria become operational and displace formal criteria.

For example, the faculty in American research universities are normally told that they are to be evaluated according to four criteria: research or creative work, teaching, university governance service, and public service. Within the various subcultures of the faculty, it is generally believed that research publications count far more than teaching or participation in university committee work or in public service activities. These perceptions will be stronger among the younger faculty who have not yet been tenured and are subject to dismissal: "It is well known on this campus that if you are not tenured and win the 'Best Teacher Award,' you have a good chance of being denied."

Management Tools and Perceptions of Criteria. Management tools influence perceptions of criteria. The fact that selected criteria are known to be important to management makes them important to the professional staff. Let me illustrate further with the criteria of teaching in research universities and the impact of management formulas that are enrollment-driven.

Teaching is not perceived as the most important criteria in most research universities. Teaching evaluations are conducted, students fill evaluation questionnaires at the end of the term, and some faculty may observe the teaching of their colleagues. However, faculty committees that decide on promotions and tenure tend to be far more concerned with the potential contribution of their colleagues to the overall status and external professional recognition of their departments and campus. Therefore, research publications and other creative works matter more in their eyes. But another factor affects faculty decisions. State funding for most public universities is provided through formulas that are enrollment-driven. This means that funding is related to head counts: so much money per full-time-equivalent student enrolled. When money is distributed within a campus, among competing subunits, there is a normal tendency to look at course enrollment. Thus course enrollment begins to take an importance that results directly from its relevance to funding formulas. One consequence is that some faculty begin to pay more attention to class enrollments in peer evaluations, even if they do not pay as much attention to the quality of teaching. This may result in both desirable and undesirable consequences.

Sampling Performance

Before rewards or punishments can be given, performance has to be observed. There may be a formal or informal sampling procedure. At Applied Research, the staff was aware that the manager would check who came in and at what time. Formal procedures provide for sampling performance and comparing with the criteria. In research universities, formal faculty peer evaluations depend on various "samples." Faculty are invited to submit their published output. This sample represents their entire intellectual effort. Letters evaluating this work are obtained from colleagues and other evaluators. This will be a sample to represent professional appraisal. Various teaching evaluations provided by students will assess the teaching effort. Later, the ad hoc faculty committees will also rely on their own knowledge of the case. Ultimately, a report of faculty discussion and vote during a departmental promotion meeting, together with the recommendation of the department chair, will compose the dossier that is sent for further review by other faculty and administrators.

For some faculty, publications provide a valid indication of their intellectual output. For others, they do not. But publications are relatively convenient to review; this is why they are used. It is more difficult for faculty to sample and evaluate the quality of teaching of their colleagues since they rarely attend their classes. Student evaluations and gossip, while indicative, do not substitute completely for evaluation that peers can conduct directly.

Characteristics of the sampling procedure affect faculty performance. When the review process is secret, younger faculty, up for tenure, are careful to avoid unseemly arguments with any and all senior members of the faculty since any one of them may be appointed to review their work. The frequency of sampling also affects faculty performance. If faculty come up for evaluation every two or three years, this tends to affect the scope of research and publications produced. The committed professional who does not care about organizational rewards may stick to one research project for ten or fifteen years. Most of the others will select research topics or books that can be produced in the available time frame.

In organizations where criteria and sampling procedures are not formalized, there may still emerge a widespread perception of what seems to be sampled. At Applied Research, it was assumed that timely production of reports and individual presence and availability mattered. Since it was not always clear when the manager would call on staff members, many made certain to be on hand when he was known to be in the office. Staff members whose time might be spent more profitably outside agency headquarters instead stayed in the office, to be seen and be available. Few people were around when the manager was known to be out of town.

Very strict adherence to report production schedules had undesirable consequences. Since it was well known that the manager wanted reports on time, and seemed extremely insistent, the staff tended to avoid telling him about serious data analysis problems. In instances when he should have been informed that the quality of the work would suffer without a time extension, the staff did not inform him. They assumed, correctly or incorrectly, that he would evaluate them negatively and penalize them.

Perceived criteria and sampling procedures have consequences. The staff responds by transmitting what they think management wants to hear. Professional standards are eroded by perceptions of the way the system of rewards and punishment functions.

Comparing Performance and Criteria

In the next step performance samples are compared with criteria. Even if the comparison is formalized, the professional staff will acquire perceptions of its own. They may come to believe that they are not made or at least not the way the formal procedure says they should be made.

Some criteria are perceived to be more important than others because they happen to be the only ones that lend themselves to comparison. Quantitative criteria are easier to compare than qualitative criteria. This may explain why quantitative measures may be expected to displace qualitative judgments in some evaluative schemes and why perceptions that the contrary is happening will surface in others.

This dimension of the process is particularly significant in professional organizations because comparisons between criteria and sampled performance inevitably entail professional judgments. The question then becomes, who is making these judgments and do they possess the necessary professional expertise?

When it is known that evaluations are conducted by nonprofessionals, nonprofessional values may tend to dominate. As we saw, the Applied Research manager was known to be a stickler on the timing of report production. This was more a managerial than a professional issue. The fact that he ran the evaluations and made assessments influenced staff perceptions of what was supposed to be relevant. It also affected their level of commitment. They perceived that professional values were downgraded and professional incentives diminished.

Shared perception that evaluations are made on inappropriate criteria can lead to strong dissatisfaction. For example, faculty may come to believe that they were denied or promoted because of political beliefs, race, or gender. Faculty and administration in universities are always attentive to such issues, and grievance procedures are established to maintain the credence and legitimacy of the review process.

Applying Rewards or Punishments

Finally, the control system operates because rewards or punishments are actually given. Such control works most effectively when

- Positive rewards are used in preference to negative sanctions.
- Rewards are given very soon after the desired performance is achieved, so there is no doubt why one is rewarded or sanctioned.
- Rewards and sanctions are strong enough and correspond to performance achievement.
- Achievements are challenging and rewards imply recognition of strong achievements.

Scarcity of Rewards. Professional motivators are both intrinsic and extrinsic. Extrinsic motivators, such as salary and other economic benefits, may be scarce. Management's task is to create an effective system of R&P that is more than the mere application of good personnel management techniques. Management has to figure out how intrinsic motivators can complement or even replace extrinsic motivators. For example, in the research university these motivators are many. They not only include promotions or tenure appointments, but a vast gamut of "goods" such as research money, support staff, research space, status, travel monies, parking spaces, invitations to official functions, and so on. The management of intrinsic professional motivators requires familiarity with professional values and goals. The way to avoid losing a valued professor may not be as simple as giving her a raise (although it will help). It may involve giving her enough money to organize a research conference on her latest research topic and showing interest in her work, her hopes, and her ambitions.

Because economic benefits are not always available, intrinsic benefits may have far more importance in day-to-day management. This may explain, at least partially, U.S. data on performance. Research on the links between worker performance and economic rewards shows that salary increases are better explained by seniority than by performance (Lawler, 1971; Medoff and Abraham, 1980, 1981; Abraham and Medoff, 1983; Stern, 1986).

The situation in public education is illustrative. In the public schools performance pay is still used rarely, although attempts have been made in the past and will be in the future (Stern, 1986). Teachers are generally given salary increases for two reasons: seniority and completion of staff development activities (taking courses at the university, in-service programs, completing requirements for advanced degrees). But teacher salary structures tend to be relatively flat: there is not much progression from initial beginning salary to top salary. Moreover, the number of steps is limited so that most teachers reach the top of the salary scale at an early age. As a result, teachers are generally not motivated by extrinsic rewards because they know that such rewards are not available.

Short of reforming the level of pay and salary structures used in the public schools, the management of teaching has to depend far more on intrinsic rewards. The use of management controls, such as emphasis on performance indicators, controls on what and how teachers teach, and the routinization of teaching, inevitably makes teaching a less attractive profession. These controls are sometimes intended to guarantee minimum performance (Bridges, 1984). We may attempt to design a "teacher-proof" curriculum that would allow even the most inept teacher to manage to teach, but these controls remove sources of intrinsic motivation—namely, professional motivations. As a result, the system of reward and punishment is ineffective. There are insufficient rewards in the system. Motivating professionals purely on the basis of negative sanctions does not seem to be effective (Beck and Hillmar, 1986; Shapero, 1985; Wlodkowski, 1985).

The Timing of Rewards. Professional roles do not lend themselves to short-term, repetitive formal rewarding and sanctioning. Professional tasks have longer time horizons. Constant formal performance evaluations do not fit well with concepts of discretion and autonomy. Nor do they encourage risk taking and learning behavior. This is why informal rewarding is more significant in the professional organization. The longer the time span between formal evaluations and rewarding (extrinsic rewards—salary increases, promotions, and so on), the more often informal rewards have to be used (invitations, praise during staff meetings, opportunities for meeting colleagues, for discussing important work issues, and others).

Feedback. Given the importance of spacing formal evaluations, monitoring and feedback take on further importance. The research literature emphasizes the importance of feedback in situations of uncertainty. When professionals undertake difficult tasks, constant and positive feedback will reduce anxiety and increase confidence (Ilgen, Fisher, and Taylor, 1979; Larson, 1984; Nadler, 1976). The successful manager of professionals knows this and is always in close contact with the staff. Feedback takes many forms, both formal and informal. Close monitoring and feedback imply that managers circulate around, meet with the staff, establish necessary trust to elicit information, and show concern with the work of the staff.

Problem of Reward Legitimacy. The professional organization is more heavily affected by issues of reward legitimacy. Since intrinsic informal reward mechanisms are more significant, there is more danger that the staff will perceive these rewards are given for the wrong reasons. Put another way, the more rewarding is routinized, the more it will appear to be legitimate: "We all get these reviews, and there is nothing different in this case." The less rewarding is routinized, the more it may be perceived to be not legitimate: "The principal has his pets, and those teachers get all the good assignments." Therefore, a management problem consists in protecting the legitimacy of the informal rewarding process without complicating it.

One approach is to use secrecy. Many firms that use strong economic incentives (for example, financial management firms) decide to keep actual incentive awards secret. You are not supposed to discuss your end-of-year bonus with your colleagues to avoid jealous comparisons. Arguments as to the desirability and liabilities of secrecy are many. Obviously, rewards can lead to jealousy or to a sense of unfairness. It can also be argued that rewards *should* be awarded unfairly because different people are motivated differentially. Therefore, the wise use of resources requires different use of rewards to maximize motivation.

I see it differently. I would argue that the profession-oriented organization has to nurture trust. Secrecy, rumors, and perceived unfairness will not increase trust. There is no reason to keep awards secret. It is more important for managers to design a scheme they and the staff can live with.

Management Tools

Management tools are the eyes and ears of management. We will review a number of them to highlight their utility and dysfunctions.

In general, management tools are always useful for monitoring as long as they are not perceived, rightly or wrongly, to be tied to the system of rewards and punishment. The fact that data are collected—even if used for totally different purposes—can affect professional behavior. The manager of the profession-oriented organization cannot afford to ignore this potential, but very real, danger.

Some management tools may be dangerous if they are linked to the system of R&P. We shall examine six such dangers. A major difference between the overbureaucratic and the effective profession-oriented organization is that the first relies too much on routinized use of management tools that are linked to the system of R&P. The effective profession-oriented organization pays far more attention to professional motivation. It uses management tools for monitoring, but is far more cautious in using routinized evaluations.

Management tools are intended to inform and monitor, to reorient action, and to justify action. When they are used to inform, monitor, or justify action, managements tools are not linked—at least not formally—to the system of rewards and punishments. But when they are intended to reorient action, they are directly linked to rewards or punishments.

For example, if we assess performance to justify what we are doing or to inform about what we are doing, we do not need to link the results of the assessment with any reward or punishment. However, if we want to raise performance, we find that informing is not enough. A carrot or a stick is more effective. We link performance with rewards or punishments.

Our concern here is with this linkage. Do management tools that are intended only to inform or justify action also reorient professional behavior? More important still, do management tools that are intended to modify or redirect action have undesirable consequences? We are concerned here with the way excessive or improper use of managerial tools causes them to be perceived as obstacles that render professional work more difficult and, therefore, less attractive. Ultimately, we are concerned with professional dissatisfaction, with job stress, alienation, and burnout (Cherniss, 1980; Maslach, 1982; Paine, 1982).

Programming and Program Budgeting. Programming is the selection of target objectives and the elaboration of means to reach these objectives. Typical techniques include PERT (program evaluation and review technique) and CPM (critical path methods). These two techniques specify time dimensions for goal achievement. Given a specific target to be accomplished by a specified time future, the analyst works backward to determine when and how activities have to be initiated, scheduled, and meshed together so that the goal will be achieved. These techniques are useful in complex projects, such as preparation for a space probe, where many different components have to be designed, tested, and produced before the probe can be brought together. An important aspect of these techniques is lead time analysis, the study of inevitable delays, which can be taken into account when scheduling component activities.

Program budgeting is the elaboration of budgets that are linked to specific programming activities. It is a leftover residue of larger scale (entire organization or entire federal system) planning, programming, and budgeting systems (PPBS) that came into disuse in the early 1970s (see Chapter Four). Program budgets, as we saw in the previous chapter, break down line itemization (so many pencils, so many workers, so many tons of coal) into component programs. Programs are justified by their goal objectives and specifications.

These techniques can be used to set priorities and optimize the use of scarce resources toward objectives. In complex technical projects (space probes), they provide opportunities for making allocative decisions (time and resources) that reflect both the relative importance and the uncertainties associated with components of the mission. All these techniques are useful in situations where goals are specific, the technology is sufficiently understood to permit handling of uncertainty, and analysis can be used to minimize risk while achieving target objectives effectively and efficiently.

Management by Objectives (MBO). This programming technique emphasizes strong management-staff contact and discussion. A purpose of MBO is to have management and staff discuss their work assignment and agree to specific objectives for a given time frame. In general, MBO requires periodic review meetings where past assignments and accomplishments are discussed and evaluated and future objectives set. In contrast to programming and program budgeting, MBO is less analytical and more supervisory in content. Time frame, selection of targets, and techniques of evaluation depend both on the nature of the tasks and on supervisory objectives. Again, this technique may be highly effective in work situations where professed goals are few and congruent with major organizational activities or where management has a good understanding and is sensitive to relevant transactions (Levinson, 1970; Odiorne, 1969).

The technique is not effective when too many objectives

are pursued and the relationships between means and ends are not well understood. As a teacher reported in a study I conducted: "My principal wanted each teacher to spell out objectives for themselves and then assign how much time they would devote to each. That exercise collapsed because once we began listing objectives, we had a difficult time deciding how important each was. We knew we had to do all of it. We had to teach, maintain discipline, deal with that overenergized youngster in the class, assign and grade homework, meet parents, patrol the halls, and do playground duty. Who would tell us exactly how to spell out objectives? We bogged down just trying to describe all the things we had to do."

Shapero, after reviewing considerable research on MBO, concludes (1985) that the mixed results of the research suggest that the main explanation for its success is management commitment. But this is probably an oversimplification. Commitment, while important, is not sufficient to explain success or failure. MBO works well when the future can be easily defined, understood, and packaged—less well when it cannot.

Management Information System (MIS). Generally, MIS is a computerized system providing management and staff with information, but it can be more. MIS can be the sum of all the intellectual tools that management and staff can use to establish what the organization is doing and how it can reach desired goals. MIS has become far more important with the advent of low-cost computers. With the availability of a data base and the design of data collection, processing and distribution are influenced, in part, by goal specifications (Atherton, 1978; Kraemer, Dutton, and Northrop, 1981; Gruber, 1981; Riley, 1981).

MIS has important uses in most professional organizations. These systems emphasize quantifiable data in contrast to qualitative judgment information. They tend to centralize information and to produce enormous amounts of data that cannot always be digested. When management and staff professionals do not participate in the design of the MIS—as is often the case —the utility of the collected data is not always apparent.

A potential problem with quantifiable data is that it tends to focus managerial attention on those issues that are better understood and documented and lessen attention or concern with issues that are not as well documented. Another problem is that data can be collected for different purposes: to evaluate, to justify, to bargain, to plan. Unless professionals participate closely in the elaboration of the MIS, there may be considerable suspicion as to its utility and function.

Performance Monitoring Systems (PMS). We include here any systematic and repetitive monitoring of programs and activities, whether generated internally or in response to external demands. External PMS often go under the general terminology of accountability. External PMS have become increasingly important in education, health, and many other services as a result of rising costs, increasing public dissatisfaction with services, and competition for scarce resources. PMS rely on key effectiveness or efficiency indicators. In general, PMS, including evaluation, rely heavily on output measures related to goal achievement (Ghorpade, 1971; Hatry, 1979; Suchman, 1967; Usher and Cornia, 1981; Washnis, 1980).

Performance monitoring systems are used to evaluate performance for two main purposes: to reward and to show how to perform better. They may also be used for other less important purposes, such as to justify and protect. Management task consists in creating PMS that reward without endangering professional ability to experiment, take risks, and make mistakes. This means that performance monitoring systems designed to monitor organizational learning have to be segregated from those used to assess individual performance. We discuss this at greater length in Chapter Seven.

Cost-Benefit Analysis. This widely used technique provides systematic comparisons of alternative ways of reaching goals. It is also used to monitor and justify specific programs. It provides systematic ways of tabulating costs of undertakings and comparing these with expected benefits. Cost-benefit analysis is also increasingly used in government regulatory practice to justify the use of regulatory controls. It is a useful management tool when both costs and benefits can be attributed to specific activities and when values can be attributed to these costs and benefits (Gramlich, 1981; Kneese and Schultze, 1975; Mishan, 1976; Ray, 1984).

Systems Analysis. This is a powerful way of conceptualizing complex processes. Essentially, it examines five areas (Churchman, 1968):

1. Defining the system. For example, we can define the electric system as the grid of electric transmission and distribution lines linking plants and load centers.
2. Defining goals. We produce electricity and want to make a profit sufficient to attract new investors so that we can finance the expansion of the system.
3. Understanding the processes involved in reaching goals. We understand the relationships between resources and production. We know how much it costs to generate in different plants and to transmit and distribute current.
4. Assessing resources. How much coal, oil, and water power are available?
5. Selecting preferable or optimal ways of using resources to reach the desired goals. Given alternative ways of reaching the goal of meeting the demand for electricity, which production and transmission pattern will allow the electric utility to maintain electric rates at the lowest level?

Systems analysis rose in importance starting in the 1950s when computers became more widely available and large volumes of data could be processed rapidly and economically. Systems analysis, operations research, and other similar techniques depend on two principal elements. First, there is an understanding of the structure, model, or order. Thus, we are able to conceptualize both an electric system and a system of rewards and punishments. We can describe the first fairly accurately but not the second. Second, there is a problem-solving, decision-making aspect. We may want to understand how to operate the system of rewards and punishments so that professional workers are motivated to perform better. The usefulness of the technique depends on the knowledge we have about the system. Do we understand how each input variable affects outputs? Do we have a theory about the system process?

Systems analysis, like many of the other management tools we have described, orients management thinking toward quantifiable data and structured thinking. Its utility has been criticized when it tends to displace other forms of thinking that would be more appropriate (Hoos, 1972; Kinder and Weiss, 1978; Taylor, 1984).

Six Dangers

Widespread use of management tools entails six dangers: (1) management tools do not address relevant effectiveness issues; (2) they are used as a defensive strategy; (3) they lead to goal displacement; (4) they result in corrupt practices; (5) they do not enhance the image of the profession; and (6) they result in bureaucratization.

Inattention to Effectiveness. Any management tool is incomplete. It may provide valuable data and information, but judgment will still have to be exercised. The list of criteria used in defining organizational effectiveness reminds us of the complexities involved. It may seem reasonable to want to set specific goals, monitor performance, and see if results are attained. In many conventional task situations, such approaches work well, but they do not necessarily work well in all professional organizations.

They do not work well when:

- They reorient management thinking away from important effectiveness issues that are not easily quantified or described.
- They result in the selection of narrow target specifications based on professed goals but downgrade important external transactions.
- They seem to assume that means toward goals or transactions are well understood and that the professional staff knows what to do when such knowledge is not available.
- They tend to be perceived as sources of rewards and result in professional behavior that avoids experimentation, risk taking, and error making—which are essential for organizational learning and adaptability.

The first manager of Applied Research illustrates over-reliance on programming. He kept close control on project progress. He was a stickler on completion dates. But he did not put nearly as much time on developing research strategies or allocating research funds. One might surmise that he was mesmerized by target specifications, but far less interested in figuring out how to increase the quality of the research.

Applied Research also illustrates overreliance on apparent rationality. At one level we may want to simply dismiss the case as an example of insensitive management. The first manager was task-oriented, orderly, and not sufficiently people-oriented, but there is more to be said: he used a rational model of his own situation and he stuck to it. He used this rational model in his own decision-making process. He defined what he wanted to accomplish: he focused on the quality and timing of the reports. He used the best means he knew to reach his goal: he spent much of his own energy and time to complete the reports. He disregarded the professional values of the staff, lost good people, and so on. The important point is that his rational model made him incapable of learning from his mistakes. He disregarded or downgraded information about unhappy staff members, annoyance of sponsors, or the poor professional reputation of Applied Research. His model served as justification. It seemed to work, and he stuck with it. The following criticism, from a staff member who remained on after his departure, illustrates the dilemma:

> He did a lot of good things. He worked hard, he had his facts together, and he was an admirable manager in many respects. He kept a very difficult set of sponsors at bay, he recruited good people [at the beginning], and he placed this organization on the map. But he seemed stuck in his vision. He was so intent on the reports that he never paid attention to the other dimensions of our work. We would suggest we run more conferences on policy issues, but he did not care so much about that. He liked to count the number of reports we had produced. He identified with them, referred to them all the time. They took on a lot of importance for him, but, in fact, they were not always that important to the sponsors. What really mattered to them

was access to other sources of information. It was the flow of ideas they were after, not the reports per se.

Defensive Strategy. Management tools can be used as a bureaucratic protective strategy. They are first used to enlighten management or staff, to improve decision making, to monitor, or even to inform. However, later these techniques serve to justify. They are used to give the appearance of effectiveness.

The manager of Applied Research would assign and reassign the staff to the different ongoing projects. He would monitor the research and report preparation. He constantly monitored every activity, and he read, corrected, and rewrote most of the reports. The quality of the reports suffered from his excessive preoccupation with meeting deadlines. But he always had the information at the tip of his fingers. He remained at Applied Research for four years. One reason was that he did issue reports that satisfied the sponsors. They were sufficiently documented and well written, if not particularly creative.

Another reason was that he appeared to be on top of things. He was able to respond to the demands of his sponsors. In his small organization, he maintained the appearance of rationality. He came to board meetings with well-documented accounts of the use of Applied Research resources. Even if he did not pay much attention to resource choices and strategies, he would demonstrate to each sponsor how he had allocated staff resources to meet their research needs. He used his PERT charts and data to give the appearance of performance. He used his managerial techniques to his advantage. He used them to justify himself.

His main problem during his last years was the professional reputation of Applied Research. The professional community had defined it as a badly managed think tank. Too many stories circulated about the problems with this manager: how he would rewrite reports, how he delayed work but was fanatic about meeting deadlines, how he mishandled the many demands of the sponsors. Maybe the stories were untrue or unfair, but they contributed to his demise.

Goal Displacement. If management tools are linked to the

system of rewards and punishment (R&P), and if they highlight wrong or incomplete objectives, and if R&P are strong enough, management will reorient professional behavior in the wrong direction. This results in goal displacement. For example, the teacher is rewarded if pupils perform well on standardized skill tests. The teacher drops many parts of the curriculum and trains pupils to take tests. Teaching to the test increases pupil test performance but reduces educational quality.

As mentioned previously, perceptions of linkage may be sufficient to cause goal displacement. The professional staff double-guesses how management is making decisions and pursues strategies that fit the imagery. The perceptions may be erroneous, but the consequences are significant. There is little doubt that the professional staff at Applied Research knew that the manager wanted strict adherence to bureaucratic disciplines that were not relevant to professional performance.

The staff claimed that the manager was more interested in their being on time than in their ideas. They were discouraged by his insensitivity. Some of them would simply come in, be seen, and leave again to attend to personal matters. There was a deep sense of alienation because the work seemed less important than the accoutrements of work—namely, who came in early and appeared to be busily writing. An informal normative order prevailed among the staff: there was not much point in overdoing it. All that was necessary was to obtain some data, analyze it, provide conclusions, and deliver on time. Goal displacement was tangible at Applied Research. Timing was more important than quality.

Corrupt Practices. Management tools may increase levels of professional corruption. If the R&P are powerful, there will be a strong desire to show good results. The classic case is teachers whose pupils are tested at the beginning and end of the school year to show "value-added learning." The teachers are tempted to obstruct the fall test and to facilitate the spring test, so that the difference between the two scores, the "value-added learning," is high.

How do teachers obstruct the fall test without breaking the rules? They give the test at recess time. Pupils are notified at the last minute. Instructions are given hurriedly. No one is allowed to leave the room to go to the bathroom. No one is allowed to talk. Tests are collected as soon as a child has finished, and those who have finished are allowed to join their companions in the recess playground. In the spring, the test is given during class time. Everyone is given a snack and allowed to go to the bathroom first. Instructions are read slowly. Questions are answered in a low, confident voice. Permissions to leave and return to the room are given. All children are encouraged to stay and work on tests until allowed time elapses.

What is interesting is that the rules have not been broken. The professionals have obeyed the instructions to the letter. The official length of the tests was respected, no cheating was allowed, and so on. In areas where teachers had no discretion, they performed as told. Where they had discretion, they used their discretion to corrupt the results. They justify this by pointing out that the tests are meaningless or inappropriate to their pupils. They do not see their act as "unprofessional." On the contrary, they would argue that they remedied the inadequacies of the tests.

The consequence is clear. The profession is perceived with suspicion. The fact that it engages in such practices weakens its legitimacy and authority.

Tarnished Image. Some management tools may downgrade the external image of the profession. A good example again is the use of standardized tests in education. Organizational effectiveness is measured in terms of pupil achievement on standardized tests. But what is a standardized test? What does the word *standardized* mean? It means that test questions are modified, the questions are made more or less difficult until successive samples of test takers distribute normally along a normal, bell-shaped statistical curve. A few do very well, a few do very poorly, and the majority are distributed around the mean. Therefore, the management tool is designed to show that half the population does poorly and half does better.

Test scores can be improved or decreased, and they change over time. The reasons for this are many: better or worse education, the population taking the tests may be different, the abil-

ity and motivation to take tests may change over time, there
may be more or less corruption, and so on. If the tests are restan-
dardized, the same distribution is achieved again. The tests do
not determine what pupils should know. They only provide
comparative information: these pupils do better than those
pupils.

Such management tools are negative. They tell half the
population that they are doing poorly when no one has defined
what doing well and doing poorly means. Moreover, there is
nothing the profession can do to alter this negative image. Even
if American education had achieved high levels of proficiency,
standardized tests would still show half the population doing
work below the mean and half above.

Increased Bureaucratization. Management tools provide
routines. These routines can easily be used to help management
see and hear. They can also result in lesser discretion, greater
alienation, and staff reluctance to take risks.

To the extent they routinize professional behavior, they
reduce valuable intrinsic motivators. This is particularly significant in professions that do not have access to significant economic incentives. A cycle of poverty is generated.

Management tools are used to routinize professional
work. Since economic incentives are scarce, this reduces valuable intrinsic motivators. As a result, the quality of work life
goes down. At the same time, more controls are imposed on the
organization and on the professional staff. This, in turn, results
in a further reduction of intrinsic motivation.

This is the prevalent situation in American education today. It is obvious that current organizational arrangements for
teaching are not challenging. Not enough responsibility is given
teachers. They do not have the right to decide how to run their
schools, they do not have any available time to govern themselves, and they do not have time to plan what they can do collectively. They usually have no time or money to undertake research and experimentation. Their work is highly routinized and
is being routinized more as their autonomy is further reduced.
As Gifford (1985, p. 67) points out: "It is difficult to imagine
how this reduced autonomy and increased [routinized] role

playing will attract more able and, one would surmise, more imaginative and creative college graduates to the teaching profession."

Conclusion

Management tools are here to stay. Our purpose is to warn about their limitations and unforeseen consequences. We have paid attention to the linkage between management tools and the system of rewards and punishments. Too often these linkages are disregarded. Let us therefore conclude by examining the way management tools are used in an excessively bureaucratized organization and contrast this with the way they are used in a profession-oriented organization.

What are the characteristics of an excessively bureaucratized organization employing professionals?

1. Centralized top-down decision making. The center controls. Top management is in charge. Information and decision requests flow upward. Decisions and directives flow downward.

2. Layered hierarchy. To process large flows of information and decisions, there exist many hierarchical levels between the field, where the actual professional work is carried out, and top management. Internal resource allocation shows a disproportionate share going into these overhead positions. The cost of centralized control is high. Fewer resources are available for the professional staff in the field.

3. Tight coupling. Links between the various hierarchical levels are tight. Not much discretion is left to the field. When decisions are taken, they are taken at higher levels.

4. Orientation to professed goals. The center is obliged to use professed goals to define the rules it uses to control. Routinized management controls are goal oriented.

5. Management controls tied to rewards and punishments. Centralized management ensures compliance by tying specific rewards or punishments to desired performance. Management routinizes control by setting performance objectives and rewarding or punishing accordingly.

In contrast, what are the characteristics of effective profession-oriented organizations?

1. Decentralized decision making. Decisions are made as close as possible to the field. Much more discretion is given to the professional staff. Therefore there is less need for information flows upward and fewer directives flow downward.

2. Fewer layered hierarchies. The formal organization has fewer hierarchies. It is leaner. Many decisions are made by professional groups or by joint managerial-professional task groups. Managerial overhead costs are lower.

3. Loose coupling. There is enough free play to allow innovation at all levels of the organization.

4. Orientation to broad professional and organizational values. Management is more concerned with effectiveness than control. It defines effectiveness both in organizational and professional terms. It trusts the professional staff. It monitors performance closely, but leaves considerable discretion and responsibility where it should reside: with the professional staff in the field.

Applied Research under the first manager provides a good example of what not to do. Yet, that first manager was eminently rational and practical. You recall, Applied Research produced research reports for a set of government bureaus that had created the agency to work for them. The first manager was very concerned with quality. His criteria of effectiveness were centered on the quality of the reports: "Maybe the staff is unhappy, but my policy at Applied Research has worked. We have survived. From the start, I knew that our only chance to remain in business depended on the excellence of our performance. All along, I've seen to it that our research reports were of the highest quality. That was my most important goal when we started, and it is still my most important goal today. I may have lost some good people, but they were leaving in any case for greener pastures. No, I do not believe I was wrong. It is the quality of the reports that mattered. This is why our sponsors have renewed their support contracts."

How are management tools linked to the system of rewards and punishments? Again Applied Research provides an illustration: The manager set specific objectives for the staff. He assigned research reports. He evaluated the quality of each report and gave rewards and punishments accordingly.

Two issues interest us: First, how are rewards and punishments actually linked to management tools? What kind of processes are involved? Who participates? How effective is the system? If we want to motivate the research staff to perform better, to write better reports and still complete them on time do we have the means of reorienting their behavior? How do we know what they are accomplishing?

Second, are we nurturing our supply of rewards? Since professional rewards are both extrinsic and intrinsic, are we imposing controls that affect professional motivation? This second question is relevant because in the public and not-for-profit sector there are fewer economic rewards to provide. With salary schedules regulated and subject to collective contracts, extrinsic rewards are less important. Management is left with intrinsic rewards or with a wide range of negative sanctions: frowning (as contrasted to smiling), admonitions, warnings, assignments to dull projects, removal of discretionary budgets, transfer to less desirable offices, and so on.

Too often, management tools reduce the intrinsic rewards associated with professional work. The system of R&P obliges professional workers to play nonprofessional roles: "I fail to see why anyone would want to become a teacher these days. The pay is bad, there are few, if any, career growth opportunities, we are criticized by everyone, we are obliged to do all sorts of Mickey Mouse stuff like lesson plans and report writing, not to mention testing that has nothing to do with my image of teaching."

Other questions remain to be answered:

• How can rewards be enhanced to achieve higher degrees of professional motivation? Given the importance of intrinsic motivators, what kind of managerial control will enhance professional performance?

- Given the importance of learning, risk taking, and error correcting, how can management enhance this kind of professional role playing?
- Given the basic need to control and the deficiencies of the management tools we have surveyed, what are the alternatives?

We will explore these and other questions in the following chapters.

6

Choosing Management Structures and Incentives That Ensure Professional Commitment

————————————◆━◆━◆━————————————

This chapter pursues two important themes. In Chapter Three we presented descriptions of various governance models. Here we examine in greater detail the advantages and disadvantages of both formal and informal governance approaches. We have also emphasized the importance of professional motivation. In this chapter we discuss in greater detail how management can increase incentives for performance.

I realize that people differ. What works for some managers may not work for others. Much is said in this book about joint managerial-professional tasks. Different personalities will do better with some arrangements than with others. Much is said in this chapter about incentives. People respond differently to incentives. My purpose is to sharpen issues, not to prescribe.

This chapter focuses on the choice of management structure. How much voice is given to professionals? When does management have the final word? Should these structures be permanent? Should they be formalized? We start with the material presented in previous chapters. We use the concepts of joint managerial-professional tasks and envelope supervision discussed in Chapter Three. How much voice is given to professionals depends also on personalities. I do not address these issues, but the reader will have to consider such factors.

The chapter also discusses further issues in incentive management, particularly the importance of professional career structures in the more bureaucratized professions. I am more concerned with intrinsic (work) than extrinsic (money) motivators. I assume that, where available, management knows how to use extrinsic economic rewards, but intrinsic rewards are far more complex and require attention. It is obviously difficult to generalize about the way incentives work. For example, I stress the importance of career ladders as a motivating factor, but we need to keep in mind that a few profession-oriented organizations thrive on democratic egalitarian principles where formal career ladders have no place or justification.

Structure and incentives are intertwined. Structure affects the way work is performed, and the way work is performed is a motivator. Similarly, motivators affect how work is performed. This, in turn, affects the choice of structure. If we create a career path that gives professionals an increasing role in joint managerial-professional tasks, we create an incentive that affects the management structure. If professionals are involved in managerial tasks, it affects the way the organization is operated. The implementations of these approaches have intertwined consequences.

Choosing a Governance Structure

The conventional view of bureaucracy assumes that management and professionals are in conflict. Blau and Scott, in their classic study of the organization (1962), pointed out that while professional and bureaucratic modes share common principles, there are important contrasts. They stressed the differences in control structure. They pointed to the source of discipline in the bureaucracy. Discipline does not come from the peer professional group but from the hierarchy. Similarly, Kornhauser (1962) showed that autonomy was important to professionals and yet they had to contribute to the goals of the organization and submit to organizational control.

Since these early writings, the research literature on the subject has repeatedly addressed the subject. It tells us that appropriate governance structures and incentives can decrease conflict and alienation. For example, several years later, Miller (1967) conducted a major study of scientific and engineering personnel employed in two divisions of one of the United States' largest aerospace companies. He showed that differences in type of supervision, freedom of research choice, professional climate, and company encouragement were associated with degree of work alienation. The more supervision was participatory, the more engineers and scientists could select research topics and publish their findings, the more the company provided opportunities to obtain professional recognition outside the company, the less alienation was found.

Since then, two trends have been evident in the research literature. Some studies stress the potential or reality of conflicts (Benson, 1973; Elliot and Kuhn, 1978; Layton, 1971; Lawler and Hage, 1973; Sorensen and Sorensen, 1974). Others emphasize opportunities for accommodation. These later studies stress the complementarities between bureaucracy and professionalism. For example, they highlight how discretion is achieved in routinized environments (envelope supervision), or how bureaucratic structures actually support and provide opportunities for professional work, development, and careers (Engel, 1969, 1970; Guy, 1985; Malone and Wedel, 1969; Michael, 1974; Montagna, 1968; Morrissey and Gillespie, 1975).

Our concern is with organizational effectiveness, but the concept of organizational effectiveness is also changing. As mentioned in Chapter Five, it is often described in terms of organizational adaptability and flexibility, profitability, efficiency, and ability to acquire resources, ability to meet external needs. It is also described in terms of employee development and retention, job satisfaction, and integration of individuals with organizational goals (Steers, 1975).

What is changing is the relative emphasis of some of these variables. Where profitability and efficiency may have dominated earlier discussions, today, new constraints are emphasized. Employee development and job satisfaction are far more important. We realize that people spend a good deal of their life in the organization. Their job defines their standard of living,

not only in terms of their pay but in terms of their work satisfaction. We realize also that integration of individual and organizational goals is a two-way street. This is particularly relevant
to professional organizations where professional values can
dominate and even replace some organizational values. The definition of clients is also changing as we begin to pay far more
attention to the larger social impacts of organizational action.
There is far more recognition of the values of individuals and
groups both in and out of the organization. Equity has emerged
to compete with efficiency (Wilenski, 1980–1981; McGowan,
1982).

The current "excellence" literature emphasizes certain
themes. These authors tell us to pay attention to customer
needs, to develop a strong internal organizational set of core
values, to promote risk taking, to design simple structures, to
keep the staff lean, and to keep the organization on target
(Peters and Waterman, 1982; Hickman and Silva, 1984; Kanter,
1983; Deal and Kennedy, 1982). Many of these themes reinter-
pret changing values and changing concepts of effectiveness.
These authors pay much less attention to narrow definitions of
efficiency. They emphasize the importance of the human spirit,
commitment, excitement, and entrepreneurship. To be sure,
some of this may be wishful thinking, but there is little doubt
that our concept of the organization has moved away from the
well-oiled machine to an organic and terribly human endeavor.

Potential for Bureaucratization. Let us not be carried
away by this florid imagery of bushy-tailed Schumpeterian
entrepreneurs in the bureaucracy. Let us return to the starker
realities of professional management. We want to discuss management structures and immediately we have to realize that professional participation in governance entails further bureaucratization. If we have an academic senate, it will soon acquire
bureaucratic traits. There will be questions of jurisdiction, turf
protection, status puffing, and propensities to blame everyone
else.

The creation of new structures inevitably implies routinization. The executive committee of the medical staff acquires a
routinized domain with its own rights and privileges. It invents
routines to protect turf. Moreover, since professionals are not

always good managers, they may not even realize what they are doing.

Delegating authority to professionals works well when this delegation is narrowly task oriented. It does not work as well when too many professionals have to participate in large-scale management decision-making processes. Unfortunately, the problem is not that simple because professional institutions acquire their legitimacy in different ways. Professional authority requires more consensus building than managerial authority. Therefore, professionals in the governance of the organization can easily become a liability.

How does management integrate professional and organizational goals? How does it stimulate professional participation in decision making without bogging down? How does it increase professional staff capacity for networking? For linking across organizational boundaries? How does it motivate professional responsibility?

In Chapter Three we described five professional management models: the professional partnership model, the senior staff model, the dual governance model, the collegial model, and the bureaucratic model. You will recall these distinctions:

- The partnership model vests managerial responsibility in a self-selected group of professionals.
- The senior staff model uses the single manager surrounded by selected senior professionals.
- The dual governance model vests selected managerial responsibilities into a professional body (say, an academic senate or a medical staff) and keeps other managerial responsibilities for the administration.
- The collegial model vests all managerial responsibilities into the entire participatory professional membership.
- The bureaucratic model vests managerial responsibility into an administrative hierarchy without formal professional participation.

We also described the concepts of envelope supervision and of joint managerial-professional tasks. Both these approaches distinguish among areas of professional autonomy, areas of joint

professional-management responsibility, and areas that remain
managerial responsibility.

The choice of model depends on the nature of the environment and tasks performed, the size of the organization, the
technology used, and the impact of participation on professional motivation.

Senior Staff Versus Dual Governance. How much of management's daily responsibilities require professional knowledge?
Let us compare two different kinds of organizations. First, take
the example of museum management. Most museum directors
and their staffs are originally trained in art, not management.
The fact is, it is much more difficult to train good managers in
art history and appreciation than it is to find and rapidly train
capable art professionals in management practice. Thus, museum management usually comes from the arts and is commonly
trained, if at all, in intensive short-term specialized management
programs.

As a result, museum management tends to use the senior
staff model. That model is well adapted to situations where
managerial and professional decisions are made by the same
people.

In contrast, university or hospital management tends to
split managerial and professional roles. Public and nonprofit
community hospitals are typically headed by two distinct
groups and in some cases may have two directors: an administrative medical director and a corporate manager. The professional staff will be broken down into administrative departments (obstetrics, cardiology, and so on) and participate in
professional-managerial committees at the department level. In
addition, there may typically be a hospitalwide medical staff
with an executive committee and a series of working committees (quality control, ethics, pharmacy, nursing, utilization, cap-
ital budget, infection control). The medical staff will have
considerable influence on those joint managerial tasks where
professional knowledge is important. On the other side, management will run the nonmedical end of the hospital without much
consultation with the medical staff.

These structures can be very effective if management

knows how to use them, but they are ponderous and not easily manipulated. Moreover, participatory professional committees can easily serve many different functions that have nothing to do with professional knowledge. They can be used to defend narrow interests, to provide status, and to justify mistakes. All the sins of bureaucracy can befall the professional governance structure.

In the museum structure, the director of the museum may have a central role in selecting the senior staff and assigning tasks. Flexibility is more easily achieved because the senior staff model parallels more exactly the existing administrative structure. Any time the existing structure happens to be deficient and bridges across boundaries are needed, management and senior staff can readily use matrix management approaches. They can establish projects, assign staff from different departments, and achieve flexible structures. Thus, in the museum, running major exhibitions requires efforts from all departments and the senior staff facilitates the process.

The problem is more arduous in the university or the hospital. Management can always adopt matrix approaches. The matrix structure may even be formalized (Davis and Lawrence, 1977), but the dual governance structure inevitably entails jurisdictional disputes. If management goes too far duplicating the work of the academic senate or medical staff, it reduces its effectiveness. If it waits for the academic senate and medical staff to act, it may be too late.

Management is inevitably concerned with the effectiveness of the professional governance body. Even in public and not-for-profit hospitals, it is not uncommon for management to have representatives on the various medical staff committees. These representatives might not vote, but their function is to keep the profession informed of management problems and to transmit back professional concerns to management. In the university, such participation is less important, but campus administrators do not fail to inform academic senates of their views, and good administrators keep open channels of communication with the faculty. Universities are designed for permanence, not for rapid change. Their internal institutions reflect this.

The resolution of professional-management conflicts is more difficult in the dual governance than in the senior staff model. There are again important distinctions between the university and the hospital. In the university, there is no locus for conflict resolution. The process is political. The campus administration uses its power and influence to seduce, cajole, and otherwise acquire the support of faculty groups. It is at the campus level that many of these exchanges will take place. The privileges and rights of the faculty are both assets and deterrents to effectiveness. Faculty committees may be quite unresponsive to administrative guidance. The formal authority structure is weak because there is not that much the administration can exchange to acquire influence over the faculty. Therefore, successful university administration has to rely heavily on faculty support. It becomes more facilitation than leadership. On many campuses, good management consists in making the faculty aware of its responsibilities and obliging it to meet its own standards. The administration may certainly lead, but it leads where the faculty was going, clearing the underbrush as it goes along.

The hospital is very different. First, the administration has more control over valued resources (equipment, facilities) and is therefore far more influential in its dealings with the medical staff. Second, hospital boards are often directly involved in the internal operations, in contrast to their university counterparts. Even in public, and certainly in nonprofit or for-profit, hospitals, the boards will include both physicians and administrators. Conflicts that are not readily resolved at the dual governance level can be resolved by the board. Obviously, the composition of these boards makes a big difference. Some may be heavily oriented to physician concerns; some may be more heavily oriented to administrative or even community needs. As a result, although both the university and the hospital use the dual governance structure, their management differs on important dimensions.

There will also be considerable variation across organizations. Not all academic senates are powerful. In universities or colleges where the administration controls appointments and budgets, the senates may have a purely decorative function. In hospitals, the participation of the various professions and their influence may differ. We also need keep in mind that in many professional organizations, formal professional institutions do not exist. The only formal structure is the administrative structure. Teachers very rarely have strong academic bodies of their own. Some principals may use informal senior staffs, but, in general, teachers have fewer opportunities for participation in formal professional bodies than nurses in hospitals who may have a nursing committee within the medical staff.

Similarly, professionals in think tanks (economists, engineers, scientists) are rarely formally organized, nor are their counterparts in corporate firms. In those organizations, problems can arise because professionals do not have formal institutions through which they can express themselves. This leads to relative poverty of managerial insight into the preoccupations of the professional staff. At Applied Research there was no mechanism for the staff to take a collective stand on certain issues. The first manager might have greatly benefited if the senior staff had had opportunities to let their hair down and make collective suggestions for improvements. But he kept them from joining forces, and most members of the staff did not have the courage to confront their superior on their own.

The lesson is clear. Professional participation can go all the way from nothing to ponderous bureaucratized institutions. Management cannot be unconcerned. The senior staff model is leaner; fewer professionals need be involved. Therefore it is far more flexible. The dual governance model is more ponderous, better suited to situations where professional consensus is important, and where the life-or-death importance of decisions requires high levels of professional scrutiny and legitimacy. But in the final analysis, management's attitude toward the professional staff will make the difference between deaf ears or enlightened cooperation.

Relevance of Professional Knowledge. All organizations are broken down into compartments or units. Within each unit, professional views may be consulted, but not beyond. For example, the scientist who runs the research laboratories of the chemical company is not a marketing expert, need not be one, and would probably do poorly if he or she spent time at it. Management, and other units, deal with the external environment, yet there may be issues about which the scientist, and other colleagues, have something to say that could affect management decisions. There may be issues of safety, public interest, or other professional concerns. The existing organizational hierarchy does not facilitate this kind of communication. The scientist and colleagues can organize themselves and send information up through the chain of command, but this may look like insurrection. They may have little impact, because either management is not really interested or their views as individuals are not perceived to have legitimacy.

An informal dual governance structure is sometimes used. For example, there may be a professional forum where company scientists and engineers sit down to discuss professional issues with management. Even a scheduled meeting can provide a legitimate mechanism to surface and expose professional concerns.

In contrast, in other organizations professional knowledge is known to be relevant across the board. The museum curator, organizing an exhibit, needs to know about art, but also about the art market, community attitudes, public wants, and philanthropic interests. Success with the environment is known to require, and be dependent on, joint professional-managerial thinking. The formal hierarchy will tend to facilitate it. This explains why the senior staff model is more appropriate. There is less need to legitimize professional viewpoints to management since management is imbued with professional values.

Organizations that do not readily control their external environment, and do not have access to guaranteed resources, rely on more unitary models—the bureaucratic, senior staff, collegial, or partnership model. If they use dual governance, they tend to have a strong administration. This is certainly the case in for-profit hospitals where the administration often uses profit sharing and other economic motivators to tighten its control on the professional staffs.

Proportion of Internal Management Tasks. As mentioned in Chapter Three, some models work best in situations where collective decisions are few and managerial skills less relevant than professional skills. The partnership model works best where management of the organizational environment depends on professional knowledge and management of the internal environment is relatively simple or even amenable to routinization. The law partnership may make many collective decisions, but most of the important decisions will have to do with the external world. The daily running of the office will not present difficulties because most managerial decisions can be left to each partner to handle.

In contrast, running the hospital requires conventional managerial skills. This is why large hospitals are not run on the partnership model. However, small health facilities, involving a few professionals, are often organized that way.

For example, let us take coordination. If internal coordination is complex and professional consensus not easily achieved, the partnership will not work well. On the other hand, the partnership will be effective if consensus is readily reached and the problem is limited to exchanging information. Where overall professional consensus is needed to coordinate, the dual governance model might still be preferable to the partnership or the senior staff model as long as speed is not important. The collegial model may be best in terms of consensus building, but will not be useful in large organizations or in situations where rapid decision making is required.

The senior staff model will probably be most effective in terms of time cost versus legitimacy. Commonly, a senior staff approach is grafted on the dual governance model. When decisions have to be made rapidly, the administration calls the relevant professional leaders, explains the problem, seeks advice, obtains support, and moves ahead. Obviously, this is how university administration deals with ponderous academic senates. But even the academic senate leadership cannot always deliver the votes of the senate and, on some occasions, the administration may be rebuffed for moving too fast and not consulting sufficiently.

Cost containment and resource management usually require far more managerial than professional skills. The partnership handles these issues relatively well when it is small and each professional is responsible for resource acquisition and expenditure control.

In contrast, the dual governance structure provides opportunities for professional resistance to cost containment and resource management. The ability of professional bodies to respond to managerial concerns depends, in part, on their identification with organizational goals. Or, turned around, the success of cost containment and resource management depends on managerial ability to formulate approaches that blend organizational and professional concerns.

One difficulty with the dual governance model is that it tends to pit management against the professions: "They want us to reduce costs by twenty percent, but they do not care about the service. They do not see patients, they do not have to tell the old lady in Ward Two that, while she is still sick, she has to be discharged tomorrow morning."

For-profit hospitals tend to rely more on the senior staff model than on the dual governance model. They may use a formal dual governance model, but other relationships are also established. Physicians may also be stockholders or may participate in hospital profit-sharing schemes. Managerial concerns are therefore shared with some members of the profession and managerial power and influence are enhanced because strong common interests link managers and professionals. Or turned around, we could assert that managerial power is enhanced because it is much more informed and sympathetic to professional concerns and interests. Somewhat similar effects also take place in the not-for-profit health sector as a result of organizational diversification. Not-for-profit community hospitals create profit-making health-related ventures in which some of their staff participate. New relationships and linkages alter past conflict relationships.

The advantage of the senior staff model is that it is both more selective and unitary. It places management and professionals in face-to-face contact. Negotiations are simplified because the structure allows professionals to identify both with management and with the profession. Similarly, management is sufficiently in charge to be able to listen to professional viewpoints without losing prestige. In contrast, the resolution of management-professional differences in the dual governance model entails loss of prestige: "They won, we lost."

A good example of these problems arises when university administrators impose appointments or promotions on the faculty. In research universities faculty appointments are a prerogative of the faculty. Searches and selection are conducted by the faculty. But there will be occasions when, for one reason or another, the administration will not concur with the faculty and impose an undesired appointment or make different promotion decisions. These acts are usually resented because they are not understood. Often there is not sufficient trust between the administration and the academic senate to discuss these issues openly. In contrast, similar situations in a think tank or research laboratory on the senior staff model would lead to franker exchanges between management and staff if only because fewer individuals are involved.

Informal Approaches. Dual governance is cumbersome but provides for professional legitimacy. Senior staff is unitary and more flexible. When both legitimacy and flexibility are required, a senior staff approach is grafted to a dual governance model.

The formal structure of committees is replaced or displaced by informal managerial-professional groups that actually run the organization. In the hospital or the campus, a number of senior professionals come to be known as leaders. They are brought into the confidence of management, or they may even have selected and appointed the managers and brought them into their confidence.

A problem with grafting an informal senior staff model upon a dual governance model is that this semisecret society tends to erode the legitimacy of the formal structure. Professionals in committees become quite bored when they realize that their mandate is vacuous and that decisions are made elsewhere. On the other hand, management may need prompt decisions. Senior staff and dual governance can cohabit, and they do. The executive committee of the medical staff, or the chairs of senate committees, can act as senior staff and act expeditiously. When management does not appoint and trust the leadership of the professional body, it inevitably turns elsewhere. When management appoints, the professional body acquires less legitimacy.

Informal approaches are used in most professional organizations. Management selects friends from the professional staff. Gradually it begins to trust and use them informally as the need arises. As management acquires confidence in the leadership and managerial skills of selected professionals, it uses them to undertake any number of joint tasks: planning, organizing, staffing, and evaluating.

Management may be sorely tempted to assume that informal approaches are all that is needed. Informal approaches are unitary, flexible, and lean. If management is wise in selecting good people, they can be energetic. Good people can form the basis of networks cutting across jurisdictions. Specific projects and task assignments can create effective teams. The informal approach can be part of matrix management. Why would this not be preferable? We will return to the question in a moment.

Hierarchical Level. A single governance model may be used in the entire organization, including the board, from level-one management down the hierarchical pyramid. But, in most organizations, different governance models are used at different levels. A centralized bureaucracy may still use the senior staff model in various bureaus although level-one management may not be participatory. School districts may have a bureaucratic structure at the central office level while principals foment informal participatory collegial approaches at school sites.

Professional discretion may be important at service delivery points and envelope supervision is relevant at that level. Level-two management may require considerable interaction between professionals and managers while level one may remain far less participatory.

The choice of level is affected both by task considerations and the impact of the model on professional motivation. For example, organizations that rely on unpaid professional volunteers tend to shift the participatory model upward because effective participation motivates commitment. This explains why the collegial model tends to be used in volunteer organizations and is relatively effective as long as these organizations are small, consensus is reached relatively easily, and the time cost of joint managerial-professional tasks is low.

In most hospitals, a large share of the medical staff is affiliated. This means that doctors who maintain a private practice use the hospital facilities and refer their patients to it. Participation in the governance of the organization is important because these doctors are loosely linked to the hospital and not readily subject to conventional managerial control. On the other hand, the time cost of this participation cannot be high since these doctors have their own practice to attend to. This explains why the dual governance model is generally used in these organizations. The model provides participatory incentives to all the members of the medical staff.

One conclusion, therefore, is that the choice and hierarchical level of the governance model has to do with professional motivation. In some organizations, formalization is important because it enhances participation. In others, it is irrelevant—other motivators are more relevant. For example, different individuals have different propensities to participate in the governance of their organization. In a certain department of a leading university I know well, I can easily list those faculty who produce good research, help their students, teach well, and enjoy, or at least contribute to, committee work. I can also list very good researchers and teachers who are hopeless on committees, and I can describe individuals who never produce any research but are very active in the governance of the department and the university. The former tend to be satisfied with participation at lower levels while the latter tend to prefer the visibility of higher-level participation.

Formal Versus Informal Models. The advantages of formalization have already been mentioned. They are legitimacy and motivational effect. But, as pointed out earlier, formalization is routinization. When a formal, official executive committee is established, rules are invented to define what it does and does not do. These rules define roles and clarify expectations.

Professionals or managers know what to expect. These formal arrangements provide legitimacy for the decision-making process.

The rules can be very detailed. For example, they may specify how decisions are made, who can participate, whether votes are taken, and how binding the votes are. They can, therefore, determine the relative influence of management and of the professions. The advantage of rules is that they help settle power conflicts. If management and professionals are at loggerheads on an issue, the rule settles the outcome: "Management always makes the final decision," or "The votes are counted and the majority decides," or "Unanimous votes are required for action."

As is well known by now, rules are useful when events are predictable or when they stand for consensual values. We may espouse a management value orientation and decide that management should have the final say on all issues. Or, we may decide that the organization should be designed to reflect professional values and that professionals should have the final say on some, or even on many, issues.

Management can be leery of formal mechanisms because the professionals in the organization might become or are already unionized. But unionization is not necessarily a deterrent to closer management-professional linkages. Professional unions understand, or should understand, professional values. Effective formal arrangements can be established in a unionized framework. Academic senates operate in universities where the faculty is unionized. Cooperation takes place because the functions and tasks to be performed require it.

Cape Canaveral: The Failure of Challenger. It is tempting to pass judgment on decision processes after the facts. For example, if we examine the failure of the *Challenger* launching of January 1986, we may conclude that the decision-making process was flawed. The professional staff of the booster manufacturer (Morton Thiokol) was against the launch and that staff, in retrospect, was correct (see Chapter Three). However, Morton Thiokol management made a different judgment and recommended proceeding. The rules under which they operated gave the final say to management.

Under a different governance model the same engineers might have made the decision. Undoubtedly, Morton Thiokol management made an important error and so did NASA, but on the day before the launch the decision-making process was not necessarily flawed. The decision rule had worked in enough cases in the past to justify its use.

What might have been flawed was the ability of top management at NASA to receive negative information from the bottom. Bad news does not travel easily in hierarchical structures, as has been well documented in numerous research studies (Wilensky, 1967). Indeed, as subsequently shown by the investigating bodies, the failure at Cape Canaveral might be better explained in terms of communication blockage and the reluctance of lower levels to send bad news upward, or the reluctance of upper levels to listen to bad news. These are evaluation problems, not necessarily decision rule problems. They may require structural modifications—better communication channels, more reviewing bodies, greater emphasis on the goal of safety and less on frequency of launches, and so on—but no modification of the decision rule.

On the other hand, we might want to reexamine that decision rule again and argue that the structure of most corporate professional organizations does not provide mechanisms for creating consensual professional judgments or for giving legitimacy to these judgments.

Layton, in his study of engineers in corporations (1971), shows the effect of lack of formal professional institutional structure. Engineers in corporate organizations tend to identify either with the profession (they want to stress scientific values) or they identify with the business end of their work. They form different factions and each of these factions revolt against mindless bureaucratic controls. This pattern does not incite consensus building and, therefore, weakens the ability of the professionals to reach consensus on important issues.

Confirming this, Pelz and Andrews show, in their research (1976), that with few exceptions, the performance of scientists in organizations is highest when project decisions are shared with managers. It is the interaction with top management that seems to make the difference. The problem, of course, is that while management may be inclined to informal contacts with the staff, the absence of permanent formal institutions means that these contacts and consultations are left to the vagaries of managerial style or preference. Even the existence of formal structures does not guarantee that managers will talk to professionals and vice versa. Managers may not be inclined to reveal their hand or simply hate to lose time discussing issues with the professional staff. As we saw earlier, there exist many reasons for managerial suspicions of the professional staff.

The problem is further complicated by hierarchical structures within the organization. If management itself did not rely on formal rules and hierarchies, the need for formalization of professional participation would be lessened. Turning back to the Morton Thiokol decision, what would have happened if that corporation had had a very weak hierarchical structure? We can only surmise that leadership would have emerged from felt needs in the task situations. The more charismatic leaders among the engineers would be heard. These vocal engineers would be able to dominate discussions and might sway management, but as Swidler shows us in her study of organizations without authority structures (1979) these organizations cannot cope with most problems and that alternative is not realistic.

As already discussed, but worth repeating, lack of formalization has distinct advantages: legitimacy of managerial decision making remains intact; time cost of participation can be reduced; assignments can be flexible and varied; bureaucratization of committee work can be avoided; management can select the leadership of the profession; and renovation of team membership can be used to increase participatory opportunities.

A Case Example: A Drug Addiction Clinic. Edward runs a community agency that deals with drug addiction. It is funded partially from city and government funds, donations, and foundation grants. It also charges fees to its clients. The agency runs a detoxification program, an intensive education program in the public schools, and a general information program. It is staffed by a variety of professionals including psychiatrists, psychologists, doctors, pharmacists, social workers, nurses, and educators.

The agency appears to be highly centralized. There is a lay board, the director (Edward), and three assistant directors. The professional staff has no formal organization and is assigned to one or more of the three programs.

Edward is continually creating task forces to deal with specific management issues. He involves the professional staff to fit needs and capabilities. Thus, a task force is looking into the characteristics of their clientele and is studying the social context of addiction. Another task force is dealing with fund raising. Edward keeps an eye on all the task forces. He keeps them small and gives them specific assignments. Edward is well aware that large committees tend to be inefficient and that professionals avoid work when too many participants are involved (Latane, Williams, and Harkins, 1979; Leibowitz and Tollison, 1980).

Edward runs a small program. Legitimacy is not as important because he can have face-to-face relations with all his staff. He has enough time to assign tasks and supervise the teams.

The excellence in management literature we quoted at the beginning of the chapter would tell us that formalization makes no sense. They would say "right on" to Edward, but what about legitimacy? What about the need for a mechanism to network and create professional consensus (Boland, 1982; Luegenbiehl, 1983)?

The Case of Whistleblowing. Why does professional whistleblowing arise in organizations? Is it empirical evidence of the need for internal professional bodies? Some organizations, such as the Bank of America, attempt to solve the problem of whistleblowing by creating confidential internal communication paths to the administration ("Can Your Employees . . . ," 1980, p. 26). Others use ombudspersons or fight against whistleblowers and attempt to punish those who do it (Bogen, 1979; Parmerlee, 1982).

The issue becomes who protects the whistleblower (Carter, 1980; Chalk and von Hippel, 1979; Perrucci, Anderson, Schendel, and Trachtman, 1980). But is that all? Should management create or promote formal professional bodies to handle these issues?

Whistleblowing is a political act. It is the attempt to use power, to create leverage by getting external forces (the press, the courts, public opinion, Congress) involved in internal issues. Whistleblowing will not stop because better channels of communication are created between professionals and management. Such proposals do not take into account the issue of relative distribution of power. Better communications are helpful, but will not alter decisions taken with other considerations in mind. In some situations, there is no substitute for enhancing professional power and authority to match the need for professional responsibility. And, while it may seem strange at first, it is in management's interest to want professional responsibility and authority (Boland, 1982). Even if management has the final say, giving a formal role to the profession obliges the profession to consider issues and reach a consensus, and obliges management to consider the profession's position.

Formal professional structures have distinct advantages and disadvantages. They provide legitimacy, networks, and engender costs, but management need not be stymied by ponderous professional structures. Management can also interact and activate professional structures. In Chapter Four we discussed planning. Management can involve the professional in planning and activate formal professional governance bodies. It can use matrix management techniques to increase internal networking. What Edward is doing informally could also be done formally, with similar results, but with higher visibility and legitimacy. The shrewd manager I introduced earlier (the one who does not trust planners) happens to believe deeply in frank discussions with his professional staff. He runs a small chemical company involved in processes that can have high risks. The company employs fewer than 300 professionals and workers. Yet management has established a formal staff forum that meets periodically to consider safety and research implications of new processes. One function of the forum is to inform the staff of ongoing activities and plans. Another is to provide a formal mechanism for staff views to surface. Both management and local unions support the forum.

As another member of the management team put it when

I visited them a few years back: "It's better for us to kill rumors as soon as they surface. We try to be frank about what we know we are doing. The forum works relatively well. Because we are serious, the staff has to be serious also. We really explore what goes on, and we want to be open. For us it works. But we put in the time and the effort."

As I said in the beginning of the chapter, I do not prescribe, but I do suggest. In my opinion, to support not having a formal professional structure, management has to be quite convinced it would be undesirable to have one. The question of whether to create a formal professional structure should certainly be asked, and answered.

Incentive Management

Incentive management is crucial in the profession-oriented organization because professionals are subject to complex sets of rewards and punishments. As pointed out in Chapter Two, motivation is not limited to organizational boundaries. The hospital relies on the medical staff to make recommendations on large equipment purchases because it realizes, quite correctly, that motivation for equipment purchase can be dictated by many different needs: professional research, the contribution of the equipment to personal career goals versus hospital needs, status, and other mercantile reasons. Participation of many professionals protects management from the power and influence of individuals or groups.

Management cannot disregard incentives and maintain control. In some organizations, external incentives are far more powerful than internal ones. Faculty in some fields may use their position to obtain lucrative consulting contracts. Scientists in think tanks may be more responsive to the desires and instructions of external sponsors than to the standards and goals of their employer. Physicians in the hospital may be more concerned with their private practice.

In other organizations economic incentives are available and can be used. These are most effective when they are substantial enough to make an important difference. For example, some for-profit firms have incentive schemes that affect as much as 30 to 50 percent of the normal salary of their professional employees. Such incentives cannot be easily disregarded.

In some organizations, the problem is the absence of economic incentives. Management has to focus on intrinsic motivators and on noneconomic incentives such as status and recognition.

Inventing Incentives. Incentives can be invented. Take the case of the Lakeside school district and the Rosemary schools. Lakeside encourages teacher performance. They have an annual prize for the six best teachers. Competition for the prize is announced each year, and candidates are nominated by most of the schools. As many as 100 candidates are nominated each year. A jury of teachers and administrators review the documents submitted and the letters of support. Each year, they select the six best teachers among their total staff of some 6,000, but they send a dry form letter to those who do not make it. They give a poorly publicized dinner for the six winners.

Rosemary schools also encourages performance, and they also have an annual prize. The same process takes place, except they give two prizes each year. They are a smaller district with 300 teachers. They receive about 20 to 30 nominations each year. There is a difference. Rosemary does not send a dry form letter to the nominees that do not make it. Instead, they also invite them to the annual dinner, which is publicized. They invite civic leaders to join them. They all share this brief recognition: losers and winners. At Lakeside, for six winners, there are about 94 disappointed nominees with a form letter. At Rosemary, there are two dozen nominees and two winners in the limelight. Costwise, Rosemary is doing much better. They manage their incentives. They do pay for additional dinners, but the cost of the food is contributed.

Staff Involvement in Planning. Managing professional incentives requires close managerial contact with professionals. It can be a joint managerial-professional task. At Rosemary, it is done by a joint committee of the administration and teachers. It is not called the incentive committee, but it could have been. It is called the teacher excellence committee. Many incentives are discussed. They do not include bread-and-butter issues because the district is unionized, but they discuss staff development, career plans, teacher evaluation, the various prizes, teacher research and publications, teachers' participation in special projects, and so on.

Rosemary has a private foundation that raises money for the district. These unattached funds are distributed by the teacher excellence committee. The committee is composed of four teachers and two administrators. The teachers receive release time to serve and rotate every two years. Two of the teachers are elected; two are appointed by the administration.

There is nothing magical about the foundation. It is composed of civic leaders and experienced fund raisers. The annual income it generates is not large, but its use can make important differences. Some of the money is used to provide the release time that allows the teachers on the teacher excellence committee to do far more than pursue their own preferences. They circulate in the various schools of the district, discussing opportunities for improving professional roles.

In cooperation with a local university, they have initiated several research activities on reading in the elementary schools. They have provided funds for a teacher publication and have encouraged teachers to attend workshops and conferences in their fields of specialization. Some of their work is fairly conventional, but the motivation of the district superintendent who created the committee is not:

> When the foundation was created six years ago, we realized that we would never receive large sums from them. . . . We decided that the money should be used to enhance the professional work of our teachers. We realize that teacher salaries are low and will probably always be low. But, teachers do not go into teaching to make a fortune. They go into teaching because they like to teach. . . . We know that when teaching is made more challenging, we attract and keep better teachers. The excellence committee involves the teachers. They

tell us what matters. They tell us what the challenges are. The money creates opportunities. . . .
Our teachers feel good about their work. When
they feel good, they teach better.

The superintendent at Rosemary has taken a step—a small
but significant step—to share managerial responsibilities with
the profession. He tells us that it works.

Some Dimensions of Incentive Management. There are
no magical formulas that explain how to create and manage incentives. Some professional organizations do not seem to practice the art. Management does not seem to realize that professionals are highly respondent to positive stroking and feedback.
They disregard professional aspirations to upgrade their professional qualifications and abilities. They do not see the relationship between work assignment and motivation.

Those who know, do practice the art. They are aware of
the characteristics of professional knowledge. They understand
that task assignments can become a progression, that giving increasingly more difficult assignments, stroking, and providing
feedback are the backbone of professional incentive and therefore the backbone of the organizational system of rewards and
punishment.

They also realize that repetitive work and routinization
are not valued professional work goals. They therefore seek to
diversify professional work and give opportunities for experimentation and for learning behavior because these motivate
participation.

They also know that professionals are sensitive to credit
fairness. They want credit when it is due. If a professional
should be credited, that individual will be highly sensitive if his
or her name is dropped when credits are given. Substitutions are
even worse. If the manager insists on his name on the report instead of the person who did the work, that manager is not managing organizational incentives. He may be managing his own
career instead.

When team credit is relevant, team credit reinforces links
within the organization, but giving team credit always needs to

be sensitive to individual contributions. Yes, it is a fact that many professionals have large egos. They are convinced their contribution is most important and they want their name to appear in big letters. Managing incentives is the art of calming down the overambitious and placing their contribution in perspective. Giving team credit and individual credit takes time, but it is essential to the management of incentives.

There are many potential incentives within work situations. Management does not always know what they are. This is why participation of the staff in the design is useful.

Status is another source of motivation. There is much management can do to enhance the status of the professions. For example, I have decried the impact of standardized tests on the teaching profession: how these tests are designed so that half the population taking them do less well than the other half and how this inevitably has an impact on the profession of teaching. The more we are told our schools are bad, the more the status of the profession is downgraded. This does not mean that management should cover up, but it does mean that management needs to be able to present all sides of the picture, including achievements. Standardized tests do not help that profession. It is more effective to establish standards that can be met by large portions of the relevant population, thus raising both status and motivation for action.

In the case of education, it means dropping standardized tests and substituting instead examinations based on standards established by the profession. This means deciding what knowledge is relevant and what minimum standard is needed to pass. In some domains the standard might be higher—say, the ability to write sentences. In other areas the choice of standard might be geared to its motivational impact. What is the most effective way to motivate student performance? What percentage might be told they did well? What percentage told they have to do better? What percentage told they failed? I do not know the answer, and it will differ according to the material and situation, but the answer is certainly not a fast and dry 50 percent rule.

Professional Career Paths. In an early work, Peter Drucker suggested that professionals make bad managers, not because they are not trained or not capable, but because they get bored with management. Professionals are narrow specialists, whereas managers are generalists. Professionals are not interested in management issues and should be kept out.

Drucker (1954) also realized that professionals needed to be able to climb a hierarchical ladder. Since they are not oriented to managerial issues, he argued they needed a parallel ladder. Thus, the position of chief of the metallurgy division, which is managerial, should parallel a position of senior metallurgist that would be strictly professional. Both would receive increased compensation, but their roles would differ sharply. The first would be filled by generalists on the managerial track while the second would remain in the hands of narrow specialists who become the great experts in their chosen specialties.

This sharp distinction between managerial and professional work is no longer accurate. As we have seen, the professions have evolved, management has changed, and problems are different.

However, Drucker's early position is partly correct. Some professionals make bad managers while others are capable and successful. Drucker is also correct to suggest that career paths are needed for those professionals who do not go into management. Should managerial and professional tasks be sharply differentiated? If the school principal decides on teacher class assignments, is this managerial work? If the teachers decide how to share classes, is this professional work? Obviously, the concept of joint managerial-professional tasks obliges us to reconsider Drucker's early warnings.

Management has to answer two questions: what are the motivational needs for professional career paths within the organization, and, is it desirable to tie professional career paths to joint managerial-professional tasks?

An affiliated doctor at Community Hospital acquires status from the fame of her private practice. Her role on the executive committee of the medical staff may be a tribute to her outside reputation and recognition of her managerial and political skills. It is not particularly relevant to her income stream, although there may be side benefits. It provides her with additional status and this happens to be something she cares about. Yes, she is motivated to work on the executive committee because she depends on the hospital and needs it for her own ends. But she is also motivated because her external reputation is reinforced and amplified by her status at the hospital. She cares very much about the appointment.

A teacher at an urban school has recently been promoted to become a mentor teacher. To be frank, there is not much difference between what he did before the promotion and after. Now he has a little release time to assist other teachers and receives a small pay increase. Nevertheless, it has meant a lot to him. It is the recognition of twenty years of devoted service. He no longer says, "I teach at Rosemary High." He puffs a bit and says, "I'm a mentor teacher at Rosemary."

In most professional organizations, strictly professional career structures are common. Thus, one may rise from assistant engineer to senior engineer without much involvement in management. Steps on the ladder are determined in part by seniority, in part by increased professional experience and knowledge, and in part by increased professional discretion and responsibility. The relative weight of these factors differs across organizations and across professions.

Some professions, such as teaching, do not emphasize increased professional responsibility. These professions are bureaucratized—professional discretion remains highly restricted at all levels of the professional career. To emphasize the absence of increased discretion and responsibility, the profession rarely uses differentiated titles. Thus, a new teacher fresh out of school is appointed as a teacher and a veteran of twenty years is accorded the same rank.

Formal professional governance structures provide opportunities to reinforce the status ladder. The physician who has become a member of the executive committee of the medical staff has acquired a differentiated title. The senior economist on the senior staff of Applied Research is recognized both for his professional and his managerial responsibilities.

It is possible to modify and strengthen career structures, particularly when increased discretion and professional responsibility are desired. Status does not derive from titles, it derives from altered responsibility. Even small role differences may be valued, as demonstrated by our mentor teacher.

Two-Stream Structure: Strictly Professional and Joint Managerial. If we want to create a career structure that has powerful motivational impact, we have to base this structure on more fundamental role differentiation. In a purely professional stream, increased self-governance is the apex of the structure. The senior researchers at the think tank select their own problems while the junior staff are assigned research tasks.

In the joint managerial stream, participation in collective governance is the apex of the structure. The members of the senior staff decide with management how to spend the equipment budget.

Higher levels of discretion and autonomy and higher levels of responsibility differentiate roles. Linking the professional and joint managerial streams is an asset because it enhances internal career opportunities.

Formal and stronger professional participation inevitably implies fundamental modifications of the governance structure. These changes may require fundamental changes on management's part. Management's role changes when professional responsibilities are increased. This may not be easy to think about, concede, or even admit as desirable. Most managers are reluctant to change fundamental ways of behaving.

To illustrate, it may be easier to examine a futuristic example. Let us imagine an American school in 2050 A.D. that employs highly educated teachers. These teachers have many more managerial responsibilities than their counterparts have today. The senior staff spends much more time diagnosing the needs of their pupils. They design curriculum, select textbooks, prescribe programs, assign teachers, plan the school year, and are in charge of teacher quality control and promotion. They truly participate in the management of their school. The role of the principal has been sharply altered. It has become a facilitating instead of a decision-making position. In this futuristic school, the principal shares all managerial responsibilities with the senior staff. One big contrast to today's school is that teachers can pursue many different careers. Their training is different; opportunities for varied work have been created. Joint managerial-professional tasks provide the basis for strong career motivation based on role differentiation.

Current practice and proposals for encouraging excellent teachers are weak. They give teachers limited resources to assist other teachers or to develop curricular materials, but they do not discuss the role of the professional in governance (Bell, 1983; Benningfield, 1984; Brandt and Dronka, 1985). Even our brave description of Rosemary School District reminds us that American public education remains highly bureaucratized.

Conclusion

We have not prescribed, but did pay considerable attention to, the concept of professional participation in the governance of organizations. We saw the variety of existing approaches. These go all the way from highly bureaucratized organizations with very limited formal participation (the case of American public education) to highly decentralized professional management (the case of professional partnerships). In between, there are many variations on different themes. The dual governance and senior staff models received most of our attention.

The dangers and maladies of bureaucratization can destroy the professional capability to participate in the governance of organizations. It may be convenient and expeditious to disregard failing professional participation, but wise management knows better. As we saw in earlier chapters, joint managerial-professional tasks emerge from underlying needs. Management is inevitably concerned with facilitating professional involvement.

We spent some time discussing the advantages and disadvantages of the various models. We paid attention to needs for flexibility versus needs for legitimacy. We also linked increased managerial responsibility with its motivational implications. We discussed the importance of organizational incentives within the larger set of professional motivators. We discussed the difference between internal and external incentives and the importance of creating new incentives.

We urged conscious approaches to incentive management, including participation of the professional staff. Last, we discussed internal professional career paths and their relevance to professional participation in the governance of the organization.

I will remind you of the student who came back to me and said that she thought that the concept of goals was not so useful after all. Maybe the concept of the profession-oriented organization is arduous. Managing professional organizations is certainly far more complicated than managing ordinary bureaucracies, but it is also much more fun.

7

Encouraging Risk Taking
and Professional Responsibility

Debureaucratization means fewer routines, less paperwork, and less centralized control. More important, it allows more organizational learning to occur. Organizational learning implies taking risks, finding out what works and does not work, and acting on that knowledge. Organizational learning requires time: time to seek alternatives and implement change.

Organizations do not reward risk takers. At best, they reward successful risk takers, but taking risks implies that success or failure is not known beforehand. Therefore, risk avoidance is a common bureaucratic practice (Benveniste, 1983; Bohland and Gist, 1983).

Failure implies errors. Making too many errors suggests incompetence. Fear of risk taking is linked to rewards and punishments. If organizational rewards are closely linked to success and if the organization severely punishes errors, risk-avoidance behavior dominates. When risks are inevitable and have to be taken, "sharing the blame" behavior dominates. Bureaucrats elaborate complex defenses to justify mistakes. They rely on routinization to do so. Routines can be used to justify what is done, including errors.

Organizational learning requires both discretion and additional resources. We may be following an expensive procedure that does not work well, but to replace it we have to experiment and try something else. During a period of time, we will need additional resources while we still use the expensive procedure and search for a better one.

We first discuss loose coupling, slack resources, and redundancy—three important concepts in risk-taking management. We proceed to discuss error management, particularly the relationship among errors, evaluation, and risk taking. We examine how evaluation for organizational learning has to be differentiated from evaluation for career promotion purposes.

We then proceed to look at professional participation in risk taking. How do conflicts between professions affect risk taking? How do we identify leaders among the professional staff? We conclude by listing four areas where greater professional responsibility can be encouraged by management.

Loose Coupling

Loose coupling implies discretion. It also implies self-sufficiency and autonomy. If you give me considerable discretion, but you depend on my work output and cannot do without it, sooner or later I will discover I really do not have much discretion. I have to perform and meet your needs. Loose coupling implies that work is so arranged that there are enough time and resources to allow for autonomy. I am able to take risks because you do not control every motion I make and you do not need me every minute of the day (Glassman, 1973; Weick, 1976).

Tight coupling is due either to system design or distrust or both. Work on the assembly line is tightly coupled to achieve efficiency. The operations of each worker affect the operations of other workers. If I am on the assembly line and begin to experiment on my own, the supervisor will come quickly and ask if I have lost my mind.

Work is closely supervised and discretion is constrained when there is considerable distrust. This, of course, is the perennial problem in many organizations but is particularly visible

and vivid in Third World countries. Visit a government ministry, say, in a South American country. You will not find much
loose coupling. The ministry is bureaucratized and centralized.
One reason is corruption. The center fears scandal at the periphery. The center wants control to reduce overall corruption or to
keep it close at hand. Another reason is scarcity of qualified
workers. The center fears incompetence, the top does not trust
the bottom. As a result, there is the typical overflow of information and decisions going to the top. Your typical Third World
manager is overwhelmed by the work.

The consequence is clear. Routinized controls or over-
worked managers do not encourage risk taking and organizational learning.

Organizational Slack

Risk taking and organizational learning require additional
resources. To be able to experiment, you need leeway, the possibility to correct small errors, to adjust course, or to use alternative paths. A detailed, precise budget with no allowance for
the unforeseen is a routine that restricts opportunities for
change. The efficient operation where everything is accounted
for, where every routine is precisely set and budgeted, does not
provide opportunities for questioning and testing.

Organizational slack is unused capabilities. It is the extra
reservoir of good will and energy that can be used by the organization to survive during crisis periods. It is also the capability to
experiment to test out new ideas.

As March and Simon point out (1965), organizational
slack helps maintain internal cohesion. When resources are restricted and there is less organizational slack, increased competition and conflict arise. Organizational slack is important for
organizational learning because learning behavior cannot always
be programmed and scheduled ahead of time. To be sure, we
may have enough experience with our organization to be able to
routinize our own organizational learning behavior and even
budget for some of it. The research and development budget of
any organization is part of the organization's effort to learn and

adapt, but organizational slack is the oil that allows the machinery to function. It provides the daily opportunities for innovation. This is a fundamental difference between adaptive organizations and mindless routinized bureaucracy.

Visit the atelier of the painter or the laboratory of the researcher. There is considerable order and purpose. You may not see it, but it is there. Resources are not squandered, they are used knowledgeably, but there is considerable slack. There are enough chemicals and equipment to vary the experiment. The painter has enough paint, canvas, brushes, and palette knives to change course, to repair, to search for alternatives: "That blue did not work at all. Let's get rid of it, try a darker, more intense shade. Yes, that does it." The painter did not have to write six memoranda to justify the shift from cadmium blue to ultramarine.

The rhetoric of bureaucracies is antiorganizational slack. What cannot be justified immediately is labeled waste. Distrust within organizations translates into tight controls designed to eliminate the "fat." The rhetoric of efficiency presupposes that organizational learning can be programmed and rationalized like any other activity.

How much organizational slack is desirable? There is no precise answer, but experience and costs provide guidelines (Scott, 1981). Taking risks is costly. Sooner or later, a general sense of the effectiveness of the organization will prevail. If we keep taking risks, and innovate but never succeed in improving performance, sooner or later we will have to decide that this strategy is getting nowhere. But if we sense that we are improving our performance, we will continue.

How much slack do we need? We can make approximations. If we contrast early estimates of how long a professional task should take with the actual time spent, we may be looking at our need for slack. That difference includes dimensions that have nothing to do with risk taking and innovation. It includes unforeseen delays, mistakes, and so on where learning behavior is negligible, but it does include learning behavior. It is common practice on large projects (construction, space exploration, military procurement) to conduct detailed delay and cost-overrun studies. The main purpose is to provide new standards for estimating or to provide insights on past errors to be avoided. These studies also provide comparative information about the extent to which learning behavior is required in the course of these projects.

Past experience with delays and overruns reveals problems that cannot be taken into account and planned ahead of time, problems that have to be solved as work progresses. An understanding of the general nature of these problems, their frequency and consequences, is the beginning of an understanding of the need for organizational slack.

Maybe we use the wrong language. The term *organizational slack* has been in the literature for so long that we forget its connotations. Slack implies waste. Fear of waste engenders tight coupling and tight coupling reduces discretion.

From management's point of view, it might be more sensible to define slack as the necessary cost of effective professional performance. Might it be called organizational innovative capability instead of organizational slack?

Redundancy

Redundancy is linked to organizational slack. Redundant capability is the availability of additional parallel means to achieve desirable ends. It is an important concept in safety design (Perrow, 1984). We may install two extra fuel pumps to ensure that a jet engine will continue to perform even if both the first and second fuel pumps fail. Redundancy can have different dimensions and aspects. We may assign the same task to various teams, we may go over the same task twice or more, we may use different kinds of meetings to generate ideas, and we may spend time looking at alternative courses of action.

Functions of Redundancy. Redundancy is an important concept for managers of profession-oriented organizations because it introduces and implies different approaches, such as internal competition between teams performing similar tasks or greater guarantees of work completion (Bendor, 1985; Cohen, 1981; Felsenthal, 1980; Landau, 1969, 1973a, 1973b; Nelson, 1961).

We assign a problem to two or three different and independent research teams. Each starts with slightly different theoretical and methodological approaches. The problem is highly important to the success of our project. By assigning three independent teams, we hope to increase our chances of success.

Redundancy has other consequences. It can reduce undesirable organizational pressures on professional workers. The single professional team working on a crucial problem is keenly aware that management is waiting for results. If pressure is too high, it engenders dysfunctional behavior. It can lead to corruption—"Let's give them the results they want"—or to dysfunctional tension—"We were so tense we could not even see what the data were telling us although it was right in front of us."

Redundancy reduces pressure on each team. "We might not succeed, but that is less important because the other teams still have a chance. That is what matters. Moreover, if we do not succeed and they fail also, then no one can succeed. If no one can succeed, no one can be blamed."

Redundancy serves to substitute professional for managerial pressure: "Management is not breathing down our necks because they do not have to. They know we are competing. They realize one of the three teams is bound to uncover what there is to uncover. All of us want to win the race. We have to publish our paper before they do."

Redundancy is particularly important when the experiment fails. It provides the capability to rectify errors. In situations where organizational learning cannot be allowed to interrupt service delivery, redundancy has to be incorporated in the design of the organization so that experimentation does not affect service.

Undesirable Characteristics of Redundancy. Redundancy is not always desirable. As Meltsner (1976) avers, redundancy can also mean that resources are used unwisely. Excessive fragmentation of available professional talent in different competing teams may weaken capability. Ambiguous territorial assignments can nourish feelings of status deprivation and ambition. Competition can become unhealthy. Fights for resources, talent, and data can be dysfunctional: "We have the data, but we are not sharing it with the other team. We will publish our results first."

Redundancy is also dysfunctional because it can create additional sources of error: "We have added research teams, but given the quality of the data, it actually increases the probability that we are making more errors." This is the classic problem in safety design: adding redundancy for safety also increases the probability of erroneous actualization. The more there are safety lights on the control panel, the more there are chances one will not operate when it should or vice versa. Yet redundancy is an important concept in professional management. Redundancy in the design of the organization may facilitate experimentation and organizational learning behavior.

Managing Errors

Organizational learning depends on making errors. Four types are relevant: marginal, articulation, commons, and control errors.

Marginal Errors. These are the customary, inevitable errors that happen once in a while: the bad pea in the peapod. In any batch, there will be imperfections; any repetitive production process generates rejects. Some technologies require high quality standards, so-called error free processes. Attempts are made to eliminate all errors by using redundant controls: we check you at the door, we check again in the lobby, and check a third time before you enter the office. But even redundant controls can fail and errors are always possible.

The technology, management philosophy, cost, consequences, and client needs determine tolerable quality standards. Some errors (individual or equipment) are tolerated. Some errors are not tolerated. Errors that are permissible in the boilers of a coal-fired plant are intolerable in the core of the nuclear reactor of an atomic plant.

Marginal errors are relevant because they are taken into account to evaluate performance. Given an accepted level of tolerable error, those that consistently seem to do worse may be considered incompetent. If I forget my lecture notes once, no one will think much about it. If I always forget my lecture notes, my dean will start worrying about my ability to teach courses.

At Applied Research under the first manager, there was considerable pressure for the professional staff to complete research reports on time. The manager considered it an error not to meet a deadline. He did not use that language, but he was adamant. He felt that the organization would lose its reputation and clients if reports were delayed. His philosophy, more than anything else, defined what was tolerable and not. The professional staff knew that any serious deviancy would result in much hair pulling and unpleasantness.

From the staff's point of view, this rigid adherence to time schedules was unjustified. There were many instances where vagaries and difficulties of research would result in inevitable delays. Moreover, it was not uncommon for planned research processes to turn out to be more complicated than originally anticipated. Most of the work required collecting data and analyzing it. It was relatively easy to estimate how long most research projects would take. But there would be occasions when data collection was slowed down; additional data might be uncovered or a different analysis might be attempted. In those cases, the research would be improved, but take longer. The manager would never want to hear about it. He held to schedules at all cost. When we interviewed him, he explained that most of the sponsors had to have reports on time, given their own decision timetables. He also indicated that if he allowed report delays, he would lose control of the staff. Once it became known that delays were acceptable, the staff would relax. Before you knew it, all reports would be late.

The strategy had costs. The staff felt it was an arbitrary top-down mandate that was not realistic. The quality of the reports and of the research was clearly affected. This was a case of tight coupling—little slack and little discretion were provided. Risk taking and error making were not encouraged. The reports were produced on time, but it was not an effective strategy. The reputation of Applied Research was lowered. The manager had created a standard for marginal errors that did not permit making learning errors. As a result, the organization was less effective than it might be.

Articulation Errors. These errors are systemic; they per-tain to the entire system. One system is not articulated to another. You manufacture round pegs for the peg market. This year demand shifted. The demand for round pegs dropped while that for square pegs increased. You are left with piles of unused and unsold round pegs. This is an articulation error.

Articulation errors are more threatening to organizations than most marginal errors. Except for high-risk technologies, where the term *marginal errors* can be a misnomer—for example, the sequence of events that led to the accident at the Three Mile Island Unit 2 nuclear power plant starting on March 28, 1979—articulation errors tend to have more serious consequences. They can jeopardize the survival capability of the organization.

If markets or clients disappear, units or entire organizations may disappear. If budgets have to be cut by 30 percent, entire departments may be eliminated. Since these errors are more threatening, there is more concern with avoiding them. At Applied Research, the manager was very concerned with delivering reports on time because he thought such routine deficiencies or marginal errors might affect some of his clients and thus create the more threatening articulation error: the clients would cancel the research service. But his fear had consequences. He generated a far more serious problem: the professional reputation of Applied Research went down, and the future of the organization was in jeopardy.

Organizational adaptability and flexibility are essential to avoid articulation errors. If we plan, sense how the environment is changing, and use our capability to experiment and adapt, we will avoid major articulation errors. As the demand shifts from round to square pegs, we experiment, redesign our processes, produce square pegs, and survive.

Excessive controls designed to reduce marginal errors can also result in increased articulation error. Conversely, increased levels of experimentation, more learning behavior, more false starts, can avoid large-scale articulation disasters.

Commons Errors. The name comes from the commons, or the community-owned land. Whereas articulation errors take place between systems that transact business together (you pro-

duce round pegs and I buy them), commons errors take place
between systems that are not customarily in exchange relations.
Economists usually call these externalities. You and I run the
factory that pollutes the river and that pollution kills the fish
that was the livelihood of the fishing industry 200 miles down-
stream. The fish, their environment, and the fishing industry
had nothing to do with our plant; we did not even know they
existed. But after the fishing village complained, environmental
groups joined them, and after they demonstrated and lobbied
the legislature, government regulation was introduced to remedy these problems.

Regulatory controls affect management and professionals differently. Management is more concerned with the costs
and uncertainties associated with regulation. Professionals may
find that regulatory controls constrain their discretion. On the
other hand, they may see them as external definitions of ethical
practice.

In any case, avoiding commons errors requires adaptability. So, once again, we see that measures intended to reduce discretion might constrain our ability to deal with commons
errors.

Control Errors. These are a survival strategy based on
ability to control the relevant environment.

If organizational learning and adaptability are insufficient,
if the organization is caught in a serious articulation error, two
outcomes are possible: the organization disappears, or the organization is able to manipulate the environment. We manage to
convince the legislature that round pegs are more American,
whereas square pegs are un-American. A bill is passed and every
citizen is obliged to own round pegs. The round peg factory is
saved.

Control errors are poor substitutes for organizational
learning and adaptability. Sooner or later, clients may complain
or revolt. Others will lobby for square pegs. In due time, the
round peg market may collapse and the organization will have
adopted the wrong strategy for too long. We did not adapt, we
did not take risks, we did not learn from errors. As a result, our
product deteriorated until it was too late to do anything. Japa-

nese competition, the revolt of our clients, and a shift of government subsidy led to the end of the round peg market.

Deliberate Error Management

Organizational learning and adaptability originate from deliberate error management. For example, analysts in financial management firms who recommend securities sales or purchases have to be allowed to make errors if they are going to be able to increase overall performance. If management rebuffs them each time an investment selection fails to meet expectations, or each time they recommended a small purchase for a stock that did very well, they will respond by adopting more cautious decision rules. Either they select those stocks that entail little risk and are also bound to entail little performance, or they will adopt protective strategies.

Level of tolerable error is determined in part by risk and desired performance. Mediating in between are professional knowledge and judgment.

Good securities analysts acquire enough knowledge about the firms and industries they invest in to be able to eliminate some risks, but information is never complete. Considerable uncertainty still remains. Therefore, desirable levels of error are determined, in part, by conscious decisions of the desired risk level.

There is an important difference between managing errors and tolerating marginal errors. Error management selects desirable error levels. Our analysts could easily select stocks that are very stable and will not fizzle out in six months. But they deliberately select riskier stocks because they expect some of these to do very well. They deliberately work at an error level higher than what might be the minimum tolerable level for marginal errors.

This can be quantified to some extent by examining how individual firms have performed in the past relative to other firms in the industry and how specific stocks have performed relative to their industry or the entire securities market. Risk indices are elaborated and, to this extent, risk management is routinized. Stocks that are more volatile due to characteristics of the industry or of the firm can be identified. Risk strategies can, to some extent, be quantified.

Routinization provides some protection. If a stock does not perform well, the analyst can point out that this error was predictable given the risk taken. If a stock does very well and was not purchased, or purchased only in small quantity, the analyst can still point out that the stock called for a greater risk strategy than was desired.

Since making recommendations for stock purchases or sales depends on incomplete knowledge, and on quantifications that illuminate but do not determine choice, the analyst is left with judgment. The success of the analyst depends also on the way he or she is able to convince portfolio managers and others in the firm of the strength and validity of the recommendation.

In the long run, management is able to identify those who make too many poor decisions and gets rid of them. It also uses strong incentive systems to reward the successful at the end of the year. But, in the short run, management expects errors to be made. It relies on the judgment and persuasive powers of the analyst. It lets it be known that it expects everyone to make some errors. It might even frown on those who never make them (Vertin, 1984).

What has to be considered when selecting deliberate error levels?

1. The potential contribution of risk and higher level of error on organizational learning and performance. The first manager at Applied Research did not believe he could improve performance by allowing report delays. He thought it would simply make life easier for the staff. He did not see how report delays could increase organizational learning and improve quality. He simply saw report delays as marginal errors to be avoided at all costs. It turned out he was wrong. In contrast, the management of the investment firm knows that higher levels of performance can be achieved only if higher risks are taken.

2. The availability of slack resources. Risk taking and increased level of errors are costly. Do these costs imperil the

organization? The Applied Research manager was convinced that sponsors would drop out if there were delays. His successor tested opportunities for delays. She approached sponsors, and discussed delays with them. We can say that she created organizational slack and used it. For the investment firm, slack is created through careful discussion of portfolio objectives with each client. The clients know that higher levels of performance also mean higher risks and that success is not guaranteed. They are prepared to absorb some losses.

3. The impact errors can have on third parties. These are the externalities or commons errors. They also present constraints on error management. When Applied Research delayed its reports, there were few consequences outside the immediate client environment. The second manager had to ascertain this. We can imagine situations where such delays might have seriously affected third parties. Coming back to our factory and river, we know that we cannot experiment with new chemicals and pollute the river. The fish will not stand it, nor will the regulatory commission.

Evaluation: Learning or Career Promotion?

Feedback, encouragement, or sanctioning are components of any learning experience. Evaluation is crucial in organizational learning since we are experimenting with new approaches. We have to know what works and what does not.

If I am to innovate and test out new approaches, I want to receive feedback and even want to be encouraged and discouraged in my pursuits. However, if my career is at stake, I may be much less willing to take additional risks I cannot control. I may even be tempted to tamper with the evaluation process. In other words, I may falsify the evaluation data to look good—even if the experiment is not working—thus hampering organizational learning while I promote myself.

Since evaluation can be used both to assist the learning process and to reward and punish, it may deter risk taking and hamper error management. Even when management is aware of this distinction, the professional staff may perceive matters dif-

ferently. It is, therefore, necessary to segregate learning evaluation from career promotion evaluation.

Desirable Risks for Organizational Learning. Discussing
and defining tolerable and desirable risks is a joint managerial-
professional task. It requires a shared understanding of both
managerial and professional attitudes, culture, and traditions as
they affect risk taking (Douglas and Wildavsky, 1982).

As pointed out, errors may be an indication of professional incompetence. The new financial analyst who makes a
big blunder the first month on the job will still have to convince management that he knows what he is doing. Professionals
will be reluctant to admit errors if they sense those who evaluate them cannot distinguish between errors due to incompetence and errors due to deliberate risk taking. Management has
to be able to make these distinctions and has to be able to convince professionals it can. It also has to induce the analyst to
avoid making choices that please management but which the
analyst does not really believe in.

Managers of financial management institutions are, or
should be, sensitive to this. They want the analyst to recommend those stocks the analyst believes in, not those the analyst
senses portfolio managers or the top brass will readily accept.
This is why they often use very strong incentive schemes tied to
specific recommendations. The analyst is inclined to recommend what he or she believes in, not what may be readily accepted (Vertin, 1984).

When errors are made, the senior partners in the financial
management firm might look over the shoulder of the junior
member to ascertain whether the blunder seemed justified. The
senior partners are accomplished professionals and their judgment is based on experience. But they will be reluctant to evaluate and prefer to see how the young analyst performs in subsequent months.

Error management requires close collaboration between
managers and professionals. Trust is important—trust based on
mutual knowledge of strengths and weaknesses. However, trust
takes time to build. It requires experience, learning to work together, and it requires honesty. Error management requires can-

dor. It requires that management reveal the rules of the game, what Pastin (1986) calls the "ethics edge." Rhetoric has to be replaced by hard-nosed reality. Management has to be convinced it understands how the professional staff is playing the game. The professional staff has to be convinced it knows the basic ground rules management is using. Ultimately, there needs to be enough trust that management will not penalize those who venture forth, and there must be enough trust that those who venture forth know what they are doing. Management needs to be reassured that they are taking reasonable risks.

Frequency of Evaluation. Taking risks, making errors, learning from them, adapting work, and finally, showing results, takes time. Evaluation for promotion has to take such time considerations into account. It is desirable to evaluate often when the staff is trying something new. These evaluations for learning have to be sharply differentiated from evaluations for promotional purposes.

It is important to design evaluation schemes that do not deter desirable innovation. For example, when we conducted research in local school districts in California, we found that statewide testing of school children was perceived to deter innovation. The following statement, made by a research-oriented principal who was discussing an experiment with us, is typical:

> District administration and the [school] board want innovation. They are even in favor of research and experimentation, but there are other problems. . . . Suppose we experiment and introduce new programs. They are going to require time to work out. Meanwhile, we are not going to do as well. Our test scores will drop at first. I know that tests are not expected to show differences, that the tests are designed independently from the curriculum, but we can still expect effects. The teachers worry about this. How will they explain lower scores? Parents have become mesmerized by test scores. They place pressure on teachers and on the board. Teachers only want to experiment if they

are convinced the experiment will not work against
them. The bottom line is that we cannot experiment very much. We are tested all the time, that is
part of the problem.

Less frequent evaluations affecting, or perceived to affect, careers or status need to be replaced by more frequent
monitoring and evaluation that are perceived to assist organizational learning. Let me give you another example. Let us visit
the second manager at Applied Research.

She gave far more autonomy and discretion to her research teams. She did not attempt to control them the way the
first manager had. She allowed them their idiosyncratic sen-
tence structure, commas, and style. She did not rewrite the research reports, although she hired a professional editor. But
these were not the more important issues.

The new manager did not believe that sponsors would
automatically respond negatively to delays. She sought to establish trust relations with them so that she could better understand their time pressure and political realities. She allowed delays in selected cases where she thought the sponsors would not
incur high costs.

She kept tight control of research progress. She insisted
on weekly reporting of work completed and of future timetables. She even visited research teams in the field to exchange
notes, discuss problems, and provide encouragement and support.

She had her own informal sources of information, using
her friends on the staff to keep an informed eye on research
progress. She would flag delays ahead of time and seek team
participation in deciding how to handle them. The team would
gather with her to discuss whether to risk delays or not. They
would assess report quality versus client problems. In many instances, report quality seemed the right answer. In others, it was
not, but the judgment was made collectively. The staff knew
that they had her support, and she understood the factors causing delays.

Her frequent monitoring was perceived to be supportive.

The staff was confident that she understood why delays were justified and did not feel threatened that she would place the blame on them if sponsors complained. In this case, monitoring and evaluation for organizational learning enhanced staff confidence.

Formal evaluations for promotions at Applied Research took place automatically every year. The second manager, like her predecessor, did not have much control over the content of these civil service evaluations leading to quasi-automatic salary increases.

The new manager would reward her best people by other means. She made it clear to the senior staff that she wanted performance but that she would judge performance over long periods of time. She also made clear the additional rewards she controlled directly—recommendations for important short-term assignments in other agencies and for career opportunities elsewhere. She was open and candid. She delivered these rewards. She recommended very good people for important assignments in other prestigious organizations. Some of her people went to work for the White House, the Office of Management and Budget, or for the Treasury. She lost them, but the reputation of Applied Research soared in professional circles. It was a good place to work because it provided career opportunities. She lost good people and acquired many talented replacements.

Professional Conflicts

Risk taking and error management require greater skill when many different professions are involved. The problem is not necessarily due to interprofessional conflicts, but to differentiated motivation.

It is often assumed that professionals are clannish, and that multidisciplinary or multiprofessional efforts are doomed to result in conflicts across professions. To be sure, conflicts do exist on a generalized basis when professions attempt to protect their prerogatives and want to constrain what other professions can do. Physicians may be concerned that nurses or other allied health workers will encroach on their autonomy and privileges.

These conflicts may create serious problems in the field, but they do not necessarily deter professional performance.

In practice, interdisciplinary work is not conflict-ridden. Experience and the research literature confirm that when two or more professions work on common tasks, the task itself provides the basis for trust (Guy, 1985). It is when there is fear of failure that defensive strategies come into play. It may be easier to blame economists if you are an engineer or to blame other professionals because your peers cannot evaluate their work as well as they can evaluate your own.

Differing Motivations for Taking Risks. One reason conflicts emerge around risk taking is that different professions have different career goals and, therefore, different motivations and commitment to organizational tasks. A common research task that is very important for the career of an engineer may have little consequence for the economist. Given different levels of motivation, willingness to take risks will differ, and willingness to provide energy and commitment will also differ. Since intrinsic motivation and status may be very important to these professionals, these different motivations can cause considerable suspicions and distrust. As a result, conflicts may emerge because different professions are interdependent but have different motivations.

Perceptions of differentiated consequences and commitment across professions can deter risk taking: "The economists want us to experiment, but it's no skin off their noses—even if we fail, they still look good, whereas we look like fools."

Genuine Differences of Opinion. Another reason conflicts emerge around risk taking derives simply from different opinions and perspectives on what can or should be done. Most risk problems are complex and genuine differences of opinion on how to proceed are bound to emerge. Differences of opinion can easily become personalized. The relative status and influence of those who disagree accentuate the conflict. What may start as a genuine difference of opinion can rapidly become a rabid fight where inviolate principles are at stake. At this point, the status, prestige, and visibility of one school of thought confront another, and the battle may rage for years.

Lack of Managerial Arbitration. A third reason conflicts emerge around risk taking results from the absence of managerial arbitration. An important function of authority figures is to arbitrate and resolve conflicts. Since much professional work requires autonomy, even team or project work tends to have less control and, therefore, fewer opportunities for arbitration. As we saw when we discussed the partnership model in Chapter Three, some governance models are less able to resolve conflicts than others. As a consequence, conflict in organizations with many professionals is an ever-present danger and can be the surest cause of the demise of the enterprise.

Management Approaches. Managers cannot afford to allow these conflicts to breed and erupt. Where they do not exist, and are needed, conflict resolution mechanisms can be established. This is particularly relevant for partnerships of dual governance models. Internal or external arbitration groups may be necessary and highly useful.

Management has to keep in touch with the professions. There is no substitute for circulating around, picking up on the early signs of dissatisfaction and opposition, and acting rapidly. Where conflicts emerge from differentiated professional commitment, management has to be aware of these differences and compensate for them. Where teamwork is important, matrix management has to ensure that managers talk with their counterparts, that team members get strong support. It also means that major and minor actors have to be taken into account.

There must be something for everyone. Rewards cannot flow in only one channel. They have to be shared across participating professions.

Finding Good People

Interview successful managers, and they will always tell you that the secret of their success is finding good people and giving them the means to do the work. But who are the good people in the professional organization?

Deadwood. Obviously, good people are not deadwood. Deadwood is that category of professionals who have reached the end of their ambition and talent. Deadwood is motivated by the status quo. Deadwood wants to stay in place. These professionals do not have ideas, nor do they produce more than told. They have no ambitions, they no longer publish, they no longer produce, but they defend the territory they occupy. They have learned the skills of bureaucratic infighting, and they understand bureaucratic defensive strategies. They are also protected by civil service regulations or by collective contract agreements. They cannot be easily removed. They locate in convenient niches. They avoid the hard work at the front line, but they can jeopardize attempts to renovate and revitalize the organization. They know their limitations and find solace in collective mediocrity.

Management wants innovation and risk taking. Deadwood insists on protection, on written, documented "share the blame" guarantees. Management does not care for their attitude. They are skilled in defending the right not to innovate. Is management asking them to experiment on defenseless clients? Has management considered the consequences this approach might have on the safety of the venture? They predict errors ahead of time, and they will be happy, later on, when errors have been made, that they were first to sound the alarm.

Management has two dilemmas. First, it needs to be able to assess the motivation for the alarm. Are these engineers against the experiment because of sound professional considerations? Or is it a strategy to protect their comfortable assignments? If it is the first, management wants to listen and understand, but if it is the second, they do not want to be deterred by mediocrity.

Second, management needs to motivate deadwood. The success of risk-taking exercises depends on trust. Those who venture forth want to be reassured that if the experiment fails, they will not automatically suffer. Dragging deadwood along is expensive because it is clear these people are opposed to the exercise and will seek advantage out of tiny failure. They have to be induced to join. There is no way to bypass them, to disregard them, because they are too numerous. Management has to spend the time, the energy, and some resources to buy their allegiance.

Formal professional bodies within the organization can provide a forum to discuss risk-taking endeavors. Here, professional leadership can surface and issues can be brought into the open. There is, nevertheless, the danger that mediocrity will prevail. Large gatherings of professionals can easily be dominated by deadwood.

One approach is to buy their allegiance. Management has to learn and understand the fears that agitate deadwood. It has to be able to dispell these fears: "No, there is no danger your job will be affected. If the experiment succeeds, we will continue producing a few round pegs for the export market." Management has to be able to provide attractive alternatives: "You will move to square peg quality control where you will have a two-window office instead of a single window."

The other approach is to remove deadwood. Reorganizations are often used for this purpose, but where will they be removed to? Can they be used at the front line of the organization, say, in client service? Can they be lodged in a different unit where they cannot possibly harm anything? Can just shuffling them around reduce their obstructionism as they have to learn different bureaucratic skills to fit different organizational realities?

Climbers. Climbers differ from deadwood in one respect: they want to succeed, to climb the prestige ladder, but they do not have the talent required. They do not have ideas, nor can they produce more than told. They are ambitious and mediocre.

They differ from deadwood in that climbers understand they have to take risks to climb. Since they are not very talented and do not have ideas of their own, they use the ideas of others. Since they have difficulty knowing which ideas will succeed, they keep an eye on what others are doing. When those they admire and emulate seem ready to venture forth, they are ready to climb and jump on the bandwagon.

Climbers are dangerous because they tend to follow leaders and give the impression of a wide professional consensus when only a few have had the idea and understand the experiment. Where deadwood sound too many alarms, climbers obliterate them. Management calls a meeting of the professional staff: "Should we proceed with the experiment?" A single committed voice answers, "Yes." That would not be enough to convince management. The others in the room look around—is that the path? They admire their leader. "Yes," they say one after the other, "yes, let us proceed." The alarm is never sounded, and management is left with the impression of wide professional consensus when only one committed voice determined the outcome.

Management has to learn to recognize climbers for what they are. They need not be counted. Once their strategies are understood, they need not cause confusion. The point is that one should not let the blind lead the blind.

They represent far less problem than deadwood because they want to play the game, they want to take chances. They may be mediocre, but they will do their best, and that is what matters.

Prima Donnas. Prima donnas are climbers with ideas. They are leaders who can do, but they are self-centered. What matters to them are their career, visibility, and status. Moreover, they know they have ideas; they know they can produce. They have a profound disdain for those who cannot and a profound suspicion of those who can. Those who cannot will steal their ideas. Those who can are never as good as they are. The prima donna fears that others will attempt to obtain credit where credit is not due and will seek to displace them.

Prima donnas use ideas to climb, but climbing and status are more important to them than organizational effectiveness or well-being. They may direct the organization in directions that are not generally desirable but are nevertheless highly advantageous to them because their work, research, or contribution is enhanced. They may be skilled in bureaucratic infighting. They know what they want and might be able to organize support among climbers, and even deadwood.

Prima donnas are important and cannot be disregarded. In the professional organization, ideas and production count.

Management cannot afford to lose and alienate prima donnas. Management's task and challenge are to convert prima donnas into good people.

First, management has to recognize and understand their need for status and recognition, to find ways of satisfying these needs without alienating the rest of the professional staff. Second, management has to learn to understand and recognize an individual prima donna's motivations as distinct from larger organizational interests. Management has to be able to judge when to disregard a prima donna's advice. Third, management has to establish clear *quid pro quo* relations with prima donnas. Can we define issues and topics of mutual interest where broad organizational objectives mesh with specific prima donna aspirations? Can we agree to work together on these issues and topics? Can we agree not to pursue specific interests of the prima donna that will cause trouble for the rest of the organization?

Some prima donnas convert. They learn to understand the organization. They find a role for themselves that is not destructive, and they contribute tremendously to the collective task. Other prima donnas remain on a destructive course. They continue to battle the talented members of the professional staff. They increasingly challenge management's authority. They continue to pursue narrow personal interests and seek to divert more resources for their own work. Finally, they attempt to displace management and reconstruct the organization to fit their image of what the organization should do.

Fortunately, prima donnas do not stay where they are not welcome. Since they have talent and produce, they will be invited elsewhere. Management can always get rid of prima donnas by making life difficult for them, by denying them the resources and status they crave. However, the battle is not an easy one. Management must take care not to be destroyed in the process. Getting rid of prima donnas is an act of last resort. First, they are valuable, and second, they bite.

The Silent Virtuosos. The silent virtuosos have ideas, produce, and are not frantically climbing. But they have no managerial interest or talent. Organizational politics are an abomination to be avoided at all costs. They became professionals to avoid politics. One can count on them to deal with professional issues, but never expect them to take leadership, to organize, to act or participate in joint managerial-professional tasks.

They have a name and a reputation in their narrow professional field. They may even have a following and are proud of it. They recognize prima donnas for what they are, but are not affected by their performance. The silent virtuosos appreciate the professional work of the prima donnas. They consider their ambitions to be amusing or childish. They do not mind being bypassed on joint managerial-professional tasks because they do not care to waste time. They expect management to be fair. Since they prefer to work on professional problems, they expect management to recognize their worth to the enterprise, to control the prima donnas, and to handle credits and rewards fairly. In their view, this is what managers are paid for.

They have ideas, they produce, and they do not mind being consulted. They are not managers, they do not want to be, and will balk if asked to spend too much time on managerial issues. But management can use them from time to time to push projects and ideas.

Good People. Good people are rare. Therefore, they are immensely valuable. They have ideas and they produce, but they have broad interests. They work well with others because they do not have exaggerated perceptions of their own worth. They do not fear managerial tasks. They are concerned with the organization, what it accomplishes and how it survives. They treat their colleagues well and are liked by most. They have professional interests of their own, but they make distinctions between organizational and personal interests. They work well on teams because they lead and do not dominate.

Good people bridge the gap between the profession and management. They have the potential to do both. They may ultimately be a threat to management because they are talented, but management may well be made of similar talent and background.

Good people are the potential members of the senior staff. They are the ones who should be selected for joint managerial-professional tasks. To do so requires alternatives for prima donnas and silent virtuosos. The senior staff might have two branches with distinct assignments. The managerial branch tackles joint tasks; the professional branch deals with professional issues. A role is found for prima donnas and silent virtuosos. Good people are allowed to contribute.

Good people are as ambitious as climbers or prima donnas, perhaps more so. This ambition is centered on their professional work. It has less to do with appearance and more to do with the quality and visibility of the work. They make less noise than prima donnas, but are no less sensitive. They expect management to deal with prima donnas, and they resent it when management does not. They resent prima donnas' encroachment and domination. They sometimes decide to leave when they sense that prima donnas have succeeded in taking over the organization.

Good people are attracted to profession-oriented organizations with career opportunities. They are centered on work as it relates to them and to the organization. They want to innovate because they see opportunities both for improving professional and organizational performance and for their own advancement. They can be the mobilizers of deadwood, climbers, and silent virtuosos. They do not threaten deadwood, they assist climbers, and they appreciate silent virtuosos. They acquire a following among those, but are not effective with prima donnas. Good people, silent virtuosos, and prima donnas are the generators of ideas and producers, but prima donnas want all the limelight. It is management's function to ensure that prima donnas are kept in place, that good people and silent virtuosos are supported and not trampled.

Good people leave when new opportunities emerge. Their visible success in the organization is noticed. It is not wise to attempt to hide their success in the hopes they might be less visible and stay. They will go sooner or later if better pastures exist elsewhere. They will stay when there is no better place to go to. The surest way to keep them is to make the organization the best in the nation and to give them an important role in this task.

Good people are not always located where they can best

contribute to the organization. They may be located in peripheral departments while they are needed in the core. Some departments may be blessed with several, while others have none. In the profession-oriented organization, mobility is limited by professional domains, but opportunities to move good people around do exist. They can advise on joint managerial-professional tasks, they can be assigned monitoring roles, and they can sometimes transfer to different units. Good people need challenges and they readily take them.

Good people need to be educated about managerial problems. They may be well trained in their profession, but quite ignorant of the larger context in which the organization operates. Management might take its own vision of the organization for granted, but the talented professionals who have ideas, produce, and are attracted to management can still be quite naive about politics, the external environment, and the realities of budgets and accountability. It is management's task to identify them, protect them, assign roles to them, and train them.

Professional Responsibility and Function

Good people are organizers. They can organize the professional body if asked to do so, but as we saw in the preceding chapter, different structures fit different needs. If a professional body is created, it can have various functions.

Maintain Quality Standards. The professional body may be asked to set program quality standards, review work, and recommend remedies. One advantage of using internal professional reviews, independent of individual career promotion reviews, is that these professional reviews are perceived to be friendly, divorced from career promotion functions, and solely concerned with upgrading work standards. Program review processes are focused on teams, units, or departments and address organizational as well as professional issues.

Universities, hospitals, and other professional organizations have long traditions of using both internal and external review processes. Their impact and success depend, in part, on the support they receive from management, and on the care with which they are briefed, the time they have to perform their task, and the resources they use for this purpose (Barak, 1982; Wilson, 1982; U.S. General Accounting Office, 1978).

Provide a Forum for Ethical Issues. The professional body can be charged with setting ethical norms and with handling individual complaints. There are several advantages in having the professional body deal with ethical issues. First, it obliges the profession to define an internal code of ethics. It can discuss and define what kind of work is acceptable, what kind is not, what procedures are accepted, and what procedures are not. Management should want to know the ethical considerations that motivate the profession. The profession needs the opportunity to discuss, select, and defend an ethical stance. Moreover, the profession can enforce the stance it has selected, and it can process complaints, review them, and intervene directly with management.

This is particularly significant in professions such as engineering, medicine, or scientific research where new ethical issues emerge quite independently, but neither management nor existing national professional associations have valid experience in dealing with them. The profuse literature on the ethical dilemmas of engineers illustrates the potential role of internal professional organizations. New ethical issues can first be resolved in front-line organizations where they emerge in the first place. The professions need sufficient authority within the organization to attack these issues. As they do, and practice evolves, it also becomes more generalized. Ultimately, it becomes part of accepted norms, but management has the responsibility of making this possible (Barber, 1970; Buzzati-Traverso, 1977; Doderlein, 1976; Flores, 1982; Nelkin, 1977; Perrucci, 1971).

Attend to Professional Development. The profession can help improve itself if asked to do so. The professional body will need resources for these and other tasks, but the profession is best qualified to deal with the issue of professional obsolescence.

Professional obsolescence is the gradual loss of relevant professional knowledge. It can be due to change in knowledge base as a result of advances in sciences; change in practice; change in job requirements; change in client needs; or change stemming from individual lapses and failures due to aging and other factors (Cherniss, 1980; Kaufman, 1974).

Management is not always best informed about needs and changes in professional knowledge and practice. Moreover, some professionals are suspicious of management-directed professional development programs since participation in these programs can suggest one's own admission of failure.

Asking the profession to attend to the problem places the responsibility where it should be lodged—in the hands of those who should know, or should want to know, what is happening to their profession. Can a professional body run successful staff development programs? Yes, if it is organized to do so. It will need a staff and a manager, but the activity can be supervised by a committee of the professional staff. Management will want to monitor progress, but it will be far more effective if it monitors instead of runs the activity.

Participate in Joint Tasks. Last, but not least, the professional body can be asked to participate in joint managerial-professional tasks. This means joining management in sharing policy decisions where professional knowledge is relevant.

We have already reviewed many aspects of joint managerial-professional tasks—how they can be an important motivator of professional participation, how they can address risk-taking issues where professional knowledge is essential, how important it is to find "good people" to undertake this work, and so on.

As pointed out at the beginning, different approaches fit different circumstances. The following guidelines are useful:

- Choose capable people. Avoid the deadwood and climbers. Be careful to select no more than one prima donna. There is no point trying to recruit silent virtuosos; they are not interested in management and will not produce.
- Create small teams. Large committees never function effectively. Five, six, or seven people can accomplish a lot. Give them specific assignments. If need be, they can report to a larger professional body or consult more staff members.
- Provide resources. Managerial-professional task groups will need to have access to minimal "thinking" resources: space to meet, secretarial help, communication facilities, data han-

dling, and report production. There is no quicker way to destroy such groups than to give them a task and oblige them to find the minimal resources needed.
- Attack tough problems. All sorts of problems can be attacked. How can the organization become less bureaucratic? How could we innovate more? What activities present special risk problems? Could we handle risk better? How do we mobilize for greater professional responsibility?
- Pay attention to advice. Act on what the professionals have to say. If they are wrong, tell them why you think their judgment should not prevail. If they are right, act upon it. Do not treat the exercise as a game or as pseudoparticipation.
- Create trust through success. The easiest way to establish trust is to succeed at joint tasks. There is no point assigning impossible tasks to incompetent groups. There is no point letting the professional body assume roles it cannot handle. Successful management of the professional body requires constant watch and monitoring. As groups succeed and management and professionals learn to work together, trust increases. As trust increases, capability to innovate also increases.

Conclusion

We approached professional management from a different angle. We asked: what conditions facilitate adaptability? Risk taking? Avoidance of routine?

We found that we have to understand errors. Making errors engenders sanctions. Fear of error engenders defensive strategies. We have to understand the difference between errors of incompetence and inevitable errors associated with competent risk taking. We have to remove the fear of sanctions from competent risk taking.

This may sound simple on paper, but it is not. This is a complex managerial-professional task. To know how to release control, how to take risks, and how to manage risk-taking performance requires close trust relations between management and the professionals in the organization.

We were reminded again that not all professionals are

suited for joint tasks. We described some of our potential friends, including the desirable "good people," whose talents may not be fully utilized, but who can be mobilized to help.

We ended by suggesting four tasks for a formal body of the profession within the organization: maintain quality standards, provide a forum for setting ethical issues, attend to professional development, and participate in joint managerial-professional tasks.

How does management reduce bureaucracy to increase effectiveness? Surprisingly, there is a very simple answer: by increasing trust.

8

How External Controls
Adversely Affect
Today's Organizations

External bureaucratic controls are imposed for a variety of reasons: to control the costs of professional public services, to achieve higher professional standards, to protect clients, to promote equity principles such as affirmative action, to regulate commerce and industry, to initiate broad reforms, to avoid corruption, to oversee and account for the use of public monies, and to protect the environment. The list can be made much longer. All professional organizations, whether public, not-for-profit, or private, are subject to external bureaucratic controls imposed by government agencies, legislatures, or the courts, or arising from contracts and negotiated agreements with other organizations such as philanthropies, accrediting organizations, unions, or client, professional, or public citizen groups (Anderson, 1962; Bernstein, 1955; Bardach and Kagan, 1982; Cary, 1967; Kagan, 1978).

Who Are the External Controllers?

External controllers are either donors or regulators. Donors transfer resources. For example, a federal agency transfers resources to state and on to local agencies in the field. A philanthropy transfers resources to grantees. Donors exercise controls since they are responsible for the funding they transfer. Regulators have a mandate to control. A statute or an agreement gives the regulator the right to impose controls on the organization. For example, the regulator might control compliance with safety codes or with pollution standards. A major reform may involve both donors and regulators.

Donors and regulators have common characteristics:

1. *Limited authority.* Regulators and donors have only limited authority over the organization. They do not control all aspects of the implementation of programs or activities they are concerned with. Since their authority is limited, they have to devise external controls that protect their interests and allow them to carry out their mandate.

2. *Small staffs.* Donors and regulators usually have very small staffs and resources given the magnitude of the tasks and responsibilities they are charged with. As a consequence, they depend on routinized controls. Routines provide them with much greater scope and coverage.

3. *Legalistic orientation.* Government donors and regulators interpret legislative mandates that are often subject to judicial challenge. The more the courts intervene in regulatory or allocative resource controversies, the more donors and regulators emphasize legal considerations in the design of controls. This results in controls that rely heavily on procedural content. Similarly, control arising from negotiated settlements with unions and others are also legalistic and procedural. Again, this translates into an emphasis on detailed rules and regulations.

4. *Weak professional capability.* Donors and regulators may employ professionals, but in most instances, the stronger professional capability resides in the operational organizations that are regulated or receive resources. These are the organizations where most of the professional work is performed, this is where the ideas and most of the talent reside, this is where the data is generated, and this is where the experiments are conducted. Given this power imbalance, regulators and donors tend to rely more on their knowledge of the law, of regulation practice, and on control procedures to influence outcomes.

5. *Concern with identity domain.* Donors and regulators have to justify their existence. They need to be able to show results. If they depend on the good will of legislatures, they need to be able to demonstrate they are doing what they are supposed to do. The grant officer in the private foundation faces the foundation board. The union leader faces the membership. Controllers need visible results. They are, therefore, concerned with professed goals. They overemphasize professed goals because those are the only goals that justify the relationship they have with the organizations they control.

6. *Short-term instead of long-term concerns.* Controllers operate in time horizons that are quite different from those of profession-oriented organizations. The next budget hearing in Congress may be the relevant horizon for decision making. In contrast, the profession-oriented organization may be here to stay. Controllers may overemphasize short-term objectives, to the detriment of long-term strategies pursued by those they control.

To conclude, external controls tend to be heavily bureaucratized. They focus on professed goals and on rules and regulations. In most instances, external controls are not designed to fit profession-oriented organizations. Are poorly designed external controls dysfunctional? They probably are if they hamper professional judgment unduly. Poorly designed controls undoubtedly result in lowered organizational effectiveness, in lowered productivity, but this does not mean society can dispense with controls.

To be sure, unnecessary controls can or should be eliminated. Much work can still be done to streamline external controls. It is often the case that an organization—say, a school district—will be reporting and documenting separately on hundreds of different activities to external agencies. Such excessive duplication of controls across federal and state agencies can be reduced, even eliminated, but controls are here to stay.

Managers of profession-oriented organizations have a special responsibility. They have to understand how controls affect professional work. They are the only effective pressure group that can argue for external controls designed for professional

work. Lawyers in Washington, D.C., or bureaucrats in state capitals are not sensitive to the issues discussed in this book. They
will pay attention to legal concerns and they will have an ear for
politics, but not for professional values. Controls can be imposed top down. At times, top down may be desirable, but it is
management's responsibility to ensure that bottom-up consensus building be allowed to take place when this is the desirable
approach.

Characteristics of "Good" External Controls

Based on our coverage of profession-oriented organizations, we find eleven principal characteristics of "good" external controls for professional organizations.

Parsimonious. External controllers have an appetite to control as much as possible. Designers are easily induced to apply
controls on any variable that can be described and measured.
Obviously, choices are made, but from the viewpoint of the
controller, not the operating professional agency. The emphasis
is on professed goals. Routinized controls cannot possibly address all the subtleties of operational transactions. There has to
be an emphasis on procedural dimensions, particularly those
that lend themselves to measurement. All this can lead to very
serious goal displacement. In the research university, a measure
of contact hours with students is used. However, this measures
classroom encounters and does not include hours spent advis-
ing, lecturing informally, meeting student groups, and reading
and improving term papers or dissertations. A procedural control is used that either incorrectly assesses or distorts faculty
behavior. How useful it might be to controllers is another
matter.

Parsimony in control design has to be based on the
awareness that in some professional organizations the only
"good" control is an input control. We may not be able, nor
should we attempt, to control process and output variables because we will distort internal performance. Before we can use
such controls, we should know the consequences.

Simple. Parsimony and simplicity go hand in hand. Complicated controls are used to achieve complex objectives. If we invent a control formula to finance the university, we want this formula to take into account the fact that different programs have different costs. Using micro-information, the formula can become very complicated. On the other hand, if we use macro-information, we can design a much simpler formula that takes into account average costs of many programs. We substitute macro- for micro-information. If the formula is a good one, it approximates expenditures sufficiently but also allows for more discretion in the field.

If controls are too complex, no one in the organization understands how they operate and no one can figure out the consequences of choices. At this point, a specialized staff is needed. Lawyers and analysts have to be employed to understand and negotiate how the controls operate, but professionals remain in the dark about how they might adjust their behavior.

Complicated rules give rise to different interpretations, conflicts, and possible litigation. In this perspective, simpler rules are always preferable. Where routinization is necessary, macro- seems preferable to micro-routinization. The danger with micro-routinization is that it can result in organizational adaptations that have undesirable professional consequences. Let us assume the finance formula for the university is based on student enrollments and we use an average cost per student to arrive at budgets. Once the formula is set, the organization will pursue strategies to maximize its access to resources. It will tend to encourage low-cost, high-enrollment programs to the detriment of high-cost, low-enrollment programs. Yet the latter programs may be highly important to the economy of the state or to the culture of the nation. Policy choices that should be determined on the basis of much wider professional or political acumen are determined by the choice of a routinized control.

In other words, simplicity is desirable as long as it does not distort. Designing formulas for university financing requires considerable knowledge of their potential impact on the university. They cannot be too complicated, but oversimplified formulas will not work either.

Based on Useful Measures. "Good" control measures

what is significant and can also be measured. If the controls are goal oriented, we have to be able to say that the outputs we are measuring are those that matter to us. If we use proxy measures, these proxy measures approximate sufficiently what we want to achieve.

In control, measurement is neither villain nor saint. The question is whether it is useful. If we measure faculty-student contact hours, is this significant? If we use hours teaching as a proxy, are we measuring what we want to measure? If we finance the university with enrollment-driven formulas, are we neglecting other factors we should take into account?

The design of external controls has to originate in a policy orientation. We need to ask questions and measure for a purpose. Do we understand client needs better? Do we understand how agencies allocate their resources? Do we understand what mix of resources seems to be more effective? Can we make better choices?

Control design has to also take account of and be based on an understanding of its consequences. If we collect certain data, we must ask whether these data are going to affect the way professionals in the organization carry on their work. Is it going to affect them in desirable directions? If we ask the physician to document procedures used in operations, we have to be satisfied there is widespread professional consensus on the use of these procedures. There is no point attempting to control, and therefore impose, procedures that are not yet well understood or about which various schools of thought disagree. What has to be controlled in those cases is the decision to use the procedure.

The point to be made is that measurement is an interactive process. We are not dealing with inanimate particles in physical science experiments. We are dealing with intelligent, well-educated professionals. The controller needs to understand how the act of measuring affects both the ability to control and the way professional work is performed.

Limited. All the arguments made in Chapter Four about the futility of comprehensive planning can be made about the futility of comprehensive control. This is where the legal mind may be somewhat dysfunctional in the design of external controls. Legal training orients lawyers to consider all eventualities, to be in a position to deal with them when they happen. External controls, however, should be logical, but they need not be comprehensive.

Partial control is preferable to comprehensive control anytime control distorts performance. At some point in organizational life, it is necessary to recognize that there will be many activities, choices, or decisions that cannot be controlled. Trust is the alternative to control. Finding ways to increase trust between controllers and controllees may be the more effective approach.

Knowing that controls are incomplete obliges us to set priorities. We ask questions: What are core concerns of the controller? How can they be met?

Oriented Toward Achievable Objectives. External controls should encourage behavior to seek or accomplish objectives that can be met. If we impose external controls to oblige a profession to perform tasks it cannot possibly perform, or does not know how to perform, these controls are never going to be implemented. We may feel virtuous in imposing them, but we will only frustrate the public or clients and discredit ourselves and the profession.

Where there is knowledge of how to achieve social, economic, technical, or scientific objectives, external controls may be used to oblige the professionals in the organization to respond. We may, for example, understand enough about the nature of chemical pollutants in industrial processes to be able to define standards that can be met by the industry. We do not know enough about bilingual education to be able to expect immediate implementation of directives. Here, setting standards is far more risky. If we decide to use standardized tests to measure pupil achievement, we enter into a different set of problems. Pupil achievement is affected by many variables teachers cannot always do something about: the child's IQ, parent and home conditions, cultural attitudes, not to mention availability of drugs on school premises. It would be far preferable to control variables teachers or managers can do something about: per-

centage of school district resources going into teaching, length
of school year, availability of antidrug programs, availability of
books and teaching materials, adequacy of salary scale, opportunities for career advancement, and so on.

Stable. External controls cannot be changed all the time
and still be effective. If the professional staff receives different
instructions every week, it soon loses interest and disregards the
controller.

Controls are altered for many reasons. New controllers
are appointed and they want to make a difference. Conflicts between controllers and controllees result in changes. Some learning takes place and controllers realize that the controls do not
work and have to be modified. New knowledge, new scientific
or technological advances create new control needs or possibilities.

External control management has to pay attention to stability. How often can controls be changed without confusing
the staff? How will constant rule changes affect the perceived
legitimacy of the controllers? "They keep changing our instructions. After six months of this we hardly pay attention to them
—they clearly do not know what they are doing." How will constant changes affect propensities toward corruption? "Since
they change the rules all the time, we have given up. We try to
tell them whatever they want to hear."

Implementable. "Good" controls can be put in place relatively rapidly. The information can be processed and transmitted to those who need to know. Corrective action can be
taken either by the controller or the controllee. There is little
use in discussing controls that cannot be implemented either because valid measures are not available or because the information arrives too late to be acted upon or because there is no way
to act upon it once you have it.

Control strategies have to also take into account the availability of resources that can be used to control. Routinized controls cost less than professional peer controls, but if they are
not effective, it may be preferable to control less but do so
properly.

Targeted. "Good" controls are targeted to meet the different needs of all the various actors in and around the organiza-

tion. If controls are intended to protect clients or the general public, they are also designed to protect the rights of the professionals involved in the service. "Good" controls do not disregard clients in favor of the profession or vice versa. They are designed on the basis of realistic assessments of the relationships between all participants.

This means that there needs to be considerable information available on the nature of these relationships, how they will be affected by proposed controls. This is particularly important when client or citizen participation is used in a "watchdog" function. How and when do client and citizen participation work? When might they hamper professional roles?

Controls result in routinization of professional work. The best sources of information on the effect of proposed controls are those who will be affected. It is management's task to elicit responses from the professional staff, clients, and other parties.

We do know, beforehand, that professionals resent controls that challenge their judgment. They may ultimately accept controls that are justified in terms of collective needs: "Papers have to be processed this way because if we all do the work differently, there will be much confusion. We understand that you are an expert in your field and quite genuinely indignant that we might suggest how to process your reports. Nevertheless, you can understand that we need to classify these reports. If we all do what we want, disorder will reign."

Professionals will not readily accept routinized controls that challenge their autonomy: "They are asking us to recognize the rights of the community, but the rights of the community do not give these leaders authority to tell us what to do. They are not trained. We have to keep that in mind. We are obliged to have periodic meetings. They can be useful, but we have to make clear who is responsible. In the last analysis, we are responsible for the safety of the building; they are not."

Conceived to Facilitate. Controls are not an end in themselves. Yet, as we well know, controls are a source of power. Weak and petty controllers can use controls to exercise power, to demonstrate their importance, to briefly strut and fret upon the stage of organizational life.

Tying external controls to policy objectives obliges controllers to pay attention to the real tasks and choices confronted by the operating field agencies. When we say that controls are conceived to facilitate and enable, we mean that we expect controllers to ask themselves what it is exactly they are to accomplish. Are they attempting to enforce laws and regulations? Are they attempting to guide or coordinate the work of the field agencies? Are they attempting to help with the work, to assist the field agencies? These are different functions with different control needs and strategies.

Enforcement is different from coordination. The two are quite different from technical assistance. The controller may be pursuing all three objectives and use only enforcement techniques. Our previous discussion of evaluation for learning and evaluation to exercise rewards and sanctions applies equally to external controls. Requests for technical assistance may not be made if it is known the donor is reviewing the project for next year's funding.

External controllers may find it far easier to avoid responsibilities for what happens in the field. As we saw, their natural defense strategy consists in distancing themselves from the nitty-gritty day-to-day problems of implementation. After all, it is far easier to routinize enforcement than to pay close attention to real problems. But when real problems surface, the discourse has to change. As long as the rhetoric of external control is allowed to be dominated by vague calls for excellence, nothing much will happen. When real problems are discussed involving top and bottom, the rhetoric fades away and workable solutions are found.

Equitable. When professional organizations compete to provide services, external controls may be perceived to have a differential effect and to modify relative competitive positions. If external controls are perceived to affect competing purveyors equally, the industry will have less trouble accepting these controls. If external controls favor some but affect others negatively, opposition can be expected.

The most common situation is one where it is not known how proposed controls affect competing purveyors. This creates uncertainty and opposition. As long as consequences are unknown, opposition will be widespread as each organization attempts to figure out what the impact may be.

Desirable or "good" controls are often abandoned because the control designer encounters widespread opposition from the industry, but the problem is not with the control. The problem is with insufficient research or knowledge of its probable differentiated impact on competing firms.

Since controllers do not have strong authority rights, they cannot sustain large-scale opposition from those they control. The legislatures that appropriate funds or provide the regulatory mandate are rarely going to support the controllers in the face of a widespread insurrection of their flock. It is much more sensible to spend the necessary time and effort to find out what these impacts might be.

Low-Cost. Last, but not least, it is not possible to discuss controls without discussing costs. All external controls have costs. In general, these costs are passed on to customers or to taxpayers. They are a form of invisible taxation since government can impose controls without having to appropriate funds to cover most of these costs.

External control is the pursuit of collective objectives. We may decide collectively that we want to protect old people in nursing homes, that we want to control health care costs, that we want cleaner air or safer nuclear plants, but one cannot make collective choices without considering alternatives. We need to make judgments about costs. As a result, it is customary in regulatory practice to undertake cost-benefit analyses of proposed regulations prior to their enactment. Presumably, expected benefits should approximate or be higher than expected costs. Much ingenuity goes into allocating values or prices to benefits and costs that are not generally traded in the marketplace (Chase, 1968; Jones-Lee, 1976; Pearse, 1978).

These analyses have to ask difficult questions. What is the value of cleaner air? How much is a life saved worth? How much do we value the esthetic beauty of the landscape? But such analyses will probably miss costs or benefits that interest us. We have described, at some length, the fragile values and characteristics of profession-oriented organizations. External controls that affect professional performance have invisible or poorly documented costs.

Reducing professional discretion is a cost. Reducing organizational ability to innovate is a cost. Reducing professional commitment or obliging professionals to play nonprofessional roles is a cost. From our point of view, external controls have to take into account professional values and culture. Otherwise, they will not be cost effective.

"Bad" Controls and Bureaucracy

"Bad" controls are imposed for two main additional reasons: either because they are a protective strategy or because they are not intended to have any impact.

Controls as Protective Strategy. Controls are rules. As we well know by now, rules are used as protective strategies. Controls are often enacted not to protect the client or the public but to protect the bureaucracy.

A federal agency receives appropriations for state and local programs. The federal agency is concerned in maintaining the visibility and success of its activities. It responds to a political environment that is quite different from that of each of the local operating agencies. The donor is concerned that the local agencies will respond too much to local political realities. These realities do not mesh with larger national political reality. What is permissible in Henley, Missouri, or in Altadena, California, may not be acceptable in Washington, D.C.

The donor uses controls to ensure that the local agencies do not engage in embarrassing activities. Turf and domain protection are the relevant considerations. The donor also keeps at a distance from the operating agencies. The donor does not want to be dragged into troubles and difficulties of the grantee —difficulties that the donor might not be able to deal with in any case.

Rules in the form of controls provide justifications: "We did everything we could to avoid these problems including setting standards of performance."

Rules provide for distancing: "They are responsible for

those decisions. They are taken in the field, not in Washington. We approve the standards but cannot be responsible for day-to-day decisions."

Rules provide turf and domain control: "These programs fall under our jurisdiction. We are responsible to Congress for their successes and failures."

Controls imposed to protect controllers instead of protecting clients, public, or the involved profession tend to disregard the nature of problems in the field. If the main purpose of the standard is to protect the controller, it matters less whether the profession can or cannot meet it. These become professional problems, not controller problems. The controller can always claim that it pursues the lofty objectives of protecting public and client interests.

In fact, it pursues neither, but who can tell?

Trivial or Utopian Controls. Trivial controls are not expected to make any difference. What is happening will happen. The controller does not expect to have any impact. The controls have no bite. Trivial controls are those that satisfy the controllee. They do not take into account the needs of clients or public.

Utopian controls are more flamboyant. They are announced widely as intended to protect all the needs of clients and public, but they too have no bite. Nothing different happens. The controllee behaves as before.

Trivial or utopian controls are enacted when the controller is controlled by the controllee. In terms of power dependencies, controllers are more dependent on controllees than vice versa. The donor agency—say, the agency in charge of foreign aid—is more dependent on foreign governments than the foreign governments receiving the aid are on the agency. This runs against common sense. But a look at mutual dependencies will clarify the point. If foreign aid is cancelled, the foreign governments may experience trouble but will continue to function. In contrast, if the foreign governments reject the aid, the foreign aid bureau for that country is abolished. This does not mean that controllers are completely under the influence of the controllee. They can still cause considerable trouble. The weaker they are, the more annoyance they will create to attempt to appear powerful. But the controller cannot afford to destroy the controllee.

Trivial or utopian controls are designed for show. They are designed to accommodate those who want them. They will be numerous and visible to appease those they do not serve. They will be petty and irrelevant and will not help professional performance.

Controls without bite may also be costly to the profession because they provide a false sense of security. They shelter undesirable or deficient performance. Clients, or the public, will be kept at bay for a while, at least until they are able to organize and insist on real controls and better service. Meanwhile, the profession has not learned how to adapt and deal with its client environment.

One might wonder, therefore, why controls without bite are used. If they are bad for the public, clients, and the profession, whose interests are pursued? The controllers may be protecting the profession in situations where legislatures are heavy on expectations but lean on resources, they may be protecting the owners of profession-oriented organizations, or they may be protecting themselves. They may even go as far as to argue they are protecting clients or the public on the grounds that appearances provide confidence and that is all that is really needed.

Implementing External Controls

Let us assume we are sitting in Washington, D.C. We are in a federal agency charged with monitoring more than 3,000 ongoing programs dispersed in small and medium-size professional delivery systems throughout the country. What control strategies can we use?

Routinized Trust. A first possible approach relies on generalized trust. We trust the implementing delivery agencies to do what they are supposed to do. We have been in close contact with them. They participated in the elaboration of the controls. We have relied on a bottom-up approach. As a consequence, our agreement with them is clear. They are to use our funds for specific purposes that are spelled out in the grant award. We know what they want and can perform. We can, therefore, routinize input controls. Funds are disbursed in accordance to agreed procedures. We do not involve ourselves in process controls except for an annual site visit carried out by hired consultants who happen to be experts in the field. We also routinize output controls. Each agency reports yearly on the results of their activities. We also watch for the utilization of expenditures. A comprehensive report is issued at the end of the grant.

Our philosophy is to leave considerable discretion to the field. To the limited extent we intervene in professional assessment, this is done by outside consultants in an annual site visit. Do the controls have bite? Yes, we can always terminate the program and not renew the grant. However, we trust the implementers and our strategy is to keep the programs on course. Basically, we have told them: "Here are resources, we are watching you, get some results, and report to us." But we are assuming that all is well. Discreet control across the board will ensure that the program remains on course.

Bad Apple Strategy. Trust is no longer generalized. We know that some implementers are inefficient and have to be encouraged to do better. We are concerned that public money will be used in ineffective local agencies. Since we cannot pay close attention to all 3,000 agencies, our task is to identify the bad apples. Which agencies are not performing as well, which ones are the worse offenders?

We have or devise a management information system to provide salient macro-information about performance in the field. How are they spending their resources? How does their failure rate compare across agencies? What do comparative cost-benefit data show?

Once we identify the bad apples, we focus on them. At this point, we no longer use routinized controls. We use outside experts to review what they are doing, and we use our clout to get them to mend their ways. Maybe we provide help, maybe we supervise them. In due time, if they fail to respond, we terminate the grant. We also publicize our intervention so that other agencies in similar straits know what we are doing. In due time, we bring the rear up to higher standards. Overall performance is improved.

This strategy works well when there are few bad apples, and when most other professional agencies are performing adequately. We spend our limited resources on the few offenders. Our interventions are not routinized. We use what experts are needed to identify problems and suggest remedies. We do pay a cost. We do get involved in local issues, but our purpose is to upgrade performance and we are willing to take the risk. We want to facilitate performance.

Lead Sheep Strategy. This strategy fits situations where the number of deficient agencies is very large. Most of our 3,000 professional organizations are doing poorly. They do not use their resources wisely, the professional staff is often poorly trained, some local managers are inexperienced, and lay boards do not know how to govern, much less manage.

Our own control resources are finite. We could routinize but we do not know what impact we might have. It is clear that many agencies are deficient, and the causes of these deficiencies vary greatly. In some cases, it is the staff; in other cases, it is the clients; in other cases, it is bad management. We do not have a model of the problem. Any routine interventions may work on a few cases and not in others. It will take too long to experiment with routinized controls.

In this case, the alternative to routinization is the lead sheep strategy. Instead of focusing on the bad apples—there are too many—we focus on the few centers of excellence. The lead sheep will jump the fence and the rear will follow. We will provide additional resources to those who are already doing well so they can share their experience with the others. We will establish centers of excellence and demonstration projects, bring people from the region, discuss issues, and thus initiate an internal learning process. In due time, we hope the centers of excellence will influence practice in their periphery. Meanwhile, we may know more about the problems and might be able to devise routinized controls.

Pretty Packaging Strategy. We have discussed relatively simple cases. When all was going well and when we knew what was going on, we routinized appropriate controls to gently direct the programs in the right direction. In the two instances when we encountered problems, we used approaches that allowed us to avoid routines and use professional knowledge to control. In the bad apple case, we concentrated our control resources on the rear. We tried to find ways to upgrade those who were not performing. In the lead sheep case, we concentrated on the vanguard, hoping the rear would follow.

Now the situation is different. The controls were enacted with very little consultation with the field. In addition, we are totally underfinanced. We have very few control resources. We are expected to monitor these 3,000 agencies with a total staff of five: two secretaries, one assistant file clerk, and two administrative officers. We also have a budget that permits us to have three consultant-months a year. In other words, we are totally underfinanced. Moreover, the problems in the field are numerous and neither routinized trust, bad apple, nor lead sheep will work.

One answer is that we cannot do the job properly but we can appear to do it. Appearances matter more than reality. We will not be able to control, but we will go through the motions as if we were.

Another answer is that, while we cannot afford to do what is needed, we can still influence the situation. We can generate information about what is going on in the hope that others, including local interests, will be able to act on it.

The pretty packaging strategy pursues these dual objectives. Pretty packaging will protect us, giving the impression we are going through the motions of control when in fact we can hardly read our mail. It also provides an avenue for action: we are using our few resources to generate information. We hope to influence grassroot reform.

We will use our few consultants to design a questionnaire, ask for routine reports that provide information on the variables we think grassroot groups can use, and ask the agencies to list staff qualifications, costs and budget allocations, information on client load, and success and failure rates. To be sure, the information will tend to pile up in the back office, but we will issue annual comparative data. We will also make sure that local community or citizen groups are informed and have a chance to use the data and act upon it.

Change of Scenery Strategy. This strategy comes into use from time to time. The legislative mandate is clear. The funds have been appropriated, but it is obvious that the programs are in heavy trouble. The lawyers who designed the statute never foresaw field reality. Even our agency staff failed to perceive that implementation would never take place as intended. When we went through rule making, we held several hearings where a few experts did warn us of dire happenings, but there were others who supported the programs.

Preliminary reports from the field are unequivocal: the program does not work. We are attracting the wrong clients. Those we are able to handle should not be there in the first place. Those who are not there are placing political pressure on the agencies to terminate their activities. We cannot even pretend the program is successful—nearly every local newspaper has an editorial lambasting the field agencies. What control strategy might we use?

The wisest approach is to learn from the experience. Can we elaborate alternatives? Can we find new objectives, go back to the legislature, and modify the statute? It is not easy to admit defeat, but it is preferable in the long run. There is no point continuing what cannot be done. If we cannot achieve what we thought we might achieve, can we achieve something else? The change of scenery strategy is the art of retreat. It is also the art of turning the retreat into something positive. How do we express it? We tried it, we learned our lesson, we changed it. Here is our program; we ask for renewed support; it is a new incarnation.

Routines, Professionals, and Public Participation

In this fictitious account, we have used three control tools: routines, professional interventions, and public participation. In "routinized trust," routines were used to control input and output measures. We had experts' on-site visits to evaluate professional performance. This was our only process control. In "bad apple" and "lead sheep," professional interventions dominated, but we used routinized information to select our control targets. In "pretty packaging," we had to rely on public participation.

Routines, professional interventions, and client participation are the three tools of external control. In our simplified scenarios, we stressed only one or two of these, but most external controls rely on all three.

Routinized External Controls

Routinized external controls work well when the conditions listed below are present.

Clear Mandate. The mandate from the legislature or the order from the court is precise and well understood. We can easily describe and define control measures that are valid and can be readily measured.

Well-Understood Technology. The scientific or technical evidence used in setting the control routine is such that we know exactly what input and process variables have to be controlled to achieve effective results. There exists a professional consensus about how to do the work.

Equal Impact. The rule will probably affect most of the controlled organizations equally. Those who do not fit know it, and the controller can handle these special cases. There is sufficient professional capability within the staff of the controller to handle special deviant cases.

Low Cost. The costs of the controls are low. They are justified in terms of expected benefits. They are borne by the beneficiaries of the program—the taxpayers, the clients, or other third parties.

Sufficient Resources. The controllers have sufficient resources to handle and act upon the flow of routinized data. They pursue specific and broad objectives that are well understood by those they control. They have sufficient access to incentives and sanctions to achieve compliance.

No Need for Technical Assistance. Technical assistance,

research, development, and experimentation are not particularly relevant. Existing knowledge in the field is adequate to carry out the work. Control can be routinized because implementation can also be routinized. The controller needs the help of professionals only to assist in the original control design and later in handling deviant cases.

Few Deviant Cases. Routinized controls capture the vast majority of cases. Deviant cases, when professional discretion is required, are few and can be rapidly handled by the controllers. The controls affect only those aspects of the work that are predictive and repetitive. If there is much variability in individual cases, the controls focus on a large number of cases so that variability can be eliminated by averaging. Professional discretion is allowed at the micro level, but controls are provided at the macro level.

Parsimony. Routinized controls can be used sparingly. The controllers can achieve their objectives by controlling a few variables only. For example, if their objective is to cap organizational expenditures, they are able to design a control system based on input variables. A good example is health cost control. Health costs are regulated by professional standards review organizations (PSRO). These federally mandated, decentralized organizations are expected to establish standards of care, definitions of routinized acceptable length of stay in hospitals for a variety of ailments. Similarly, they establish acceptable reimbursable expenditures for a variety of medical interventions. Professionals are used in the design of the routinized control. The PSROs also intervene to deal with deviant cases, but if the formulas are good enough, they can be used routinely without too much impact on the performance of medical staff.

Whether these routines do, in fact, work well is another matter. We will want to know whether the routinization of reimbursable length of hospitalization and accepted expenditures affects the way individual physicians prescribe for their patients. Do they impose the routine when it does not fit the needs of their patients? Are they willing to assume the risk of appealing to the PSRO? If they keep a patient for a longer time in the hospital and the PSRO finally disallows the expenditure, how does this affect their future performance?

Professional Control

External professional control is more expensive. In our fictitious example, the federal agency is overseeing 3,000 separate programs in the field. It can use professional interventions only sparingly. Since professional controls are not routinized, they take longer to carry out. For example, a site visit using consultants requires time. First, we have to select the consultants, appoint a team leader, instruct the team, and send it to the field. In due time, we obtain their report. At this point, we may initiate an internal evaluation of the report and prepare policy options on the basis of their recommendations. If we are not convinced by their recommendations, we may decide to send a second team or take a look ourselves.

Professional controls are generally intended to address areas of professional discretion. We are attempting to pass judgment on the suitability and quality of professional performance. If task learning is important, our evaluation effort may have to tilt toward technical assistance instead of enforcement. Our field agencies may wish to implement our directives but not know how. If task learning is irrelevant, enforcement may be more important. Our field agencies understand perfectly well what we want but are reluctant to perform.

The composition of our professional team and the talent required varies considerably depending on whether enforcement, technical assistance, or both are needed. Enforcement requires professionals who understand managerial politics, regulatory practice, and control. They need to be able to diagnose the problem, to see that it existed in the first place. For this, they need to be trained in quantitative analysis to be able to discover and understand gross macro-discrepancies in the performance of the organization. They may also need to know something about micro-professional performance, but that may be less important. If the assignment is in education, they may need to know something about teaching; if in public health, something about medical practice; if in law enforcement, something about police work. But it is more important they also understand managerial politics to unravel why the agency is not performing, and they need to know about the relevant laws and regulations that apply to the case if they are to intervene.

In contrast, technical assistance requires a totally different breed of expert and a different orientation. Bottom-up approaches are more relevant than top-down. As a consequence, the expertise needed has to be immersed in the problem area. The experts need to know what kind of procedure works where and when. Micro-knowledge at the individual professional level will be more relevant whereas the politics of the situation may be far less important. They will also have to be able to diagnose the problem, but from then on, their approach has to be oriented to the task: they are not enforcing, they are helping. Controls that should be oriented to technical assistance are often tilted toward enforcement. When the field needs assistance to perform, it is penalized for not performing, which makes it more cautious and less anxious to ask for help the next time around.

Controllers and their experts have a much easier time instructing other professionals instead of helping them solve problems. Bureaucratic values prevail: "We told them what to do, but those people are hopeless. They never manage anything right." The controllers can keep at a safe, comfortable distance: "The law is clear. They have to mend their ways. It is their responsibility to take care of the problem. We are responsible for the enforcement of the law and nothing else."

Professional controls are useful when the circumstances listed below prevail.

In-Depth Evaluation Needed. Short-term, but in-depth, evaluations of professional performance are necessary. Routinized aggregate controls do not provide sufficient information to set policy. It is not clear whether programs should be continued or modified. In-depth evaluations can rely on both quantitative and qualitative data. Professional judgment can be focused on individual cases. Both macro- and micro-information can be used.

Technical Assistance Important. Technical assistance, research, and program development are important. The control agency has the necessary research and development resources. There is little the implementing agencies in the field can do. Moreover, centralizing technical assistance, research, and development is cost effective.

Design of Routinized Controls Needed. In-depth analyses provide the necessary information to design future routinized controls. Professionals are used to determine what macro-data is collected or analyzed, what variables can and should be measured, what variables should be used in the control system, how control might function, and most importantly, what additional consequences the controls might have on the organization.

Trust Needed. Trust relations need to be established between the controller and controllee. There is a good deal of suspicion and ignorance about conditions in the field. External professional evaluators hired by the control agency acquire the trust of their sponsors. Nevertheless, since they are professionals, they can establish closer rapport with their colleagues in the field. In due time, they may eliminate unnecessary misunderstandings between both parties.

Citizen and Client Participation

Ever since the Model Cities and War on Poverty programs of the 1960s, client and citizen participation at the local level has been used in a watchdog function. Today, many federal or state programs mandate citizen or client participation in program implementation (Aleshire, 1972; Barber, 1984; Langton, 1978; Nelkin and Pollack, 1979; Rosener, 1982; Thomas, 1983).

Citizen and client participation can vary greatly. It may have clout or it may be purely decorative. In some situations, participation is essential to permit the professional staff to understand what the issues and problems are. In other situations, participation is essential to motivate and activate client contribution to the effort. In still other situations, client or citizen participation hampers professional performance.

Functions of Participation. Generally, these participatory efforts serve many different functions.

1. Legitimacy. One function is to provide legitimacy for decision-making processes that appear to be centralized and have an excessive professional orientation. The values of the profession and those of the clients do not necessarily coincide. Since the profession serves clients, it needs to know the views of clients. Participation provides mechanisms to legitimize the confrontation and resolution of professional-client conflict.

2. Community Involvement. Another function of participation is to motivate and energize community involvement in complex transformation processes. Clients and citizens are often the target of professional interventions, but these interventions are extended by what happens around them. The professional experts may build the housing complex, but the local community will give it life. Participation provides opportunities for channeling client and citizen energies in the joint endeavor, what is now referred to as coproduction (Brudney and England, 1983; Percy, 1983; Whitaker, 1980; Susskind and Elliot, 1983).

3. Watchdog Function. The watchdog function can take various dimensions. Where the issue is enforcement and compliance with the law, the clients may or may not be in a good position to assess whether they are receiving the care and attention they are supposed to be receiving. Where they can evaluate professional performance, they may be the best informants. When it comes to technical assistance, the clients or public may not be the most relevant helpers, although they can be the source of considerable information.

Potential Conflicts Between Professionals and Citizens. One problem with citizen participation in profession-oriented organizations is that the client or citizen is, by definition, not a professional and, therefore, not expected to challenge the professional role. Participation alters the conventional relationship. The professional has been socialized to serve the best interests of the client. He or she has also been socialized to expect to make all the decisions. When clients or citizens question professional judgments, it suggests that the professionals are not serving the best interests of the client or the public. This may be factual, but is not easily accepted. Therefore, professional-client conflicts can be expected.

Another problem is that, notwithstanding the good intent of much legislation, citizens tend to be at a disadvantage in their conflict with the profession. Participation not only requires that citizens be motivated to participate and willing to spend the time and energy, but also that they be able to be informed about the issues. This means that, in many cases, participation is effective only if the citizens are instructed or assisted by advocates from the profession.

A third problem we need to pay more attention to is that serious conflicts between professionals and clients or citizens can lead to more bureaucratization. If the citizens are vocal, if they are assisted by experts, and if they have clout, the profession within the organization is going to defend itself by using bureaucratic defenses—namely, legalism and close interpretation of rules and regulations.

Let me give you an example. This is the case of the Education for All Handicapped Children Act of 1975 (PL 94-142), which gives the parents of handicapped children in the public schools considerable clout. They are expected to participate in the design of an individual education program (an IEP) for their child and they can ask that the public school pay for private services or programs when the public schools cannot meet their needs. They can bring their own experts to the meeting. In case of disagreement, they can appeal through administrative channels and ultimately through the courts. The reason they have clout is that they can ask for private services if the public school cannot accommodate their child. These outside services may be expensive, thus placing a burden on the public school.

We conducted a study that contrasted school districts that were heavily involved in litigation, with parents demanding special private programs, and school districts with very few such conflicts. Since private programs can be expensive, we assumed that school districts that experience considerable conflict would be threatened and take defensive strategies. Professional experts in those schools would be much more cautious. They would follow the rules and regulations very carefully, but they might not tell parents all they knew. They might not discuss or attempt to diagnose handicapped children, in the fear that this knowledge could then be used by the parents to obtain school payment of outside private services that would remove resources from other school priorities.

The research corroborated our suspicions (Hassell, 1981). The fact that parents were known to be able to make claims on substantial resources affected professional roles. Instead of being more concerned with the welfare of their clients, the school specialists in special education for handicapped children were obliged to pay attention to organizational realities. The schools were reluctant to divert large sums for individual needs. In the performance of their tasks, these professionals paid more attention to the rules and regulations than to assessments of the child's disability. As a consequence, those parents who were vocal, active, and had access to external expertise were more likely to obtain services and attention for their handicapped children. Those who were not, might not be helped by the professional experts in the schools.

When Is Participation Desirable? Given these facts, it is not surprising that client and citizen participation have varied effectiveness in external control. In general, the strategy is desirable when:

1. The profession needs closer ties with the public. The profession could benefit from closer systematic encounter with the client or public. This is relevant for professionals who work away from clients or the public, who do not see clients or public in the day-to-day performance of their work. For example, urban architects or planners could easily design a city and never meet a citizen. In contrast, educators, public health providers, and social workers are in constant contact with their clients and in less need of formalized participation.

2. Coproduction is possible. The profession can benefit from increased client and citizen participation in the task at hand. Again, some tasks can benefit more than others. The

learning process can greatly benefit if teachers acquire the cooperation of parents. The completion of a rural development scheme will greatly depend on the cooperation of the villagers. The success of a heart operation may not depend immediately on family support, but the long-term rehabilitation of the patient does.

3. The watchdog function is effective. Clients and citizens assess behaviors or results they can properly evaluate. They are the better judges of what is good for them. The specialized knowledge of the professional is not needed to recognize whether the service is good or bad. This will tend to constrain the extent to which this type of control is effective. Even when the citizens or clients have the necessary resources, time, and energy, the gulf between their knowledge and that of the profession will reduce their effectiveness. It will be effective when it deals with compliance that is peripheral to professional work. Was the patient admitted quickly? Did a doctor come? Was the patient's temperature taken? The client can assess these steps, but the patient cannot readily assess the quality of the diagnosis.

Conclusion

External controls tend to bureaucratize the profession-oriented organization. We have seen why routines tend to prevail, why it is expensive and difficult to substitute professional evaluations for low-cost routine control. Yet we know and understand that external controls are here to stay. Deregulation will not eliminate regulation. Attempts to decentralize will not eliminate the natural proclivity toward greater centralization. Technological advances with computers and monitoring systems will not reduce opportunities for more complex and sophisticated routinized external control systems. What can the manager of the profession-oriented organization do?

Protect the Professional Staff. Since we know that well-intended external controls can hamper professional performance, it is management's responsibility to buffer the professional staff. Whenever possible, management should handle external requests for information and reporting, and facilitate professional handling of these requests. Centralized data handling and reporting are probably cost effective in most profession-oriented organizations. But more important, management can create a sense of commitment to professional values in the face of inadequate external interventions by taking care to shelter the professional staff and by making this clear both to external controllers and to the staff.

Insist on Appropriate Controls. External controllers know little about profession-oriented organizations and the management of professionals. As we saw, they tend to be bureaucratic and legalistic, but they are not necessarily irresponsible or negligent. They can be educated. Top-down controls are usually inappropriate for profession-oriented organizations. Bottom-up participation is necessary to understand how controls might be implemented. The managers of profession-oriented organizations have a special responsibility *vis-à-vis* external controllers. If proposed controls do not work, it is the responsibility of managers of professional organizations to organize and present alternatives to controllers.

We have to keep in mind that managers are probably the only ones who can do this. The professional staff is too preoccupied with its daily tasks. Boards and other overseers are probably too far away from daily reality to assess effects. Managers are the ones who are both informed and able to act.

Insist on Controls That Protect Professional Discretion. Even if the work of professionals has to be monitored and supervised, it is nevertheless necessary to protect task discretion. The professional worker must be allowed to work unhampered even if performance is to be reviewed. Mindless, routinized controls that prescribe how the task should be performed when routinization is inappropriate cannot be left standing.

External controllers may seem very powerful indeed. Seen from field operations, they appear to have immense power, sitting as they do in Washington, D.C., or in state capitals. But they are, as we saw, dependent on the good will and support of the field. They may not respond to individual complaints, but they respond to organized action.

Since managers have a stake in achieving sensible external controls, they have a stake in organizing to achieve leverage on professional-control practice. In some professions, such as medicine and allied health, such action is commonplace. In other less prestigious and less well organized professions, much more can be done.

9

Beyond Bureaucracy: Why Profession-Oriented Organizations Are More Effective

It was four in the morning. We had landed at Orly Airport. The taxi was taking us to our hotel in Paris. The driver stopped at the red light, looked at the empty boulevard to the left and right, and drove on without waiting for it to change. "*Alors*," he said, "that light does not think, why should I wait for it?"

Lights and rules do not think, whereas people do. People invent rules and install lights at busy intersections. In the daytime, the light at our boulevard works well. The endless traffic coming from the south into Paris is regulated, while traffic going east and west is allowed to proceed. At four in the morning, the rule is unnecessary. There is no one to be seen anywhere. The driver is not going to be delayed two minutes by an unthinking light.

Bureaucracy makes widespread use of rules. As we saw in Chapter One, rules work well when the future is predictable, unvaried, and repetitive. Rules are a fantastic invention. No one has to be present to instruct. No policeman has to stand in the rain to direct traffic. All that is needed is a fair approximation of the flow of traffic going both ways so that the length of wait can be adjusted to provide for the far greater traffic coming from the south.

Rules are fantastic inventions because they allow us to organize the work of many individuals. We can centralize without having to direct and instruct each person. Thus, we can bring together the efforts of many men and women. The division of labor allows us to combine their effort and to accomplish far more than they could on their own.

But, as we also discussed in Chapter One, rules are not always useful. Rules do not work when it is not clear what should be done, how it should be done, when tasks are varied and unpredictive, and when the rule does not fit reality. We also saw how rules can be used for other purposes. They can be used as defensive strategies: we can justify our behavior on the basis of obeying the rule. When we discussed risk management in Chapter Seven, we even saw how routinized formulas can be used to document and justify risk taking. The securities analyst in the investment management firm carefully elaborates various indexes to measure relative risks of stocks. This provides a documentation, a record of how and why decisions were made. The routine provides some protection from errors.

Rules and routines can reduce or eliminate discretion. When learning and adaptability are important, rules can constrain our ability to solve problems. In our taxi, it did not really matter very much if we waited two minutes at the intersection. Our driver was more concerned with asserting his Gallic sense of independence. However, in a rush to the hospital, these two minutes would be important. The driver of the ambulance would be given discretion to use a different set of rules that allowed the use of a siren and flashing red lights. The ambulance would be able to proceed, but the heart attack victim in a private car would not be able to proceed without risking an accident. Here the rule does not work. There is no solution for the problem.

In the modern organization, it is possible to organize and direct the work of large numbers of people by three different methods. We can instruct and supervise directly; for this we may have to establish long chains of command. We can instruct indirectly by using rules and routines. Or we can delegate discretionary authority to individuals whom we trust. They can handle problems as well as if we were there to instruct them, perhaps better.

Since rules and routines work well when tasks are predictable, unvaried, and well understood, they are used extensively. However, when tasks are varied and unpredictable, when learning is important in the task situation, and when adaptability is required, discretion is necessary. Discretion and trust have to replace routines. This is where the professional in the organization takes on new importance.

Professionals are socialized to play complex roles. We discussed in Chapter Two how professions become what they are, the varieties of professions and semiprofessions. In Chapter Three we differentiated between professional and managerial authority. We saw how professional knowledge complements and overlaps managerial knowledge.

We discussed two different sets of tasks. First, there are tasks where professionals need discretion. In these cases, management uses envelope supervision. Second, there are tasks where both management and professionals need to work together. These we called joint managerial-professional tasks. This led us in Chapter Six to discuss the governance of the profession-oriented organization. We emphasized the difference between professional and worker participation in management, and we described and analyzed various governance models, including the partnership, the senior staff, the dual governance, the collegial, and the ordinary bureaucratic model.

We emphasized the important role that professionals can play to increase organizational effectiveness and their potential contribution to organizational adaptability and flexibility. We pointed out that, in an uncertain environment and task situation, the professional has the necessary knowledge and experience, from practice, to act independently. The professional can search for solutions, determine which alternative to adopt, and implement new approaches. The professional is task oriented and less committed to or deterred by organizational structures and by internal boundaries. Where considerable interdependence exists and the organization is broken down in functional units or across product, area, or service, the professional is good at networking and coordination. As we saw in Chapter Three, it is no surprise that organizations that employ many professionals often use formal or informal matrix structures.

The Concept of the Profession-Oriented Organization

The profession-oriented organization has distinct characteristics:

- It employs many professionals and they are involved in the core activities of the organization.
- It is structured in ways that permit management to have access to professional knowledge and vice versa.
- It substitutes control through rules and regulations with controls that rely on professional discretion, professional self-restraint, and professional self-regulation.

Management of the profession-oriented organization differs from management of more conventional bureaucracies. At a simplistic level, a first difference is that there is more thinking going on in the profession-oriented organization. We may not be able to document this, but there certainly are more qualified people and therefore more opinions, conflicting views, and discussions. The roles of managers and professionals are closely linked by many interdependencies. The social status separating management and workers may be smaller, eliminated, or even reversed. Management is far less autocratic and self-contained and far more concerned in motivating, guiding, or inspiring greater professional performance.

There are nine major strategies that differentiate the management of the profession-oriented organization from the conventional bureaucracy. We will look at each in turn.

Emphasis on Governance Instead of Centralized Direction. A first difference between management styles is that the profession-oriented organization is governed, not directed from above. Here, the imagery of politics is more useful than that of scientific management. As we saw in Chapter Three, the manager of the profession-oriented organization shares authority with professionals. Joint managerial-professional tasks require overlapping yet different knowledge and experience.

In Chapters Three and Six, we described various governance models. We paid more attention to three models: the partnership, the senior staff, and the dual governance. Each of these models is suited to different tasks, technologies, or environments. They operate very differently, but in all of them, management requires skills in diplomacy, negotiation, bargaining, and collective decision making. Management has to be close to the staff to understand the motivations of individuals and groups, the suspicions and the conflicts that can smoulder or erupt among them and, more importantly, to guarantee that the flow of relevant knowledge going from profession to management and vice versa is not impaired.

The manager of the profession-oriented organization has a more complicated and a more arduous task than his or her bureaucratic counterpart. The reason is straightforward: the bureaucratic authority structure is a much simpler design. But while it may be, organizationally speaking, more efficient, it is far less effective in conditions of high uncertainty.

The first lesson we derive is that approaches that rely more on professions have different costs and different benefits. Management cannot rule as intensely and directly. A change of attitude is necessary. We see that the culture of the profession-oriented organization has to differ from that of the bureaucracy. Management has to learn to share authority with the profession, and the profession has to learn to take responsibility for managerial decisions and talk and communicate with management. For management the task may be more challenging, more complex. The benefits are obvious: where bureaucratic approaches do not work well, this is the only alternative that does.

Less Reliance on Rational Controls. The manager of the profession-oriented organization is more conscious of the limitations of rational controls. We spent considerable time in Chapters Four and Five exploring the advantages and limitations of rational controls. We discussed problems of measurement and its major negative consequence: goal displacement. We made clear that excessive goal displacement can be highly dysfunctional in the profession-oriented organization.

Less reliance on rational controls does not mean that management is less rational or that the profession-oriented organization is less well managed than the bureaucracy. It does not mean that managing a profession-oriented organization requires less information or less analysis, or that one should rely more on instinct or the proverbial "gut feeling." In fact, we stressed the greater importance of monitoring and partial planning.

It means that management is more concerned with impacts. When a rational control is introduced, management pays attention to the way the control will interact with professional performance. Had we contemplated using management by objectives when everyone was doing it, we would have wanted to understand beforehand how the staff would react. Would professional tasks lend themselves to target specifications? Would it be useful to have formal discussions? Would the staff be able to implement? Would management be able to monitor? Would the process enhance or deter innovation, risk taking, and self-correcting behavior?

The characteristics of the measurements, the underlying assumptions implicit in the techniques, and the limitations of the models matter. The perceptions of the professional staff, the ambitions and status they pursue, the way the controls impinge on their performance and role are taken into account.

More Emphasis on Intrinsic Motivation. In the bureaucratic organization, management relies more on extrinsic motivation, particularly on the ability to reward economically. Given unimpaired authority to direct and control, intrinsic motivation is less important.

As we saw in Chapter Two, motivators that have to do with status and with the way work is organized and carried out are far more significant in the professional organization. The fact that management shares authority with professionals contributes to the intrinsic motivation of professional participants. Management styles differ. In the bureaucracy, management relies on routinized control. In the profession-oriented organization, management relies on motivation. Top-down authority is less important as long as management is able to generate enthusiasm and guide the staff.

Ability to use intrinsic motivators requires considerable

insight into the characteristics of the various professions in the organization. We discussed these characteristics in some detail in Chapters Two, Three, Six, and Seven. Inventing new sources of motivation requires management leadership. It requires both a keen sense of the possible and desirable, and the talent to invent what makes work and careers interesting and challenging.

In somewhat unique circumstances, Applied Research could offer career opportunities in more prestigious locations. As we saw, the professional staff was strongly motivated by long-term career opportunities in the White House and elsewhere. The second manager was able to tap into that reservoir of good will. She made it clear to her senior people that she would be fair, that she would give strong support to her best people to allow them to move to more prestigious and challenging positions elsewhere in government. She was successful because her people had to remain with her long enough to prove themselves and the outflow was manageable. She lost a few good people; she also acquired many talented new recruits. She had discovered the relevant motivators.

Greater Emphasis on Working Through Others. In the profession-oriented organization, management relies on the profession to take greater responsibility. You will recall our tabulation in Chapter Seven of five professional varietals: deadwood, climbers, prima donnas, silent virtuosos, and the good people. Management of profession-oriented organizations can less well afford to let incompetent people into positions of influence because teamwork is going to be more important. How it is organized and the extent of professional participation depends on the governance model. Managing conflicts in a partnership is quite different from managing conflict in a senior staff organization, but, in all of them, people skills are relevant.

The good managers have to become skilled diplomats and politicians. If they read management texts, maybe they should also read Machiavelli ([1513], 1952).

More Emphasis on Conflict Resolution. Taking risks and making errors implies that we do not know exactly how to proceed. If we do not know how to proceed, it is probable that different schools of thought will emerge. There will be those who want to take greater risks and those who want to avoid all risks. There will be those who believe that Florence's Refuge should deal more with feminist issues, and those who argue that it should focus more on the relationship between the battered women who came to the clinic and the men who were the cause of the trouble. Profession-oriented organizations are, because of the nature of the tasks they undertake, more prone to internal conflicts.

They are also more prone to internal conflicts because some governance structures do not provide easy means of conflict resolution. Partnerships and dual governance models can, therefore, suffer greater levels of internal conflict. Auletta (1986) has shown us, in his insightful study of the demise of a powerful financial partnership on Wall Street, that ambition and desire for power and status can easily dominate professional bodies.

Combining task complexities and structure tells us that the manager of the profession-oriented organization has to remain in close touch with the staff. Conflict has to be nipped before it becomes uncontrollable. In the partnership and dual governance models, it is important to institutionalize conflict-resolution mechanisms.

Reliance on Envelope and Matrix Management, Partial Planning, and Consensus Building. In the more deterministic bureaucratic organization, problem solving is less important. The profession-oriented organization is organized to handle learning, risk taking, and problem solving. Professional discretion depends on envelope supervision, namely, limited controls designed to allow the professional to adapt to task variability to experiment and provide solutions. Where internal interdependencies are important, the project approach and task force and more formalized matrix structures are widely used. The profession-oriented organization is better able to use matrix structures because management depends far less on routinized rational controls and more on monitoring and partial planning.

It may seem contradictory that the bureaucratic organization depends less on planning than the profession-oriented organization. In fact, they are different forms of planning. In the

more predictive environment of the bureaucracy, planning tends
to have a longer time range and deals more with events that are
not amenable to policy choices. In the less predictive environment of the profession-oriented organization, planning tends to
be short range and deals more with policy options. It has an
additional function since it is more participative: it serves to
help reach a consensus about the future.

The Mexican public utility described in the first chapter
could establish detailed plans for the future. It could forecast
the rising demand for electricity, calculate requirements for cap-
ital plant additions and replacements and the expected costs of
production and maintenance, and produce detailed analyses of
necessary electric rate increases during the next twenty years.
Florence's Refuge or Applied Research had much more trouble
discussing or describing what they might expect to accomplish
in the next few months.

Yet Florence's Refuge and Applied Research needed to
dispel uncertainty. They had to be able to talk about the future
with confidence. Even if their plans were partial and tentative,
and often used to seek external funding, they nevertheless provided opportunities to discuss the future and offer some reassur-
ance that the organization would survive.

In the profession-oriented organization, partial planning
serves the important function of consensus building. Professional participation in planning serves to stimulate coalition formation. Data gathering and analysis serve to demystify the future, to inform the professional and managerial staff of the
conditions of the organization. It provides a basis for coalition
formation.

This is why planning is always partial and incomplete.
Planning cannot have a scope that goes beyond the agreements
that can be reached and the coalitions that are created. Neither
can it go beyond the ability to predict future events with some
confidence.

More Emphasis on Symbols. In the routinized bureaucracy, the problem of long-term goals is settled. The organization does not need to assert what it will do since it is going to
continue meeting the same needs it has been meeting. Routines

reaffirm the validity of past commitments: we know what we are doing because we have been doing it all along.

In the profession-oriented organization, the future is more uncertain. The fact the organization has to adapt, learn, and perform in new ways tells us already that what was a good way to perform previously may not be good enough tomorrow.

We described in Chapter Four the eight steps the organization follows as it defines what it is, what it does and does not do, how the staff coalesces around a set of ideas, a language, and symbols of what it stands for, how the staff experiments with the environment and ultimately alters the language and symbols that it uses. We saw how Florence's Refuge went through these various phases as the staff argued and fought about the wider or narrower role the agency should assume in battered women's cases. As we saw, Florence never seemed to guide the process; she avoided conflict and failed to maintain her leadership. But the language and symbols were still important. They served to coalesce most of the staff, to keep commitment and devotion to the task. As we saw, a minority of the staff were unhappy with the prevailing ideology. You will recall that the psychiatrist felt the organization should pay more attention to clinical needs of men. But for most of the committed workers, the symbols of women's liberation from male oppression provided ample justification for their effort.

More Emphasis on Trust. The routinized bureaucracy does not depend as much on trust. Roles are clearly defined and routines are set. Since there is little discretion, we do not need to trust those who perform. If they do not perform, we will know it and be able to sanction them. Control substitutes for trust.

In the profession-oriented organization, trust is far more important. Professional discretion implies that we trust the professional. That is, clients, public, and management trust the professionals.

To trust is to allow oneself to be vulnerable (Deutsch, 1962; Zand, 1972; Barber, 1983), to give to others power over oneself. You will recall our brief discussion of the conditions for trust in Chapter Four. We trust those who play by the rules of the game, we trust those who are capable, predictable, and reliable, and we trust those who have our best interest in mind.

The manager of the profession-oriented organization, in contrast to the manager of the bureaucratic organization, is far more concerned with clarifying the rules of the game. As you may recall, the second manager of Applied Research went to some length making her position clear. She insisted on being open with the staff; she insisted on candor. Florence, in contrast, was far more secretive and could not comprehend why the staff resented her style of management. There was far more distrust on both sides. Whether Florence failed because she was unable to establish trust relations is hard to document. She probably failed for many different reasons, including her choice of accountant, but lack of trust certainly did not help her.

How is trust established and maintained? Management has a greater responsibility for consistency and fairness and a greater responsibility for defining and sticking to the rules of the game. Management has also to be far more concerned with the ethics and performance of the professional staff and of the entire organization. Trust is a difficult plant to cultivate. When lost, it is not easily retrieved. It takes time and it requires relatively stable relationships. It certainly requires a clarification of interests and purposes, an awareness that competition and ambition are always present but that the game can be played in ways that are both competitive and open. There is less tolerance for secrecy even if management requires Machiavellian skills. Politics in the successful profession-oriented organization have to be relatively open, understood with modalities or rules of the game that are respected by all.

The second manager of Applied Research did not hide her problems from anyone. She was open and accessible. To be sure, she must have kept some facts to herself. She would often say that whenever she thought it would not harm her or her shop, she felt free to talk. She would discuss any issue with any and all members of the staff. The staff reciprocated; they believed her word and were not inclined to imagine complex plots to explain her behavior. She asked them to raise issues and problems at staff meetings. She was always quick to dispose of rumors and complaints. She understood very well the need for secrecy, but her main preoccupation was to stick to the rules, to play it as she had promised she would play it. She wanted to inspire confidence. She wanted to trust the staff and, in return, to be trusted.

More Emphasis on Ethics. Management is concerned with the ethics of the organization and of the professional staff for two main reasons. First, it is important to define the internal rules of the game. Management and the professional staff need to have shared values: what is done and what is not done in the organization. Adherence to a code of behavior has much to contribute to maintenance of internal trust.

The second reason is external. Those professions that flaunt their power, do not attempt to define their relations with clients and public, and do not respect accepted practices will, sooner or later, be subject to external controls. However, as we saw in Chapter Eight, external controls tend to constrain professional discretion, to bureaucratize organizational life. Therefore, management has to be concerned with the standards adopted by the profession, and it has to ensure that the profession is monitoring and disciplining itself.

To be sure, ethical concerns can never satisfy everyone. Criticisms are always varied and come from many quarters. When we read Illich's razor-sharp attack on the medical profession (1976), we are reminded that consensus is not easily reached. I still shudder when I remember his description of the death dance around the terminal patient, and how, at a very high cost, the celebrants dressed in white and blue wrap what remains of the dying in antiseptic smells.

Illich does not approve of many conventional practices, and he stirs our imagination and critical faculties. But if management's concern with ethics cannot address all issues, it can address some. This is a joint managerial and professional task that can easily be downgraded because it does not seem to solve pressing everyday issues. Yet, in the long run, the success and survival of less bureaucratic organizations depend on greater levels of self-regulation and discipline.

Conclusion

We have discussed the profession-oriented organization. We have asserted that it is flexible and adaptive. Yet we have seen how bureaucratization tends to creep in at every opportunity. What can we say about the future? Will this concept of the profession-oriented organization become more or less important? Can we expect major changes in managerial style and strategies? Or is this a tempest in a teapot?

There exists today a general malaise about large organizations. The public still distrusts government and large corporations. The resounding title of Schumacher's early 1970s book *Small Is Beautiful* (1973) no longer has the same meaning and political reverberations it had at the time. The public attitude has evolved possibly to a more hardened cynicism with strong self-gratification overtones. Today's generation is far more fascinated with the accouterments of power, the display of success. It is also far more realistic about the possibilities of acting and doing and about the tremendous opportunities large organizations offer. The new generations of undergraduates that compete for spots in business schools or public administration programs are testimony that large organizations have a strong appeal in our society.

The malaise is still there, however. In the shining modern offices with the latest computer technology, bureaucracy remains the bad word. The literature is more often pessimistic than optimistic. Some authors argue that bureaucracy is here to stay. They argue that experiments with other approaches tend to fail and that bureaucratic forms will not change much in the future (Markert, 1979; Meyer, 1979; Miewald, 1970; Shariff, 1979). Other authors advance more optimistic views. Bennis (1966, 1969, 1973) has long argued that rigid and hierarchical organizations are poorly adapted to requirements for adaptation and self-correction. He has consistently made the case for new adaptive approaches oriented to problems and people, and has often predicted that bureaucracy would sooner or later become obsolete.

Many other authors have also argued that bureaucracy is not effective. Remedies vary. Some authors urge greater participation and democracy (Abrahamsson, 1977; Matejko, 1979; Yates, 1982; Zwerdling, 1978). Others urge more privation and self-help (Barton, 1979; Doughton, 1980) or a new doctrine (Levine, 1986). Still others urge that more humane or more diverse values should prevail (Dvorin and Simmons, 1972; Ferguson, 1984; Simpson, 1972; Weinstein, 1979). And some authors have fewer remedies to offer. They tell us, instead, of burnt-out managers (Vash, 1980) or invite us to learn how to cope in the bureaucratic maze (Budd, 1982) or simply ask us to think more creatively (Schon, 1983).

What is to be said for the profession-oriented organization? Will it become more or less bureaucratized?

Looking ahead, it is obvious that even professional work will become increasingly bureaucratized. The reason is simple. Bureaucracy controls and protects at the same time. Professionals protect themselves also. As external interventions and controls increase, we can reasonably conclude that professions will increasingly routinize their work.

The physicians who are subject to more and more negligence suits will continue to routinize and document the procedures they use to justify outcomes. The teachers who are subject to more and more external controls will routinize their procedures to demonstrate they have done all they could to raise the school's overall pupil achievement score. To reduce bureaucratic trends, we would need to be willing to reduce external controls.

For this to happen would require far greater leadership on the part of professional bodies and of managers and leaders of profession-oriented organizations. It would require far more effort on the part of professions to regulate themselves to police and correct their own errors. In a sense, it is unfortunate that the most visible government-mandated professional self-regulation in quality control—the use of PSROs discussed in Chapter Eight—is so narrowly oriented to cost containment. It would be far more refreshing if similar large-scale efforts could address the meta-issues of external intervention: how can external control be carried out without provoking bureaucratic defense mechanisms?

Meanwhile, we have to understand that rules and routines

are used because they provide the only defense strategies that individuals in organizations can readily use. To reduce the need for defense strategies, one has to pay more attention to the fears that are engendered by uncertainty and the ever-present possibility of making errors and being punished for it. In an uncertain and complex world, it is difficult to imagine how we can truly reduce uncertainty and fears of errors. Therefore, we have to assume that bureaucracy is here to stay.

The other side of the coin is that we know that the human animal is adaptive. We also know that bureaucracy does not work well and that adaptation is bound to take place. I would assume that the modern organization will evolve in many different and gradual ways to provide for greater flexibility and adaptability. I feel quite confident that the profession-oriented organization will have a more important role in the future.

We tend to take the modern organization for granted, but, historically speaking, it is a recent development. The widespread idea that individuals are appointed to organizations because of their qualifications is a nineteenth-century concept (Albrow, 1970; Jacoby, 1973). The organizational culture that preceded it was based on lineage, family relations, and personal allegiance. These prebureaucratic organizations still exist. We all know, or hear about, tightly owned family businesses or about personal allegiances, individuals who work together throughout the career of one of them. In family businesses, father, uncle, sister, and cousins run the place. Here, family ties provide the glue of trust and, therefore, allow for discretion and flexibility. In the bureaucracy a good deal of discretion has been lost because trust has to depend on control: "I trust you because I control what you do, not because I know your father or your uncle or sister."

The transformation of the bureaucracy into the profession-oriented organization is an alternative. Instead of relying on trust generated by family socialization, we rely on trust generated by professional socialization. The two approaches have commonalities. They also have important differences. Family ties are replaced by qualifications for the task. The incompetent uncle is replaced by the trained expert. More important still, the values and ethics of the profession can be oriented toward the public well-being.

The problem is complex. As I said earlier, one of the reasons bureaucracy is so successful is that it protects. It guarantees salvation as long as routines are obeyed. In the old order, one had less occasion to seek such protection. The hidden hand of the market acted as an absolute master. Those that did not adapt were wiped out. No one blamed government or industry when errors were made. The small nineteenth-century entrepreneur understood about bad luck, bad judgments, and lost markets just as well as the peasant understood about bad weather and destroyed crops. But corporations and governments have learned to control and regulate markets. Instead of taking destructive articulation errors for granted, we have learned that we can avoid some of them. The idea of planning and regulation starts in the nineteenth century but flourishes in the twentieth. Protection has become a part of our culture and an accepted value. We should know that there is no going back to the unfettered market entrepreneurship of the past centuries.

The current nostalgia for deregulation is sometimes useful and sometimes not. It disregards the causes of protection. Fear of large-scale articulation and other errors generates defensive strategies. What we are witnessing is the control of organizations by other organizations. Government regulation is only one aspect of the problem. Corporate control may create very similar bureaucratic problems. It is not capitalism or socialism that matters here, for these problems are shared by all these systems (Hodges, 1981; Mallet, 1974). What matters are defensive strategies.

This tendency to control is not brought about by greed, although greed certainly contributes, nor is it caused by excessive managerial stupidity and lack of vision. On the contrary, it is the sane and realistic response to the dangers of a very uncertain and complex world.

Faced by considerable uncertainty, good and mediocre people do what they can to cope. They join together, they link arms, they seek to form powerful groups strong enough to resist whatever might happen. This is what bureaucracy is about. It is the creation of strong, centralized organizations that can resist because they are large and powerful. They are large and powerful because they routinize and control.

However, as we saw, there is another way to resist. One can keep slim and skate rapidly on the ice. The organization we have described in this book is adaptive. It learns. It self-corrects. It thinks. It does not need to dominate as much, because it can solve problems. This is the image in which my optimism resides.

To conclude, dear reader, you see that good management is not easily defined. There is no substitute for thinking things out. Distrust fads and panaceas. Keep the problem in focus. The solution is probably self-evident, but we all wear so many blinders, we do not see it easily. Learn to remove blinders.

References

Abel, L. "Why Does the ABA Promulgate Ethical Rules?" *Texas Law Review*, 1981, *59*, 639-688.

Abraham, K. G., and Medoff, J. L. *Length of Service and the Operation of Internal Labor Markets*. Cambridge, Mass.: Sloan School of Management, Massachusetts Institute of Technology, 1983.

Abrahamson, M. *The Professional in the Organization*. Skokie, Ill.: Rand McNally, 1967.

Abrahamsson, B. *Bureaucracy or Participation: The Logic of Organizations*. Beverly Hills, Calif.: Sage, 1977.

Albrow, M. *Bureaucracy*. New York: Praeger, 1970.

Aleshire, R. A. "Power to the People: An Assessment of the Community Action and Model Cities Experience." *Public Administration Review*, 1972, *32*, 428-443.

Ammons, D. N., and King, J. C. "Local Government Professionalism." *The Bureaucrat*, 1984, *13* (2), 52-57.

Anderson, J. *The Emergence of the Modern Regulatory State*. Washington, D.C.: Public Affairs Press, 1962.

Anderson, R. M., and others. *Divided Loyalties: Whistleblowing at BART*. West Lafayette, Ind.: Purdue Research Foundation, 1980.

Antonio, J. "Domination and Production in Bureaucracy." *American Sociological Review*, 1979, *44*, 895-912.

Argyris, C. *Integrating the Individual in the Organization.* New York: Wiley, 1964.

Argyris, C., and Schon, D. A. *Theory in Practice: Increasing Professional Effectiveness.* San Francisco: Jossey-Bass, 1974.

Atherton, J. *Professional Information Services.* New York: State Mutual Books, 1978.

Auletta, K. *Greed and Glory on Wall Street: The Fall of the House of Lehman.* New York: Random House, 1986.

Baldridge, V. J., Curtis, D. V., Ecker, G., and Riley, G. L. *Policy Making and Effective Leadership: A National Study of Academic Management.* San Francisco: Jossey-Bass, 1978.

Barak, R. J. *Program Review in Higher Education: Within and Without.* Boulder, Colo.: National Center for Higher Education Management Systems, 1982.

Barber, B. "Some 'New Men of Power': The Case of Biochemical Research Scientists." *Annals of the New York Academy of Sciences,* 1970, *169,* 519-523.

Barber, B. "Control and Responsibility in the Powerful Professions." *Political Science Quarterly,* 1978, *93,* 599-615.

Barber, B. *The Logic and Limits of Trust.* New Brunswick, N.J.: Rutgers University Press, 1983.

Barber, B. *Strong Democracy: Participatory Politics for a New Age.* Berkeley: University of California Press, 1984.

Bardach, E., and Kagan, R. A. *Going by the Book: The Problem of Regulatory Unreasonableness.* Philadelphia: Temple University Press, 1982.

Barnard, C. I. *The Functions of the Executive.* Cambridge, Mass.: Harvard University Press, 1938.

Barton, A. H. "A Diagnostio of Bureaucratic Maladies." *American Behavioral Scientist,* 1979, *22,* 483-492.

Baum, H. S. *Planners and Public Expectations.* Cambridge, Mass.: Schenkman, 1983.

Bayle, M. D. *Professional Ethics.* Belmont, Calif.: Wadsworth, 1981.

Beck, A. C., and Hillmar, E. D. *Positive Management Practices: Bringing Out the Best in Organizations and People.* San Francisco: Jossey-Bass, 1986.

Becker, H. S. "The Career of the Chicago Public School Teacher." *American Journal of Sociology,* 1952, *57,* 470-477.

References

Becker, H. S. "The Teacher in the Authority System of the Public School." *The Journal of Educational Sociology,* 1953, *27* (3), 129-141.

Beetle, G. R. "Engineering and Society: A Contemporary Challenge." *Civil Engineering,* Feb. 1971, *41,* 51-53.

Bell, T. H. *The Peer Review Model for Managing a Career Ladder Master Teacher Performance Pay Program for Elementary and Secondary Schools.* Washington, D.C.: U.S. Department of Education, 1983.

Bendor, J. B. *Parallel Systems: Redundancy in Government.* Berkeley: University of California Press, 1985.

Benningfield, M., and others. *A Proposal to Establish Demonstration Schools: The Identification, Training, and Utilization of Master-Mentor and Master Teachers.* San Antonio, Tex.: American Association of Colleges for Teacher Education, Feb. 1984.

Bennis, W. G. "The Coming Death of Bureaucracy." *Think,* 1966, *32* (Nov./Dec.), 32-35.

Bennis, W. G. "Post-Bureaucratic Leadership." *Trans-Action,* 1969, *6* (July/Aug.), 44-52.

Bennis, W. G. *Beyond Bureaucracy: Essays on the Development and Evolution of Human Organizations.* New York: McGraw-Hill, 1973.

Benson, J. K. "The Analysis of Bureaucratic-Professional Conflict: Functional Versus Dialectical Approaches." *Sociological Quarterly,* 1973, *14,* 376-394.

Benveniste, G. *The Politics of Expertise.* (2nd ed.) San Francisco: Boyd & Fraser, 1977.

Benveniste, G. *Regulation and Planning: The Case of Environmental Politics.* San Francisco: Boyd & Fraser, 1981.

Benveniste, G. *Bureaucracy.* (2nd ed.) San Francisco: Boyd & Fraser, 1983.

Benveniste, G. "On a Code of Ethics for Policy Experts." *Journal of Policy Analysis and Management,* 1984, *3,* 561-572.

Benveniste, G. "The Design of School Accountability Systems." *Educational Evaluation and Policy Analysis,* 1985, *7,* 261-279.

Bernstein, M. H. *Regulating Business by Independent Commission.* Princeton, N.J.: Princeton University Press, 1955.

Bhagat, R. S., and McQuaid, S. J. "Role of Subjective Culture in Organizations: A Review and Directions for Further Research." *Journal of Applied Psychology,* 1982, *67,* 653-685.

Blankenship, R. L. (ed.). *Colleagues in Organization: The Social Construction of Professional Work.* New York: Wiley, 1977.

Blau, J. R., and Alba, R. D. "Empowering Nets of Participation." *Administrative Science Quarterly,* 1982, *27,* 363-379.

Blau, P. M., and Scott, R. W. *Formal Organizations.* San Francisco: Chandler, 1962.

Bledstein, B. J. *The Culture of Professionalism: The Middle Class and the Development of Higher Education in America.* New York: Norton, 1976.

Blumberg, P. *Industrial Democracy: The Sociology of Participation.* New York: Schocken, 1969.

Bogen, K. T. "Managing Technical Dissent in Private Industry: Societal and Corporate Strategies for Dealing with the Whistleblowing Professional." *Industrial and Labor Relations Forum,* 1979, *13,* 3-32.

Boguslaw, R. *The New Utopians: A Study of System Design and Social Change.* Englewood Cliffs, N.J.: Prentice-Hall, 1965.

Bohland, J. R., and Gist, J. "The Spatial Consequences of Bureaucratic Decision Making." *Environment and Planning,* 1983, *15,* 1489-1500.

Boland, R. J., Jr. "Organizational Control, Organizational Power and Professional Responsibility." *Business and Professional Ethics Journal,* 1982, *2* (1), 15-25.

Bowman, J. S. "Whistleblowing: Literature and Resources Material." *Public Administration Review,* 1983, *43,* 271-276.

Bowman, J. S., Elliston, F. A., and Lockhart, P. *Professional Dissent: An Annotated Bibliography and Resource Guide.* New York: Garland, 1984.

Brandt, R., and Dronka, P. (eds.). *Incentives for Excellence in American Schools.* Alexandria, Va.: American Association for Supervision and Curriculum, Task Force on Merit Pay and Career Ladders, 1985.

Bridges, E. M. *Managing the Incompetent Teacher.* Eugene, Oreg.: ERIC Clearinghouse on Educational Management, 1984.

Brudney, J. L., and England, R. L. "Toward a Definition of the Coproduction Concept." *Public Administration Review,* 1983, *43,* 59-65.

Budd, J. *The Fast Track: How to Survive in the Corporate Labyrinth.* New York: St. Martin's Press, 1982.

Burke, C. G. "The Control of Professionals in a Democracy." *International Journal of Public Administration,* 1983, *5* (3), 291-320.

Buzzati-Traverso, A. *The Scientific Enterprise: Today and Tomorrow.* Paris: United Nations Educational, Scientific, and Cultural Organization, 1977.

Caiden, N., and Wildavsky, A. *Planning and Budgeting in Poor Countries.* New York: Wiley, 1974.

Camenish, P. *Grounding Professional Ethics in a Pluralistic Society.* New York: Haven, 1983.

"Can Your Employees Blow the Whistle on Internal Wrongdoing?" *ABA Banking Journal,* Nov. 1980, p. 26.

Carr-Saunders, A. M., and Wilson, P. A. *The Professions.* Oxford: Oxford University Press, 1933.

Carter, L. J. "Job Protection for 'Whistle Blowers' Being Tested." *Science,* 1980, *210,* 1057.

Cary, W. L. *Politics and the Regulatory Agencies.* New York: McGraw-Hill, 1967.

Chalk, R., and von Hippel, F. "Due Process for Dissenting Whistle-Blowers." *Technology Review,* 1979, *81* (June/July), 49-55.

Chase, S. B. (ed.). *Problems of Public Expenditure Analysis.* Washington, D.C.: Brookings Institution, 1968.

Cherniss, C. *Professional Burnout in Human Service Organizations.* New York: Praeger, 1980.

Child, J. "Predicting and Understanding Organization Structure." *Administrative Science Quarterly,* 1973, *18,* 168-185.

Churchman, C. W. *The Systems Approach.* New York: Dell, 1968.

Clark, P. R., and Wilson, J. Q. "Incentive Systems: A Theory of Organizations." *Administrative Science Quarterly,* 1961, *6,* 129-166.

Cogan, M. L. "The Problem of Defining a Profession." *The An-*

nals of the American Academy of Political and Social Science, 1955, *297*, 105-111.

Cohen, M. "The Power of Parallel Thinking." *Journal of Economic Behavior and Organization*, 1981, *2* (4), 285-306.

Committee on the Evolution of Work. *The Changing Situation of Workers and Their Unions*. Washington, D.C.: AFL-CIO, 1985.

Crozier, M. *The Bureaucratic Phenomenon*. Chicago: University of Chicago Press, 1964.

Cunningham, J. B. "Approaches to the Evaluation of Organizational Effectiveness." *Academy of Management Review*, 1977, *2*, 463-474.

Daft, R. L. *Organizational Theory and Design*. (2nd ed.) St. Paul, Minn.: West Publishing, 1986.

Dandridge, T., and others. "Organizational Symbolism: A Topic to Expand Organizational Analysis." *Academy of Management Review*, 1980, *5*, 248-256.

Davis, S. E., and Lawrence, P. R. *Matrix*. Reading, Mass.: Addison-Wesley, 1977.

Deal, T. E., and Kennedy, A. A. *Corporate Culture: The Rights and Rituals of Corporate Life*. Reading, Mass.: Addison-Wesley, 1982.

Deutsch, M. "Cooperation and Trust: Some Theoretical Notes." In M. R. Jones (ed.), *Nebraska Symposium on Motivation*. Lincoln: University of Nebraska Press, 1962.

Dingwall, R., and Lewis, P. (eds.). *The Sociology of the Professions*. London: Macmillan, 1981.

Doderlein, J. M. "Nuclear Power, Public Interest, and the Professional." *Nature*, 1976, *264*, 202-203.

Dornbusch, S. M., and Scott, R. W. *Evaluation and the Exercise of Authority: A Theory of Control Applied to Diverse Organizations*. San Francisco: Jossey-Bass, 1975.

Doughton, M. J. "People Power: Alternatives to Runaway Bureaucracy." *Futurist*, 1980, *14* (April), 13-22.

Douglas, M., and Wildavsky, A. *Risk and Culture: An Essay on the Selection of Technical and Environmental Dangers*. Berkeley: University of California Press, 1982.

Drucker, P. F. *The Practice of Management.* New York: Harper & Row, 1954.

Duffy, N. F. *Changes in Labour-Management Relations in the Enterprise.* Paris: Organisation for Economic Co-Operation and Development, 1975.

Dvorin, E. P., and Simmons, R. H. *From Amoral to Humane Bureaucracy.* San Francisco: Canfield, 1972.

Eimickle, W. B. "Professionalism and Participation: Compatible Means to Improved Social Services?" *Public Administration Review,* 1974, *34,* 409-414.

Elliot, C., and Kuhn, D. "Professionals in Bureaucracies: Some Emerging Areas of Conflict." *University of Michigan Business Review,* 1978, *30* (January), 12-16.

Elliot, P. *The Sociology of the Professions.* New York: Heider and Heider, 1963.

Elliston, F., Keenan, J., Lockhart, P., and Schaick, J. V. *Whistle-blowing: Managing Dissent in the Workplace.* New York: Praeger, 1985.

Emerson, R. M. "Power-Dependence Relations." *American Sociological Review,* 1962, *27,* 21-32.

Engel, G. "The Effect of Bureaucracy on the Professional Autonomy of the Physician." *Journal of Health and Social Behavior,* 1969, *10,* 30-41.

Engel, G. "Professional Autonomy and Bureaucratic Organization." *Administrative Science Quarterly,* 1970, *15,* 12-21.

Etzioni, A. (ed.). *The Semi-Professions and Their Organization: Teachers, Nurses, Social Workers.* New York: Free Press, 1969.

Evangelauf, J. "Top Economists Are Bullish on Their Discipline's Future." *The Chronicle of Higher Education,* 1986, *31* (17), 13.

Ewing, D. W. *'Do It My Way or You're Fired.' Employee Rights and the Changing Role of Management Prerogatives.* New York: Wiley, 1983.

Felsenthal, D. S. "Applying the Redundancy Concept to Administrative Organizations." *Public Administration Review,* 1980, *40,* 247-252.

Ferguson, K. E. *The Feminist Case Against Bureaucracy.* Philadelphia: Temple University Press, 1984.

Fleishman, J. L., and Payne, B. L. *Ethical Dilemmas and the Education of Policy Makers.* Hastings-on-Hudson, N.Y.: Hastings Center, 1980.

Flores, A. "Organizational Influences on Engineers' Safety Attitudes." *Applied Philosophy,* 1982, *1* (2), 71-89.

Foster, G. D. "Law, Morality, and the Public Servant." *Public Administration Review,* 1981, *41,* 29-34.

Freidson, E. *Professional Dominance.* New York: Atherton, 1970.

Freidson, E. (ed.). *The Professions and Their Prospects.* Beverly Hills, Calif.: Sage, 1971.

Fretz, B. R., and Mills, D. H. *Licensing and Certification of Psychologists and Counselors: A Guide to Current Policies, Procedures, and Legislation.* San Francisco: Jossey-Bass, 1980.

Gans, H. *People and Plans: Essays on Urban Problems and Solutions.* New York: Basic Books, 1968.

Georgopoulos, B. S., and Tannenbaum, A. S. "A Study of Organizational Effectiveness." *American Sociological Review,* 1957, *22,* 534-540.

Ghorpade, J. *Assessment of Organizational Effectiveness: Issues, Analysis, and Readings.* Pacific Palisades, Calif.: Goodyear, 1971.

Gifford, B. R. "Teaching—from Occupation to Profession: The Sine Qua Non of Educational Reform." *New England Journal of Public Policy,* 1985, *1* (2), 60-75.

Glassman, R. B. "Persistence of Loose Coupling in Living Systems." *Behavioral Science,* 1973, *18,* 83-98.

Glazer, B. G. (ed.). *Organizational Careers.* Hawthorne, N.Y.: Aldine, 1968.

Goldman, A. H. *The Moral Foundations of Professional Ethics.* Totowa, N.J.: Rowman and Allenheld, 1980.

Goodman, P. S. *Assessing Organizational Change: The Rushton Quality of Work Experiment.* New York: Wiley, 1979.

Goss, M. E. W. "Influence and Authority Among Physicians in an Outpatient Clinic." *American Sociological Review,* 1961, *26,* 39-50.

Gouldner, A. "Cosmopolitans and Locals: Toward an Analysis of Latent Social Roles." *Administrative Science Quarterly,* 1957, *2,* 281-306.

Gramlich, E. M. *Benefit-Cost Analysis of Government Programs.* Englewood Cliffs, N.J.: Prentice-Hall, 1981.

Gruber, K., and Cloyd, I. *Encyclopedia of Associations.* Detroit: Gale Research, 1986.

Gruber, M. L. (ed.). *Management Systems in the Human Services.* Philadelphia: Temple University Press, 1981.

Guy, M. E. *Professionals in Organizations: Debunking a Myth.* New York: Praeger, 1985.

Hall, R. H. "Professionalization and Bureaucratization." *American Sociological Review,* 1968, *33,* 92-104.

Harris, S. E. *Economic Planning: The Plans of Fourteen Countries with Analyses of the Plans.* New York: Knopf, 1949.

Hassell, C. "A Study of the Consequences of Excessive Legal Intervention on the Local Implementation of PL 94-142." Unpublished doctoral dissertation, Department of Education, Graduate School of Education, University of California, Berkeley, 1981.

Hatry, H., and others. *Efficiency Measurement for Local Government Service: Some Initial Suggestions.* Washington, D.C.: Urban Institute, 1979.

Herrick, N. Q. *Improving Government: Experiments with Quality of Working Life Systems.* New York: Praeger, 1983.

Herzberg, F. *Work and the Nature of Man.* New York: World Publishing, 1966.

Hickman, C. R., and Silva, M. A. *Creating Excellence: Managing Corporate Culture, Strategy and Change in the New Age.* New York: New American Library, 1984.

Hickson, J. D., and Thomas, M. W. "Professionalization in Britain: A Preliminary Measurement." London: *Sociology,* 1969, *3* (June), 38-53.

Hirschman, A. O. *Exit, Voice, and Loyalty: Responses to Decline in Firms, Organizations, and States.* Cambridge, Mass.: Harvard University Press, 1970.

Hodges, D. C. *The Bureaucratization of Socialism.* Amherst: University of Massachusetts Press, 1981.

Hollander, R. "Ecologists, Ethical Codes, and the Struggles of a New Profession." *The Hastings Center Report,* 1976, *6* (Feb.), 45–46.

Hoos, I. R. *Systems Analysis in Public Policy: A Critique.* Berkeley: University of California Press, 1972.

Hopkins, A. H. *Work and Job Satisfaction in the Public Sector.* Totowa, N.J.: Rowman and Allenheld, 1983.

Horowitz, D. L. *The Courts and Social Policy.* Washington, D.C.: Brookings Institution, 1977a.

Horowitz, D. L. *The Jurocracy: Government Lawyers, Agency Programs, and Judicial Decisions.* Lexington, Mass.: Heath, 1977b.

Houle, C. O. *Continuing Learning in the Professions.* San Francisco: Jossey-Bass, 1980.

Ilgen, D. R., Fisher, C. D., and Taylor, M. S. "Consequences of Individual Feedback on Behavior in Organizations." *Journal of Applied Psychology,* 1979, *64,* 349–371.

Illich, I. *Medical Nemesis: The Expropriation of Health.* New York: Random House, 1976.

Jacoby, H. *The Bureaucratization of the World.* Berkeley: University of California Press, 1973.

James, G. J. "Whistleblowing: Its Nature and Justification." *Philosophy in Context,* 1980, *10,* 99–117.

Jaques, E. *Measurement of Responsibility: A Study of Work, Payment, and Individual Capacity.* London: Tavistock, 1956.

Jones-Lee, M. W. *The Value of Life: An Economic Analysis.* London: Martin Robertson, 1976.

Kagan, R. A. *Regulatory Justice: Implementing a Wage-Price Freeze.* New York: Russell Sage Foundation, 1978.

Kamarck, A. M. "McNamara's Bank." *Foreign Affairs,* 1982, *60,* 951–953.

Kanter, R. M. *Men and Women of the Corporation.* New York: Basic Books, 1977.

Kanter, R. M. *The Change Masters: Innovation for Productivity in the American Corporation.* New York: Simon & Schuster, 1983.

Katz, D., and Kahn, R. L. *The Social Psychology of Organizations.* New York: Wiley, 1966.

Kaufman, H. G. *Obsolescence and Professional Career Development.* New York: AMACOM, 1974.

Kelley, R. E. *The Gold Collar Worker: Harnessing the Brainpower of the New Work Force.* Reading, Mass.: Addison-Wesley, 1985.

Kets de Vries, M. F. R., and Miller, D. *The Neurotic Organization: Diagnosing and Changing Counterproductive Styles of Management.* San Francisco: Jossey-Bass, 1985.

Kinder, D., and Weiss, J. "In Lieu of Rationality: Psychological Perspectives on Foreign Policy Decision-Making." *Journal of Conflict Resolution,* 1978, *22* (4), 707–735.

Kneese, A., and Schultze, C. L. *Pollution, Prices, and Public Policy.* Washington, D.C.: Brookings Institution, 1975.

Kohn, P. M., and Hughson, R. V. "Perplexing Problems in Engineering Ethics." *Chemical Engineering,* May 5, 1980, p. 100.

Kornhauser, W. *Scientists in Industry: Conflict and Accommodation.* Berkeley: University of California Press, 1962.

Kraemer, K., Dutton, W., and Northrop, A. *The Management of Information Systems.* New York: Columbia University Press, 1981.

Krieger, M. H. *Advice and Planning.* Philadelphia: Temple University Press, 1981.

Krislov, S. *Representative Bureaucracy and the American Political System.* New York: Praeger, 1981.

Landau, M. "Redundancy, Rationality, and the Problem of Duplication and Overlap." *Public Administration Review,* 1969, *29,* 346–358.

Landau, M. "Federalism, Redundancy, and System Reliability." *Publius,* 1973a, *3* (2), 173–196.

Landau, M. "On the Concept of the Self Correcting Organization." *Public Administration Review,* 1973b, *33,* 533–542.

Landau, M., and Stout, R., Jr. "To Manage Is Not to Control: Or, the Folly of Type II Errors." *Public Administration Review,* 1979, *39,* 148–156.

Langton, S. (ed.). *Citizen Participation in America.* Lexington, Mass.: Heath, 1978.

Larson, J. R. "The Performance Feedback Process: A Preliminary Model." *Organizational Behavior and Human Performance,* 1984, *33* (1), 42-76.

Latane, B., Williams, K., and Harkins, S. "Many Hands Make Light the Work: The Causes and Consequences of Social Loafing." *Journal of Personality and Social Psychology,* 1979, *37,* 822-832.

Lawler, E. E. *Pay and Organizational Effectiveness: A Psychological View.* New York: McGraw-Hill, 1971.

Lawler, E. J., and Hage, J. "Professional-Bureaucratic Conflict and Intraorganizational Powerlessness Among Social Workers." *Journal of Sociology and Social Welfare,* 1973, *1,* 92-102.

Layton, E. *The Revolt of the Engineers.* Cleveland, Ohio: Press of Case Western Reserve University, 1971.

Lehman, E. W., and Waters, A. M. "Control in Policy Research Institutes: Some Correlates." *Policy Analysis,* 1979, *5,* 201-221.

Leibowitz, A., and Tollison, R. "Free Riding, Shirking, and Team Production in Legal Partnerships." *Economic Inquiry,* 1980, *18,* 380-394.

Levine, C. H. "The Federal Government in the Year 2000: Administrative Legacies of the Reagan Years." *Public Administration Review,* 1986, *46,* 195-206.

Levinson, H. "Management by Whose Objectives?" *Harvard Business Review,* 1970, *48,* 124-133.

Lortie, D. C. *Schoolteacher: A Sociological Study.* Chicago: University of Chicago Press, 1975.

Losk, D. "The Professional Role of Public School Teachers and State Accountability Programs." Unpublished dissertation, Graduate School of Education, University of California, Berkeley, 1986.

Luegenbiehl, H. C. "Code of Ethics and the Moral Education of Engineers." *Business and Professional Ethics Journal,* 1983, *2* (4), 41-61.

Lynn, K. S. *The Professions in America.* Boston: Houghton Mifflin, 1965.

McGowan, R. P. "The Professional in Public Organizations: Lessons from the Private Sector." *American Review of Public Administration,* 1982, *16,* 337-349.

McGregor, D. *The Human Side of Enterprise.* New York: McGraw-Hill, 1960.

Machiavelli, N. *The Prince.* New York: Mentor Books, 1952. (Written in 1513.)

Mallet, S. *Bureaucracy and Technocracy in the Socialist Countries.* Nottingham, England: Bertrand Russell Peace Foundation, 1974.

Malone, D., and Wedel, J. "Professional Orientation and Bureaucratic Forms: Variations Among Three Social Work Agencies." *Proceedings of the Southwestern Sociological Association,* 1969, *19,* 237-241.

Mannheim, K. *Freedom, Power, and Democratic Planning.* London: Routledge & Kegan Paul, 1965. (First published in Germany in 1935.)

Mansbridge, J. J. *Beyond Adversary Democracy.* New York: Basic Books, 1980.

March, J. G., and Simon, H. A. *Organizations.* New York: Wiley, 1965.

Markert, J. "Bureaucratization of the Alternative Youth Program of the Sixties: A Decade of Change." *Group and Organization Studies,* 1979, *4,* 485-495.

Marrow, A. J., Bowers, D. G., and Seashore, S. E. *Management by Participation.* New York: Harper & Row, 1967.

Martin, M. W., and Schinzinger, R. *Ethics in Engineering.* New York: McGraw-Hill, 1983.

Maslach, C. *Burnout: The Cost of Caring.* Englewood Cliffs, N.J.: Prentice-Hall, 1982.

Matejko, A. "From the Crisis of Bureaucracy to the Challenge of Participation." In R. Mohan (ed.), *Management and Complex Organizations in Comparative Perspective.* Westport, Conn.: Greenwood, 1979.

Mazmanian, D. A., and Nienaber, J. *Can Organizations Change? Environmental Protection, Citizen Participation, and the Corps of Engineers.* Washington, D.C.: Brookings Institution, 1979.

Meadow, I. S. G. "Organic Structure and Innovation in Small Groups." *Human Relations,* 1980, *33,* 369-382.

Medoff, J. L., and Abraham, K. G. "Experience, Performance, and Earnings." *Quarterly Journal of Economics*, 1980, *95*, 703–736.

Medoff, J. L., and Abraham, K. G. "Are Those Paid More Really More Productive? The Case of Experience." *Journal of Human Resources*, 1981, *16*, 186–216.

Meltsner, A. J. *Policy Analysts in the Bureaucracy.* Berkeley: University of California Press, 1976.

Meltzer, H., and Nord, W. (eds.). *Making Organizations Humane and Productive: A Handbook for Practitioners.* New York: Wiley, 1981.

Meyer, A. "How Ideologies Supplant Formal Structures and Shape Responses to Environments." *Journal of Management Studies*, 1981, *19*, 45–61.

Meyer, J. W., and Scott, R. W. *Organizational Environments: Ritual and Rationality.* Beverly Hills, Calif.: Sage, 1983.

Meyer, M. W. "Debureaucratization?" *Social Sciences Quarterly*, 1979, *60*, 25–34.

Michael, J. A. "Professional Practice in a Bureaucratic Organization." *Public Administration* (Sydney, Australia), 1974, *33*, 147–166.

Miewald, R. D. "The Greatly Exaggerated Death of Bureaucracy." *California Management Review*, 1970, *13*, 65–69.

Miller, D. B. *Managing Professionals in Research and Development: A Guide for Improving Productivity and Organizational Effectiveness.* San Francisco: Jossey-Bass, 1986.

Miller, G. "Professionals in Bureaucracies: Alienation Among Industrial Scientists and Engineers." *American Sociological Review*, 1967, *32*, 755–768.

Millward, R. E. "PPBS: Problems of Implementation." *Journal of the American Institute of Planners*, 1968, *34* (March), 88–94.

Mintzberg, H. *Structure in Fives: Designing Effective Organizations.* Englewood Cliffs, N.J.: Prentice-Hall, 1983.

Mishan, E. J. *Cost-Benefit Analysis.* (2nd ed.) New York: Praeger, 1976.

Montagna, P. "Professionalization and Bureaucratization in Large Professional Organizations." *American Journal of Sociology*, 1968, *74*, 138–145.

Moore, W. E. *The Professions: Roles and Rules.* New York: Russell Sage Foundation, 1970.

Morrissey, E., and Gillespie, D. "Technology and the Conflict of Professionals in Bureaucratic Organizations." *Sociological Quarterly,* 1975, *16,* 319-332.

Mosher, F. C., and Stillman, R., Jr. "A Symposium: The Professions in Government." *Public Administration Review,* 1977, *37,* 631-685.

Mosher, F. C., and Stillman, R., Jr. "A Symposium: The Professions in Government II." *Public Administration Review,* 1978, *38,* 105-130.

Nadler, D. A. "The Use of Feedback for Organizational Change: Promises and Pitfalls." *Group and Organizational Studies,* 1976, *1,* 177-186.

Nash, M. *Making People Productive: What Really Works in Raising Managerial and Employee Performance.* San Francisco: Jossey-Bass, 1985.

Nelkin, D. "Scientists and Professional Responsibility: The Experience of American Ecologists." *Social Studies of Science,* 1977, *7* (Feb.), 75-96.

Nelkin, D., and Pollak, N. "Public Participation in Technological Decisions: Reality or Grand Illusion?" *Technology Review,* 1979, *80* (Aug.-Sept.), 55-64.

Nelson, R. "Uncertainty, Learning, and the Economics of Parallel Research and Development Effects." *Review of Economics and Statistics,* 1961, *43,* 351-364.

Nonet, P., and Selznick, P. *Law and Society in Transition: Toward Responsive Law.* New York: Octagon Books, 1978.

Odiorne, G. *Management by Objectives: A System of Managerial Leadership.* New York: Pitman, 1969.

Orlans, H. *Private Accreditation and Public Eligibility.* Lexington, Mass.: Lexington, 1975.

Ouchi, W. G. "The Relationship Between Organizational Structure and Organizational Control." *Administrative Science Quarterly,* 1977, *22,* 95-113.

Packer, H. L., and Ehrlich, T. *New Directions in Legal Education.* New York: McGraw-Hill, 1972.

Paine, W. S. *Job Stress and Burnout: Research, Theory, and Intervention.* Beverly Hills, Calif.: Sage, 1982.

Parmerlee, M. A., and others. "Correlates of Whistleblowers: Perceptions of Organizational Retaliation." *Administrative Science Quarterly*, 1982, *27*, 17–34.

Pastin, M. *The Hard Problems of Management: Gaining the Ethics Edge*. San Francisco: Jossey-Bass, 1986.

Pearse, D. W. (ed.). *The Valuation of Social Cost*. London: Allen & Unwin, 1978.

Pelz, F. M., and Andrews, D. C. *Scientists in Organizations: Productive Climates for Research and Development*. Ann Arbor: University of Michigan Press, 1976.

Percy, S. L. "Citizen Coproduction Prospects for Improving Service Delivery." *Journal of Urban Affairs*, 1983, *5* (3), 203–210.

Perrow, C. *Normal Accidents: Living with High-Risk Technologies*. New York: Basic Books, 1984.

Perrucci, R. "Engineering: Professional Servant of Power." *American Behavioral Scientist*, 1971, *13*, 119–133.

Perrucci, R., Anderson, R. M., Schendel, D. E., and Trachtman, L. E. "Whistleblowing: Professional's Resistance to Organizational Authority." *Social Problems*, 1980, *28*, 149–164.

Peters, T. J., and Austin, N. *A Passion for Excellence: The Leadership Difference*. New York: Random House, 1985.

Peters, T. J., and Waterman, R. H., Jr. *In Search of Excellence: Lessons from America's Best Run Companies*. New York: Harper & Row, 1982.

Pinder, C. C. *Work Motivation: Theory Issues and Applications*. Glenview, Ill.: Scott, Foresman, 1984.

Prandy, K. *Professional Employees: A Study of Scientists and Engineers*. London: Faber & Faber, 1965.

Rabin, J. (ed.). "Professionalism in Public Administration: Definition, Character, and Value." *American Review of Public Administration*, 1982, *16*, 303–412.

Rabin, J. "The Future of Professionalism." *The Bureaucrat*, 1985, *14* (2), 3–4.

Rahman, F. "Medicare Makes a Wrong Diagnosis." *New York Times*, Jan. 23, 1986, p. 23.

Ray, A. *Cost-Benefit Analysis: Issues and Methodologies*. Baltimore, Md.: Johns Hopkins University Press, 1984.

Rhode, D. L. "Why Does the ABA Bother: A Functional Perspective on Professional Codes." *Texas Law Review*, 1981, *59*, 689-721.

Riedel, J. A. "Citizen Participation: Myths and Realities." *Public Administration Review*, 1972, *32*, 211-220.

Riley, M. J. (ed.). *Management Information Systems*. (2nd ed.) Oakland, Calif.: Holden Day, 1981.

Roemer, R. "Trends in Licensure, Certification, and Accreditation." *Journal of Allied Health*, 1974, *3* (1), 26-33.

Rohr, J. A. *Ethics for Bureaucrats*. New York: Dekker, 1978.

Rosener, J. B. "Making Bureaucrats Responsive: A Study of the Impact of Citizen Participation and Staff Recommendations on Regulatory Decision Making." *Public Administration Review*, 1982, *42*, 339-345.

Rourke, F. E. "Bureaucracy in Conflict: Administrators and Professionals." *Ethics*, 1960, *70*, 22-27.

Sarfatti Larson, M. *The Rise of Professionalism: A Sociological Analysis*. Berkeley: University of California Press, 1977.

Scanlon, J. N. "Profit Sharing Under Collective Bargaining: Three Case Studies." *Industrial and Labor Relations Review*, 1948, *2*, 58-75.

Schaffir, W. B. *Strategic Planning: Some Questions for the Chief Executive*. New York: AMACOM, 1976.

Schaub, J. W., and Pavlovic, K. (eds.). *Engineering, Professionalism, and Ethics*. New York: Wiley, 1983.

Schein, E. H. *Organizational Culture and Leadership: A Dynamic View*. San Francisco: Jossey-Bass, 1985.

Schick, A. "A Death in the Bureaucracy: The Demise of Federal PPB." *Public Administration Review*, 1973, *33*, 146-156.

Schon, D. A. *The Reflective Practitioner: How Professionals Think in Action*. New York: Basic Books, 1983.

Schultze, C. L. *The Politics and Economics of Public Spending*. Washington, D.C.: Brookings Institution, 1968.

Schumacher, E. F. *Small Is Beautiful: Economics As If People Mattered*. New York: Harper & Row, 1973.

Scott, R. W. *Organizations Rational, Natural, and Open Systems*. Englewood Cliffs, N.J.: Prentice-Hall, 1981.

Seashore, S. E., and Bowers, D. G. "The Durability of Organizational Change." *American Psychologist,* 1970, *25,* 227-233.

Selden, W. K. *Accreditation: A Struggle Over Standards in Higher Education.* New York: Harper & Row, 1960.

Selden, W. K. *Accreditation and the Public Interest.* Washington, D.C.: Council on Postsecondary Education, 1976.

Selden, W. K. "Accreditation in Medical and Other Health Fields." *Journal of Allied Health,* 1979, *8* (1), 69-89.

Shapero, A. *Managing Professional People: Understanding Creative Performance.* New York: Free Press, 1985.

Shariff, Z. "The Persistence of Bureaucracy." *Social Science Quarterly,* 1979, *60,* 3-19.

Shklar, J. N. *Legalism.* Cambridge, Mass.: Harvard University Press, 1964.

Simon, H. A. *Administrative Behavior: A Study of Decision-Making Processes in Administrative Organization.* (3rd ed.) New York: Free Press, 1976.

Simpson, R. L. "Beyond Rational Bureaucracy: Changing Values and Social Integration in Post-Industrial Society." *Social Forces,* 1972, *51,* 1-6.

Smircich, L. "Concepts of Culture and Organizational Analysis." *Administrative Science Quarterly,* 1983, *28,* 339-358.

Snizek, W. W. "Hall Professionalism Scale: An Empirical Reassessment." *American Sociological Review,* 1972, *37,* 109-114.

Sorensen, J. E., and Sorensen, T. L. "The Conflict of Professionals in Bureaucratic Organizations." *Administrative Science Quarterly,* 1974, *19,* 98-106.

Steers, R. M. "Problems in the Measurement of Organizational Effectiveness." *Administrative Science Quarterly,* 1975, *20,* 546-558.

Steiner, G. A. *Strategic Planning: What Every Manager Must Know.* New York: Free Press, 1979.

Stenberg, C. W. "Citizens and the Administrative State: From Participation to Power." *Public Administration Review,* 1972, *32,* 190-198.

Stern, D. "Compensation for Teachers." Berkeley: University of California, Graduate School of Education, 1986. (Mimeographed.)

Strange, J. H. "The Impact of Citizen Participation on Public Administration." *Public Administration Review*, 1972, *32*, 457–470.

Suchman, E. A. *Evaluative Research, Principles, and Practices in Public Service and Social Programs.* New York: Russell Sage Foundation, 1967.

Sumner, G. C., and others. *Federal Programs Supporting Educational Change.* Vol. VI: *Title VII. Bilingual Projects.* Santa Monica, Calif.: Rand Corporation, 1977.

Susskind, L., and Elliott, M. (eds.). *Paternalism, Conflict, and Coproduction: Learning from Citizen Action and Citizen Participation in Western Europe.* New York: Plenum, 1983.

Swidler, A. *Organizations Without Authority: Dilemmas of Social Control in Free Schools.* Cambridge, Mass.: Harvard University Press, 1979.

Taylor, S. J. *Making Bureaucracies Think: The Environmental Strategy of Administrative Reform.* Stanford, Calif.: Stanford University Press, 1984.

Thomas, J. C. "Citizen Participation and Urban Administration: From Enemies to Allies." *Journal of Urban Affairs,* 1983, *5* (3), 175–182.

Toch, H., and Grant, D. J. *Reforming Human Services: Change Through Participation.* Beverly Hills, Calif.: Sage, 1984.

Unger, S. H. *Controlling Technology: Ethics and the Responsible Engineer.* New York: Holt, Rinehart & Winston, 1982.

U.S. General Accounting Office. *Comprehensive Approach for Planning and Conducting a Program Result Review.* Washington, D.C.: Government Printing Office, 1978.

Usher, C. L., and Cornia, G. C. "Goal Setting and Performance Assessment in Municipal Budgeting." *Public Administration Review,* 1981, *41*, 229–235.

Varga, A. C. *The Main Issues in Bio-Ethics.* Ramsey, N.J.: Paulist Press, 1980.

Vash, C. L. *The Burnt-Out Administrator.* New York: Springer, 1980.

Vertin, J. R. (ed.). *Managing the Investment Professional.* Charlottesville, Va.: Institute of Chartered Financial Analysts, 1984.

Vollmer, H. M., and Mills, D. L. (eds.). *Professionalization.* Englewood Cliffs, N.J.: Prentice-Hall, 1966.

Waldman, P. "More Doctors and Lawyers Joining Unions to Fight Large Institutions." *Wall Street Journal,* May 23, 1986, p. 21.

Washnis, G. J. (ed.). *Productivity Improvement: Handbook for State and Local Government.* New York: Wiley, 1980.

Weber, M. *The Theory of Social and Economic Organization.* (A. M. Henderson and Talcott Parsons, trans.) New York: Free Press, 1964. (First published in Germany in 1922.)

Weick, K. E. "Educational Organizations as Loosely Coupled Systems." *Administrative Science Quarterly,* 1976, *21,* 1-10.

Weinstein, D. *Bureaucratic Opposition.* Elmsford, N.Y.: Pergamon Press, 1979.

Westin, A. F. *Whistleblowing: Loyalty and Dissent in the Corporation.* New York: McGraw-Hill, 1981.

Whitaker, G. P. "Coproduction: Citizen Participation in Service Delivery." *Public Administration Review,* 1980, *40,* 240-246.

Wildavsky, A. "Rescuing Policy Analysis from PPBS." *Public Administration Review,* 1969, *29,* 189-202.

Wilenski, P. "Efficiency and Equity: Competing Values in Administrative Reform." *Policy Studies Journal,* 1980-1981, *9,* 1239-1249.

Wilensky, H. L. "The Professionalization of Everyone?" *American Journal of Sociology,* 1964, *70* (2), 137-158.

Wilensky, H. L. *Organizational Intelligence: Knowledge and Policy in Government and Industry.* New York: Basic Books, 1967.

Wilkins, A. L., and Ouchi, W. G. "Efficient Cultures: Exploring the Relationship Between Culture and Organizational Performance." *Administrative Science Quarterly,* 1983, *28,* 468-481.

Wilson, R. *Professionals as Workers: An Annotated Bibliography.* Cambridge, Mass.: Policy Training Center, 1979a.

Wilson, R. *Professionals as Workers, A Selection of Readings.* Cambridge, Mass.: Policy Training Center, 1979b.

Wilson, R. F. (ed.). *Designing Academic Program Reviews.* San Francisco: Jossey-Bass, 1982.

Wlodkowski, R. J. *Enhancing Adult Motivation to Learn: A Guide to Improving Instruction and Increasing Learner Achievement.* San Francisco: Jossey-Bass, 1985.

Worthley, J. A. "PPB: Dead or Alive?" *Public Administration Review,* 1974, *34,* 392–394.

Yates, D. *Bureaucratic Democracy.* Cambridge, Mass.: Harvard University Press, 1982.

Yeager, S. J., Rabin, J., and Vocino, T. "Feedback and Administrative Behavior in the Public Sector." *Public Administration Review,* 1985, *45,* 570–575.

Yuchtman, E., and Seashore, S. E. "A System Resource Approach to Organizational Effectiveness." *American Sociological Review,* 1967, *32,* 891–903.

Zammuto, R. F. *Assessing Organizational Effectiveness.* Albany, N.Y.: State University of New York Press, 1982.

Zand, D. E. "Trust and Managerial Problem Solving." *Administrative Science Quarterly,* 1972, *17,* 229–239.

Zwerdling, D. (ed.). *Workplace Democracy.* New York: Harper & Row, 1978.

Index

A

Accountability, 25, 225-253

Adaptability, 268-270; and control errors, 204; in definition of effectiveness, 137, 167; and slack, 197-198

Ambiguity, 57, 108-109, 195-207

American Association of Marriage and Family Therapists, 37

American Association of Sex Educators, Counselors and Therapists, 37

American Mental Health Counselors Association, 37

American Psychological Association, 37

Andrews, D. C., 181

Anti-intellectualism, 21

Applied research, 4, 8, 20-21, 47, 73, 88, 125, 141, 143, 145, 155, 157, 162-163, 173, 202, 207, 210, 250, 262, 264

Art management, 170, 174

Articulation errors, 118

Artistic professions, 38

Auletta, K., 87

Authority: defined, 61; of profes-

sionals, 51, 61-68; sources of, 33-35

Autonomy, 50-51

B

Bad apple strategy, 239

Becker, H. S., 34

Bennis, W. G., 266

Bilingual education, 12

Blau, P. M., 166

Bledstein, B. J., 2

Booz Allen & Hamilton, 106

Brokers, 29

Budgets, 117, 121-122, 133, 151; and formulas, 16

Bureaucracy, 269-270; defined, 6; excessive, 8, 10, 12; and goals displacement, 107; and model of governance, 93-94; and regulation, 9; roots of word, 9-10

Bureaucratization of professions, 37, 147, 161-164, 168; linked to management tools, 149-150, 160-161; used as defensive strategies, 157

C

Caiden, N., 124